M&A Disputes and Completion Mechanisms

Arbitration in Context Series

VOLUME 3

There are by now many excellent sources on international commercial arbitration, addressing procedures and practice in general and in relation to specific arbitral institutions and rules. There are also many excellent sources on the business sectors in which commercial disputes often go to international arbitration: to name only some, construction, sports, intellectual property, energy, insurance, securities.

The purpose of Kluwer Law International's sector-by-sector *Arbitration in Context Series* is to merge these two types of sources into stand-alone guides for the busy in-house lawyer and transactional practitioner facing the prospect of specialized arbitration. We are pleased to launch the third volume of this series with *M&A Disputes and Completion Mechanisms* by Heiko Daniel Ziehms.

M&A Disputes and Completion Mechanisms

Heiko Daniel Ziehms

Wolters Kluwer

Published by:
Kluwer Law International B.V.
PO Box 316
2400 AH Alphen aan den Rijn
The Netherlands
E-mail: international-sales@wolterskluwer.com
Website: lrus.wolterskluwer.com

Sold and distributed in North, Central and South America by:
Wolters Kluwer Legal & Regulatory U.S.
7201 McKinney Circle
Frederick, MD 21704
United States of America
Email: customer.service@wolterskluwer.com

Sold and distributed in all other countries by:
Air Business Subscriptions
Rockwood House
Haywards Heath
West Sussex
RH16 3DH
United Kingdom
Email: international-customerservice@wolterskluwer.com

ISBN 978-90-411-8625-6

e-Book: ISBN 978-90-411-8637-9
web-PDF: ISBN 978-90-411-8639-3

To Alba Lucia, Laura and Sara

About the Author

Heiko Daniel Ziehms is a managing director in the London office of Berkeley Research Group. He focuses on the quantification of damages and forensic accounting analyses in M&A, joint venture and other commercial disputes and provides transaction advisory services.

Mr Ziehms was appointed as financial and accounting expert in a large number of disputes. He has worked on matters in ICC, DIS, LCIA, ICSID, and SIAC arbitration forums, ad hoc arbitrations and the courts, including some of the most complex corporate disputes in Europe with values up to several billion euros. He is experienced in giving oral expert testimony. He has advised on several hundred transactions, including 'landmark' deals.

He was listed among the world's foremost expert witnesses in the tenth edition of Global Arbitration Review's GAR 100. He has also been recognised by Who's Who Legal for several years among the leading expert witnesses for arbitration worldwide, and among the leading consulting experts for the quantum of damages and forensic accounting.

Mr Ziehms holds an MBA from the Haas School of Business at the University of California at Berkeley and a graduate degree in Business from the University of Bamberg, Germany. He is a Certified Fraud Examiner, qualified and previously worked as a Certified Public Accountant.

'Apparently there is nothing that cannot happen.' Mark Twain

Table of Contents

List of Abbreviations

ASC	Accounting Standards Codification (as issued by FASB)
ASU	Accounting Standards Update (as issued by FASB)
CAPM	Capital Asset Pricing Model
DCF	Discounted Cash Flow
EBIT	Earnings before Interest and Taxes
EBITDA	Earnings before Interest, Taxes, Depreciation and Amortisation
FASB	Financial Accounting Standards Board
IAS	International Accounting Standard
IASB	International Accounting Standards Board
ICC	International Chamber of Commerce
IFRS	International Financial Reporting Standards
M&A	Mergers and Acquisitions
MAC	Material Adverse Clause
PE	Private Equity
POC	Percentage of Completion
PPA	Purchase Price Adjustment
RIM	Residual Income Model
SPA	Sale and Purchase Agreement
US GAAP	US Generally Accepted Accounting Principles
WACC	Weighted Average Cost of Capital
WIP	Work in Progress

List of Figures

List of Tables

Acknowledgements

I would like to express my gratitude to my clients, colleagues, professors, friends, and my family.

I have a particular debt to John Winepress, a former KPMG Transaction Services partner, who went through an early draft of the manuscript word by word and made many helpful suggestions. I am grateful for the generosity with which he gave his time and inspired by the breadth and depth of his knowledge. John's contributions improved many aspects of the book (I am responsible for any mistakes that remain).

Thank you to Professor David Teece, Danny Ryan, and David Saunders of Berkeley Research Group for supporting the project and enabling me to see it through.

I am indebted to my co-authors of past publications: Maren Burtoft, Matthias Breimhorst, Myriam Birch, Erik van Duijvenvoorde, Sean Fishlock, Thomas Goslich, Phil Hersey, Abigail Harris, Anna Hartley, Dr Ekaterina Lohwasser, James Lumley, Dr Shireen Meer, Eduard Saura, Thomas Kunder, Wilhelm Mickerts and Edmond Richards. This book draws on our joint publications, at times significantly.

My appreciation also goes to my colleagues at the Berkeley Research Group and former colleagues at Accuracy as well as clients who all lent support over the almost four years it took to write this book. I have learned much from them while working on transactions and disputes and in many informal discussions. They include Chaitanya Arora, Christian Axmann, Anna Baird, Vipul Barbhaya, Stefan Bödeker, Veronica Böhmer, Thomas Brown, Alexandros Christou, Nataliya Das, Piers de Wilde, Ron Evans, Giovanni Foti, Daniel Galante, Abigail Gammie, Adam Garside, Sarah Glover, Peter Grindley, Mustafa Hadi, Roula Harfouche, John House, Julius Huckabee, Susanna Ingalls, Mark James, Ben Johnson, Sarah Keeling, Amy Kingdon, Leontine Koens-Betz, Alexander Leslie, Amy McLaughlin, Matthias Odrobina, Matthew McSheaffrey, James Rusden, Christophe Schmit, Ayumi Ukita-Schneider, Rebecca Stadward, and Sally Wilks. Thank you in particular to the experts who shared with me their experience from M&A disputes in private arbitrations that would not have been accessible otherwise. I have ensured that any details remain confidential.

I have co-presented many of the topics in this book in numerous seminars and workshops to law firms, investment banks, private equity (PE) firms, and corporate

M&A departments. I have enjoyed these presentations tremendously and benefited from the experience of my co-presenters and the participants. The most frequent co-presenters were Gregor Klenk, Dr Martin Neuhaus, and Dr Harald Selzner, all of Latham & Watkins, and Dr Dirk Oberbracht of Gibson Dunn.

Thank you also to Peter Grindley (Berkeley Research Group) for comments on transactions economics of incomplete contracts, Rolf Brien (MITCAP Partners) for his insights into bidding processes, Roula Harfouche (Accuracy) and Adam Kramer (3 Verulam Buildings) for comments on the sections on damages valuation and breaches of warranties, Professor Siegfried H. Elsing (Orrick) for pointing me to relevant literature on damages, Olaf W. John (Insight Investment) for detailed comments on the discussion of pensions, Professor Jennifer Chapman of the Haas School of Business (UC Berkeley) for pointing me to behavioural research into decision-making, Thomas Pfeiffer (Berkeley Research Group) for detailed comments on the sections on derivative securities and damages valuation, Professor Gerhard Wächter for comments on capital structure questions in disputes, Sarah Keeling (Berkeley Research Group) for comments on risks in emerging market transactions, Michael Betten (Transmed) for comments on economic aspects of transactions, Lou Tricarico (Macquarie) for helpful hints on factoring and reverse factoring, Markus Schneider (Grant Thornton) for input on derivative securities, Gregor Klenk (Latham & Watkins) and his colleagues for sharing their experiences with completion accounts processes, Dr Dirk Oberbracht (Gibson Dunn) for input on indemnities and damages valuation clauses in SPAs, Noah Ojetola (Berkeley Research Group) for comments on the section on taxes in damages valuation and Professor Stephen Penman of Columbia Business School (Columbia University) for comments on damages valuation and for writing *Financial Statement Analysis and Security Valuation*. Experiencing the generosity with which these busy professionals and academics shared their time and knowledge has been among the most rewarding aspects of writing this book. Again, all mistakes that remain are mine alone.

I'd also like to thank the team at Wolters Kluwer for their guidance and encouragement, especially Eleanor Taylor, Monique Sasson, Claire Chouzenoux, Iris L. Montesa, and the team at Newgen, including Kavya Shekar, Sudha Elangovan, R. Srinivasan and Rohini Murugesan, for guiding me through the publication process.

Most of all, I am grateful to my wife Alba Lucia for her love, support and encouragement. This book is dedicated to her and our daughters Laura and Sara.

CHAPTER 1
Introduction

§1.01 BACKGROUND AND PURPOSE OF THIS PUBLICATION

In the course of an M&A transaction, the key protagonists, be they the principals or their advisers, deal with a myriad of complex matters. They often have to make decisions against the backdrop of an unrealistic deadline, imperfect (despite, often, voluminous) information, and a shrewd other side. In making these decisions, they have to deal with complex technical issues spanning a variety of specialist fields of knowledge such as: accounting, law, taxation, corporate finance, banking, operations, environmental, and strategy. This can make decision-making tricky, and it is easy in these circumstances to create outcomes that are open to disagreement and that end up in legal disputes. The extent to which such outcomes relate to financial and accounting matters is the principal focus of this book.

Research by economists and practitioners working in the field of mergers and acquisitions (M&A) shows that a high number of deals fail.[1] The causes cited for such failure are varied: a lack of strategic fit, poorly executed integration, clash of cultures, insufficient understanding of the target company's market, to name a few. A post-M&A dispute is another factor often associated with a failed transaction: At best, it can take the gloss off a deal. At worst, it can threaten the viability of the acquirer's own business as well as that of the acquired company.

It is difficult to think of another corporate activity that wastes as much management time and costs as much money without furthering - and often, hindering - the core operating activities of the enterprise as a post-deal dispute. Disputes can take years to resolve and cost many millions of pounds, euros, or dollars. In short, they should be avoided.

1. For an overview, *see* Ioannis C. Thanos and Vassilis M. Papadakis, *Unbundling Acquisition Performance*, in David Faulkner, Satu Teerikangas, Richard J. Joseph (eds) *The Handbook of Mergers & Acquisition*, 121 (Oxford University Press, 2014).

It is not always possible in the highly charged circumstances of a deal to find the time to contemplate, much less debate, issues from a theoretical point of view, to think through a problem conceptually, to go back to basics. In this publication, it has been tried to link practical matters back to corporate finance theory and accounting conventions, to provide a grounding in these disciplines that underlie most transactions.

Understanding why disputes happen starts with the conceptual framework of the 'deal mechanics' – a term used here to embrace the completion mechanism (*see* §1.03 below) – and their interface with the valuation of the target company, the acquisition structure, and the sale and purchase agreement (SPA). Beyond this conceptual framework, the book draws on a large number of actual post-M&A disputes cases to identify precisely where things go wrong. Lessons learned from past disputes can help identify situations which might otherwise lead to their being repeated; they can also be instructive, where a dispute has already arisen, in forming a view as how to resolve it.

The principal focus of this publication is on financial and accounting matters in the context of M&A. It should be emphasised that it is not the intention to prompt a discussion of accounting issues outside this context; these are covered exhaustively elsewhere. Further, this is not a legal textbook. When legal questions are discussed, it is only to provide context and explain relevant financial or accounting aspects of completion mechanisms and their related disputes.

The book is aimed at M&A practitioners, be they corporate M&A departments, PE, sovereign wealth funds or other players, as well as the investment bankers, lawyers, accountants and other professionals who advise them. It is also intended for those who deal with post-M&A disputes: judges, arbitrators, and litigators. Whether they possess extensive or relatively little experience in the field, these busy people would find the discussion here of benefit to them.

§1.02 WHAT GOES WRONG?

The circumstances that lead to disputes often happen at the intersection of different professional disciplines. Take accounting. Much in accounting relies on professional judgment, both of the accountant and others. For example, accounting for a long-term construction project may require a technical (engineering) estimate as to the degree of completion. The estimate may affect reported earnings and working capital. These reported earnings, in turn, can be the basis of a buyer's valuation. If a buyer uses a market approach and an earnings multiple of, say, ten, a dollar increase in earnings (if considered recurring and cash-relevant) may increase the valuation of the enterprise by a similar multiple (all else being equal). The very same estimate may affect the working capital figure at closing and lead to a dollar-for-dollar purchase price adjustment. Much can go wrong here: Estimates of the degree of completion can be overly aggressive, earnings inflated, working capital overstated. The buyer overpays, possibly even more than once: The effect of the same overstated degree of completion may be included in both earnings and working capital at closing (*see* §9.03 [B]). Different professionals would have been involved in reviewing the technical estimates from those analysing the accounting, and again from those valuing the target or drafting the SPA. The exchange of information across disciplines is not always straightforward.

The occurrence of an unexpected event around closing is another important contributing factor to M&A-related disputes. This could be the disruption to a customer relationship, volatility in supplier or financial markets or changes to regulations. Examples include turmoil in the credit markets during the financial crisis that contributed to the dispute discussed in §4.04 [C], rapidly falling prices in the markets for ships (§3.04 [A]), a cyberattack (§1.05 [B]), the discovery of fraud (§10.01), amounts owed to suppliers that come to light unexpectedly after closing (§12.01), the discovery of an accounting error in the historical accounts (§3.04 [B]), unforeseen regulatory decisions (§8.03 [A] [2]), or the default of an important counterparty, to name a few.

The effect of a disruptive event can be exacerbated when it meets with ambiguous wording or vague measurement concepts in the SPA (§12.04 [D]). The combination provides a fertile feeding ground for those seeking to disagree over the determination of a purchase price adjustment (§4.04 [C] [5]), the basis of an earn-out (§8.03 [A] [1]), who an exclusivity agreement relates to (§1.05 [A]), whether a material adverse event has occurred (§1.05 [B]), or the value of shares when there is a call or put option on an ownership interest to be acquired later.[2] There is often a trade-off between, on the one hand, getting the deal done while accepting some ambiguity (which can be constructive in negotiations, (*see* §13.02 [A]), and on the other resolving difficult technical matters satisfactorily and investing enough time to ensure the wording and concepts are as clear as possible.

A response sometimes heard when particularly complex topics arise in the course of a transaction is the claim that such issues do not really matter in the context of the deal. Comments such as 'at the end of the day, there is only one purchase price and it doesn't matter how you get there', or an almost exclusive focus on 'the big picture' are not uncommon. Those who raise legitimate concerns are sometimes branded 'deal killers'. While one should not lose sight of the big picture, many disputes arise not necessarily out of 'big picture' problems, but because the parties got the technical minutiae wrong. A successful transaction can be forgiving. However, when things start going wrong, and one party starts looking – usually with more time than was available when the deal was negotiated – technical oversights and errors very often come to light. Marry in haste, litigate at leisure, to paraphrase.

Having said that, it is important to be sufficiently pragmatic to acknowledge that, however perfect the deal mechanics, some transactions cannot be saved. Factors such as the unequal balance of power between buyer and seller and behavioural biases, or a cultural mismatch can play a significant role. Even deals acclaimed as a marriage made in heaven end, sadly, in tears and, sometimes, divorce. Those are for others – perhaps behavioural economists – to analyse.

2. *Cavendish Square Holdings BV v. Makdessi* [2015] UKSC 67.

§1.03 DEFINITIONS AND COMMONLY USED TERMS

Throughout this publication the term '**deal mechanics**' is used to refer to a range of completion mechanisms, completion accounts, purchase price adjustments, and locked box arrangements. For the sake of clarity, these terms are defined below:

- Completion mechanism: a transaction procedure involving completion accounts and purchase price adjustments or alternatively a locked box.
- Completion accounts (or 'closing date accounts'): the accounts drawn up as at the completion date, by either purchaser or seller, in accordance with the provisions of the SPA, in order to establish, under the terms of the SPA, the purchase price adjustments to be made to the preliminary (or provisional) purchase price agreed by the parties.
- Purchase price adjustments: the adjustments to the preliminary purchase price to reflect the actual values in respect of, most commonly, net debt and working capital and, in some transactions, certain other defined items and which, added to or deducted from the preliminary purchase price, represent the final purchase price and from which equity value is derived.
- Locked box: the arrangement whereby the parties to a transaction agree on a fixed price with no subsequent adjustments, based on a balance sheet date before signing. The date is often that of the last audited financial statements. This avoids the necessity to prepare completion accounts. The purchase price is fixed on the basis of that historical balance sheet date and reflects, *inter alia*, the levels of cash, debt, and working capital at that date. Locked box transactions are economically, though not legally, backdated transactions.

§1.04 CASES

The cases referred to in this book have two sources:

- A proprietary data set of over sixty cases with over 1,000 individual claims. These are primarily international arbitration cases which the author and his colleagues have worked on over the last fifteen years. Given the confidentiality of these cases, they have not provided any specific information on any actual case. In all instances names and details have been changed in order to maintain confidentiality.
- Cases in the public domain which the author references as appropriate.

It should also be pointed out that the discussion of the cases in this book, which come from a variety of different legal jurisdictions, relate to financial and accounting questions, not points of law.

§1.05 TYPES OF M&A DISPUTES

An M&A-related dispute is defined here as any dispute, whether litigated, arbitrated, mediated, or prosecuted, arising from the sale of one business, or part of one business, to another or a merger of two businesses.

M&A transactions are often long processes, and disputes arise at different stages. Most M&A-related disputes occur after closing. However, this is not necessarily the case as shown in Figure 1.1.

Figure 1.1 Transaction Timeline

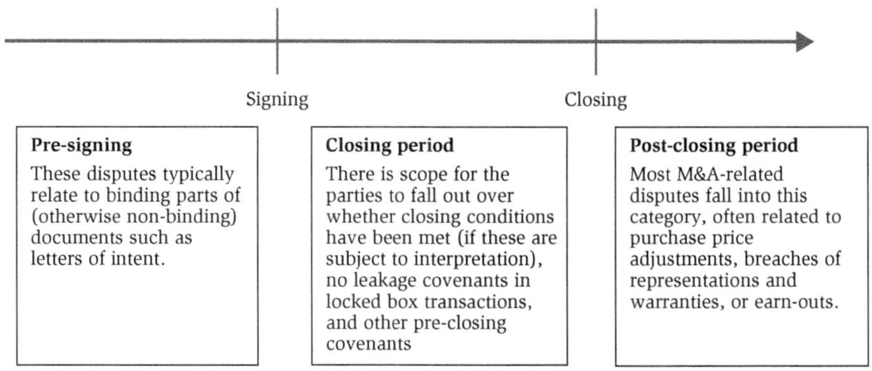

[A] Pre-signing

A typical pre-signing dispute relates to letters of intent, exclusivity, confidentiality agreements, or break-up fees. The example below is a dispute about an exclusivity agreement that is part of an otherwise non-binding indicative offer. An exclusivity agreement is an agreement used in M&A transactions to ensure that the counterparty deals only with a single, named party for a certain period.

Example of a Pre-signing Dispute over Exclusivity Agreement (United States Court of Appeal for the 1st Circuit)[3]

Gemini v. AmeriPark is a US case that relates to an exclusivity agreement entered into by buyout firm Gemini to finance the proposed acquisition by AmeriPark of MileHi, a competitor. AmeriPark and Gemini executed an 'Outline of Key Transaction Terms', which specified the terms of the proposed financing. While the rest of this term sheet was expressly non-binding, the paragraphs entitled 'Exclusivity' and 'Confidentiality' were binding. The exclusivity provision in the term sheet mirrored that in a separate arrangement between MileHi and AmeriPark. The part of the exclusivity agreement relevant here included the following wording:

3. United States Court of Appeal for the 1st Circuit, *Gemini Investors Inc.–v. Ameripark Inc.* 2011.

AmeriPark 'agrees not to discuss this opportunity or reach any agreement with *any person or entity* regarding financing for this Transaction or the pursuit of any sale or major other financing'[4] for a certain period.

The term sheet contemplated a recapitalisation of AmeriPark and a redemption of the shares of Greenfield Partners LLC, a large shareholder in AmeriPark. AmeriPark therefore required Greenfield's approval for the proposed financing.

As work on the MileHi acquisition progressed, AmeriPark management began to distrust Gemini and, before the exclusivity period expired, asked its shareholder Greenfield whether Greenfield would be interested in financing the MileHi acquisition instead of the Gemini-led financing. Also during this period, AmeriPark management approached the CEO and sole shareholder of MileHi, the acquisition target, about the possibility of seller financing. After some negotiation, the CEO and shareholder of AmeriPark agreed to finance the acquisition, and AmeriPark purchased MileHi using seller financing. Gemini had been dropped from the deal.

Gemini sued AmeriPark for breach of the exclusivity provision by pursuing financing for the MileHi acquisition from both Greenfield and the MileHi shareholder. At trial, the parties had differing views about the meaning of the exclusivity provision in the term sheet. AmeriPark argued that the phrase 'any person or entity' referred to the persons or entities expressly set forth elsewhere in the term sheet – investment banks, PE funds, etc. As the funding did not come from any of those sources, AmeriPark argued that it was not in breach.[5] Gemini's counter-argument was that the exclusivity provision was unambiguous and prohibited discussions with 'any person or entity' which included Greenfield and the shareholder.

Gemini lost in a jury trial in Federal court. The court concluded that the exclusivity provision was ambiguous (which an appeals court confirmed). Further, the court considered that the discussions with Greenfield about the Gemini financing were necessary in the context of a redemption of the Greenfield stake.

It was pointed out by attorneys Kirkland & Ellis that if the court's logic is extended, a PE sponsor 'obtaining a broadly-worded exclusivity at the end of an auction nevertheless would be exposed to being displaced, during the exclusivity period, by a management buyout or a transaction led by a significant target shareholder. Equally, a lender which bargains for exclusivity to finance an acquisition would be at risk of being dislodged by the target's or buyer's existing lender whose consent may be required'.[6] It can be important to consider carefully when drafting exclusivity agreements how to specify the parties to whom exclusivity shall apply.

[B] Closing Period

Signing and closing typically do not occur on the same day as there are usually conditions to be met prior to closing. The purpose of closing conditions is to ensure that

4. *Ibid.*, emphasis added.
5. *Ibid.*
6. 'Exclusivity' – Not as Preclusive as It Sounds?, Kirkland & Ellis LLP, Kirkland M&A update, 19 Jul. 2011.

legal and other requirements have been satisfied, and that, when control is transferred to the buyer, the business is the one that the buyer contracted to buy. Closing conditions may include regulatory approvals, financing, third-party and shareholder consent, bring down of representations and warranties, the retention of key employees, or the non-occurrence of a material adverse change (MAC) since an agreed date, just to name a few.

There is scope for the parties to fall out over whether closing conditions have been met or over breaches of pre-closing covenants if these are subject to differing interpretations.

An example of a closing condition that can lead to disagreement is the MAC clause.[7] The purpose of a MAC clause (if a closing condition) is to protect the buyer by avoiding that a deal closes if a materially adverse change has occurred. There are different types of MAC clauses. A 'Company MAC' is tested relative to the target company. It references material adverse changes in the target company, such as a reduction in sales or EBITDA by a certain percentage. A 'Market MAC' references changes in the overall market situation. A MAC clause in an SPA may be aligned with that in an acquisition debt financing agreement (especially in PE transactions), the idea being that, in the event the senior lender considers an adverse change to be a MAC event and debt financing is not available, the buyer can avoid closing.[8]

A key element of a MAC clause is the definition of what changes or events are 'material'. A MAC clause may specify specific changes or events or include only general wording (often in combination with carve-out clauses that exclude certain events). Buyers will prefer broad MAC clauses. A broad MAC clause, however, increases the scope for disagreement.

The bar to establishing a material adverse event is generally high, and most MACs do not lead to the transaction not closing. For example, Delaware courts had never allowed a MAC clause to invalidate a deal until *Akorn, Inc. v. Fresenius Kabi* (C.A. No. 2018-0300-JTL (Del. Ch. Oct. 1, 2018)) in which a combination of multiple serious misrepresentations and a sustained and substantial decline in financial performance of Akorn's business led to the court's conclusion that a material adverse event had occurred (Akorn is appealing). After signing, Akorn had announced year-over-year declines in quarterly revenues and earnings per share of 29% and 96%, respectively, followed by even greater declines in subsequent periods.

In almost all other cases, rather than leading to a transaction not closing, alleged MACs create leverage for renegotiating the price to avoid or settle a legal challenge. This is what happened in the acquisition of Yahoo by Verizon.

Example: MAC Clause in the Acquisition of Yahoo by Verizon

In Verizon's acquisition of Yahoo for USD 4.8 billion in July 2016, the SPA included a MAC clause; the MAC event was defined as one that would 'reasonably be expected to

7. MAC clauses are often closing conditions, but can also be representations (or both).
8. Even if very similar or identical wording is used, however, there can be a disconnect between the two MAC clauses. For example, cases may be heard in different courts.

have a material adverse effect on the business, assets, properties, results of operation or financial condition of the business, taken as a whole'.[9]

After signing, Yahoo disclosed that it had become aware of two cyber-attacks dating to 2013 and 2014 that compromised more than one billion of its customer accounts. The disclosures sent the parties back to talks, and Verizon renegotiated a reduction in the purchase price by USD 350 million. Reuters cited federal filings that Verizon's CEO initially proposed a discount as high as USD 925 million.[10] The question underlying this is how to value a compromised customer account.

Spelling out terms of a MAC may especially make sense in a volatile industry like technology. On the other hand, an ambiguous MAC clause that creates uncertainty over whether a MAC event has occurred may be preferable to a buyer who is then in a better position to renegotiate the price.

[C] Post-closing

Most of the cases in this book fall into this category. Post-closing disputes, other than those related to earn-outs, are usually initiated soon after closing. The trigger is often an unexpected additional liquidity need of the target business. This may be unexpected because a liability was not accounted for or a contingent liability not disclosed. This, in turn, then leads to a forensic review and, ultimately, a legal dispute may follow. It is fair to say that, in the absence of a trigger event such as this, many warranty breaches and other potential causes of post-M&A disputes go unnoticed.

9. See 'How Yahoo's Data Breach Could Affect Its Deal With Verizon', *The New York Times*, 23 Sep. 2016.
10. Verizon sought USD 925 million discount for Yahoo merger, got USD 350 million, Reuters Business News, 13 March 2017, available at: https://www.reuters.com/article/us-yahoo-m-a-verizon-idUSKBN16K2ID.

CHAPTER 2

The Value of the Firm, Capital Structure, and the Completion Mechanism

§2.01 OVERVIEW

[A] The Value of the Firm and Capital Structure

A firm engages in operating, investing, and financing activities. It does so with the intention of generating value and providing a return to investors who have acquired claims on the firm for the distribution of future surpluses. The two principal types of investors are the shareholders and the debtholders, their claims being on the firm's equity and debt, respectively.[11] These claims may be tradeable in the capital markets (such as shares on a stock exchange) or not tradeable (such as many partnership interests).

In a perfect market and in the absence of taxes, the value of the firm is independent of how the claims on it are divided among the different investors.[12] The capital structure itself is irrelevant: the present value of two potentially uncertain income streams equals the sum of their separate present values.[13] However apportioned between the respective claimants (shareholders and debtholders), the value of the firm does not change.

The relationship between firm value and the value of the claims on the firm may be set out as follows:

$$\text{Value of the firm} = \text{Value of debt} + \text{Value of equity}$$

11. There are other claims, but these two are sufficient for the purpose of this analysis.
12. Franco Modigliani and Merton Miller (Modigliani-Miller's Proposition I), *The Cost of Capital, Corporation Finance and the Theory of Investment*, American Economic Review June 1958, Vol. 48, No. 3, 261–297.
13. This is called the 'Law of the Conservation of Investment Value' by John Burr Williams, *Theory of Investment Value*, North-Holland Pub. Co., 1956. John Burr Williams preceded Modigliani-Miller. *See* Rubinstein, *A History of the Theory of Investments*, Wiley, 2006, 128.

In a transaction, the value of the firm is commonly referred to as 'enterprise value', but also as the 'headline price' (often in the letters of intent issued in the early stage of a deal), the 'value of the operations', or the 'cash and debt free price'.

[B] The Equity Value Bridge

In a share deal, the buyer and seller ultimately have to agree on the price for the equity. While a number of valuation approaches are available, the starting point for valuation in most (though not all) transactions is enterprise value, to which adjustments are made for debt and debt-like items and for cash and cash equivalents in order to arrive at a value for the equity. In practice, cash and debt-like items are usually combined under one heading, 'net debt'.

This is depicted in Figure 2.1 in a simple version of what is known as the equity value bridge:

Figure 2.1 Equity Value Bridge

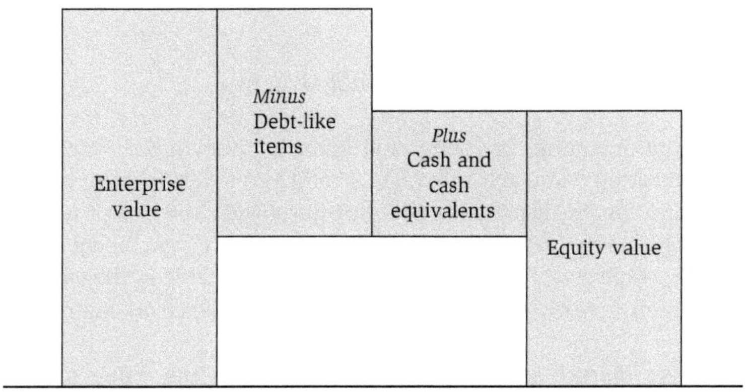

Enterprise value is typically measured by discounting free cash flows or using a multiple-based method, such as a multiple of Earnings before Interest and Taxes (EBIT) or Earnings before Interest, Taxes, Depreciation and Amortisation (EBITDA). (Some valuation approaches value the equity – for example, the dividend discount model and the discounted net abnormal earnings models – however these are less common in practice.) Common approaches to valuation are discussed in Chapter 11.

Enterprise value encompasses all the operating assets and liabilities necessary to carry on the business. It assumes, critically for transactions, an appropriate, or normal, level of working capital at the date on which closing takes place (or other relevant date). The level has to be agreed between the parties. The value they agree is commonly referred to as the 'reference values' with any variances from this being reflected in an adjustment. Enterprise value also assumes that capital and revenue expenditure have been maintained at appropriate levels and that the business is not 'underinvested'. What level of investment is considered 'appropriate' is a matter for negotiation between the parties.

Hence, as well as an adjustment in respect of net debt, the final purchase price in a transaction will typically also incorporate adjustments in respect of working capital and, less frequently, capital and revenue expenditure. These are collectively referred to as purchase price adjustments. They are discussed in outline later in this section and in depth in Chapters 4, 5 and 6.

To the layman purchase price adjustments may seem quite straightforward. However, even in a relatively uncomplicated transaction, an inordinate amount of time can be expended, particularly by the accountants and lawyers acting for each side, in rehearsing the various arguments as to whether an item should or should not be treated as an adjustment and how it should be measured.

[C] The Uncertainty Inherent in a Transaction

Ultimately, the buyer and seller have to reach agreement on the items to be treated as purchase price adjustments, namely: what items are to be treated as an adjustment, how they are to be defined and measured, and the process for doing this. All this - or at least a detailed mechanism to this end - needs to be formulated clearly in the SPA. One of the difficulties, however, is in knowing precisely what assets and liabilities will be in the balance sheet when the deal closes. A business is not static, it (and its balance sheet) changes every day: sales are made, inventory levels rise and fall, creditor accounts are settled, capital expenditure is incurred, and so on. The latest independently verified figures available to the purchaser are probably the audited financial statements prepared at the previous year end. For more up-to-date figures he or she will rely on information obtained during the course of the due diligence. Inevitably there is an element of uncertainty (in some transactions anxiety) in the mind of the buyer as to what assets and liabilities he will get when ownership transfers. This concern may become heightened once the SPA is signed: there is generally no going back.

[D] The Transaction Timeline

As indicated above, there are usually conditions to be met prior to closing, and it can take some time before these are fulfilled. A typical timeline for a transaction where signing and closing occur on different dates is shown in Figure 2.2.

Figure 2.2 Transaction Timeline

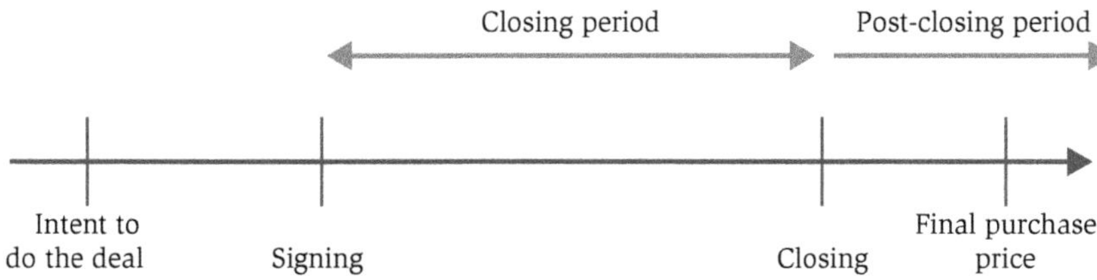

Examples of closing conditions include governmental or regulatory approvals, transaction financing, third-party and shareholder consent, bring down of representations and warranties, the retention of key employees, and the non-occurrence of material adverse changes. Closing periods can range from a few weeks to several months and can be significantly longer, for example, in regulated industries or where antitrust issues are involved.

The existence of this interval between signing and closing, which can be difficult to predict accurately, gives rise to further uncertainty as to the precise assets and liabilities to be transferred at closing. Clearly, the longer the closing period, the greater the uncertainty; however, even in a relatively short closing period, significant changes can occur.

[E] The Purpose of the Completion Mechanism

The purpose of a completion mechanism is to set out a clear and unambiguous process which will ensure that the parties to the SPA obtain what they bargained for. Ironically, many post-M&A disputes originate from disagreements over the very mechanisms that were put in place precisely for this purpose. A sound completion mechanism should ensure that both buyer and seller get what they understood they negotiated, resulting in a 'clean' transaction.

More often than not, the main concern (at least up to completion) is on the part of the buyer. The buyer will seek to incorporate into the SPA measures to safeguard his or her interests, including for the period from signing to completion, during which the target business remains under the stewardship of the seller. This is not limited to financial and accounting matters; the buyer will usually be protected by covenants concerning the operation of the business during the closing period.

One of the buyer's principal worries here is that the seller could 'extract value', or that value could 'leak', between signing and closing, and that this is not reflected in the final purchase price, resulting in the buyer taking over a business worth less than what it believed it was getting.

If the SPA does not contain a completion mechanism that adjusts the purchase price or prevents value leakage, then there are a number of ways in which a seller could potentially extract value. These include:

- dividend payments;
- adjusting transfer prices used in transactions between related parties;
- inter-company charges;
- management compensation;
- advisory fees;
- waiving liabilities.

Value leakage is discussed further in §7.03.

Leaving aside the possibility of a seller's less than honourable intentions, it is sensible for both parties to protect themselves from being disadvantaged as a result of movements in the balance sheet in the period up to closing. While the buyer's concerns probably outweigh those of the seller during that time, the boot is rather more on the other foot when it comes to the preparation of completion accounts, as shall be seen later.

Traditionally the solution to the problems outlined above has been to prepare a set of completion accounts. These incorporate the various purchase price adjustments, computed on the basis agreed by the parties and documented in the SPA, and result in the establishment of the final purchase price.

However, an alternative approach has emerged in the early 2000s, namely the 'locked box'. In this scenario, the parties agree on a fixed price in the SPA with no subsequent purchase price adjustments.

Figures 2.3 to 2.5 show the two principal completion mechanisms that are available in a private M&A transaction, the purchase price adjustment and the locked box, as well as a combination of the two, a hybrid completion mechanism. Each option is discussed further below.

Figure 2.3 Purchase Price Adjustments

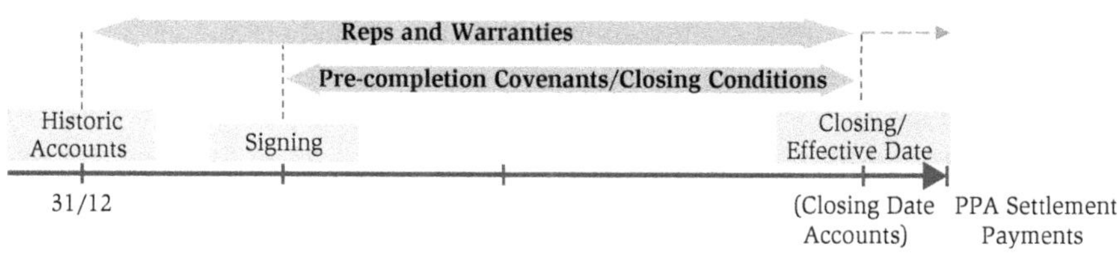

Figure 2.4 The Locked Box

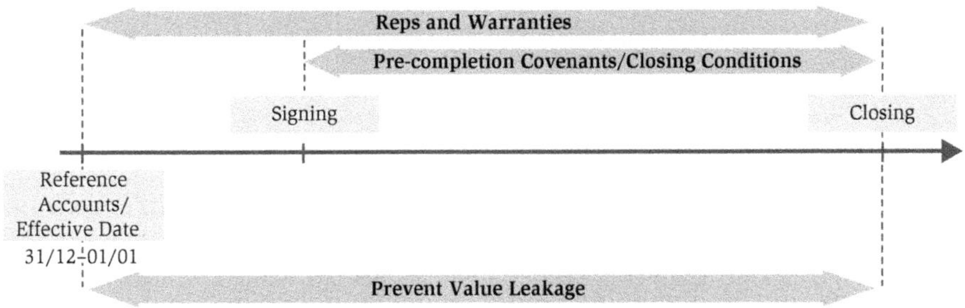

Figure 2.5 Hybrid Completion Mechanism

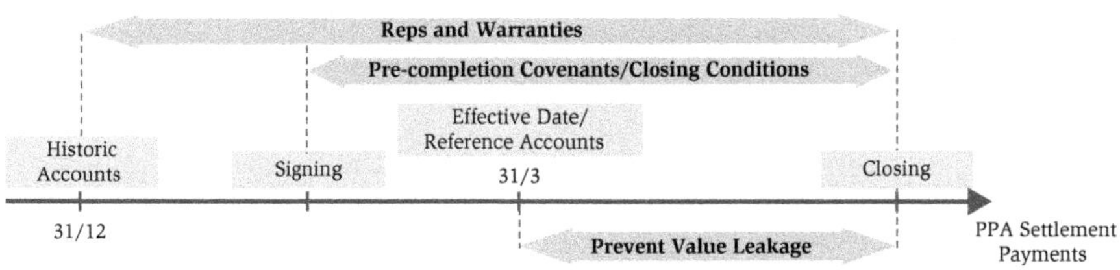

[F] Relevance of Items Leading to Purchase Price Adjustments in a Locked Box Transaction

The purpose of a locked box mechanism is to eliminate adjustments to the purchase price subsequent to closing by computing an equity value based on a historical balance sheet, i.e., *prior to* the closing date. The agreed equity value is a fixed purchase price that is not subject to any post-closing adjustments. It is a final price.

The term 'purchase price adjustments' typically refers to adjustments made to the preliminary purchase price following the completion accounts process. It should be noted that similar adjustments are made, or should be made, in agreeing the fixed purchase price in locked box transactions, only they are incorporated into the fixed purchase price.

The use of the term 'purchase price adjustments' here is therefore generic: it refers to transactions involving completion accounts as well as to those made in agreeing the fixed purchase price with a locked box mechanism.

Example of Enterprise Value, Equity Value, and Double Counting (German courts)[14]

14. BGH, 8 Sep. 2004 – XII ZR 194/01, NJW-RR 2005, 153, OLG Koblenz, 13 Jul. 2001 – UF 248/00, OLGR Koblenz 2002, 152, (simplified here). *See also* a discussion in: Wächter, M&A Litigation, 3rd Edition 2017, RWS Verlag Kommunikationsforum GmbH, p. 665.

The case shows that the interaction between the individual elements of the equity bridge in Figure 2.1 can lead to confusion and double counting. This is a divorce case, and the aspects of interest here concern the valuation of the husband's business, a machinery, and equipment maker. The owner's wife was entitled to one-half of the value of the husband's increase in net assets over the duration of the marriage. The dispute was over the valuation of the increase in the value of the shares in the business which were part of the husband's net assets.

The balance sheet of the husband's company is shown in Table 2.1.

Table 2.1 Balance Sheet as of 31 December 1995

	EUR Thousand
Manufacturing facility (building)	132
Other assets	54
Total liabilities	-492
Net assets	-306

On 31 December 1995, the company reported negative net assets of EUR 306,000. According to a property expert, the fair value of the manufacturing facility (with a book value of EUR 132,000) amounted to EUR 319,000.

An expert valued the business at EUR 260,000 (enterprise value). The expert then deducted the negative net assets, arguing that a buyer of the business would be willing to pay a positive amount only if the net asset value was not negative. On this basis he determined the equity value to be -EUR 46,000 (=260,000-306,000). Note that this figure included the same net operating assets - in particular, the facility - twice: in enterprise value and in the deduction of the book value of net assets. However, possibly because this was a negative number, the judge at first instance decided to add to the equity value the fair value of the manufacturing facility of EUR 319,000. The value of the shares was thus determined as -EUR 46,000 + EUR 319,000 = EUR 273,000. By adding the fair value of the facility, this value now included the manufacturing facility three times, with three different values:

- book value of EUR 132,000;
- the value included in the enterprise value of EUR 260,000;
- property value of EUR 319,000.

The first Court of Appeals[15] decided to eliminate the book value of the facility from the negative net assets which is calculated as -EUR 306,000 - EUR 132,000 = -EUR 438,000. It determined that the equity value amounted to EUR 260,000 (EV) - EUR 438,000 = -EUR 178,000. The court then added the fair value of the manufacturing facility of EUR 319,000 to obtain EUR 141,000. As the book value of the facility had been removed, this valuation of EUR 141,000 included the facility two times.

15. OLGR Koblenz 2002, 152 - FamRZ 2002, 1190.

The German Federal Court of Justice (BGH) sent the case back to the lower court instructing the court to review whether the manufacturing facility was a necessary part of the operations. This suggests that the value of the facility could only be added if it was determined that it was not part of normal operations. It is not known how the lower court ruled.[16]

§2.02 PURCHASE PRICE ADJUSTMENTS: OVERVIEW

[A] Introduction

As discussed above, purchase price adjustments represent adjustments between enterprise value (a debt and cash-free basis with a normal level of working capital and investments in fixed assets) and equity value (after the deduction of net debt at closing).

In a 'traditional' transaction involving a completion accounts process, purchase price adjustments are made to a preliminary purchase price by measuring (subsequent to completion) the relevant balance sheet at the closing date. In a locked box transaction, such adjustments are made to a historical balance sheet, i.e., at a date prior to closing. Purchase price adjustments are summarised in Table 2.2.

Table 2.2 Purchase Price Adjustments

Adjustment	*Purpose*
Net debt	To arrive at a debt-free, cash-free valuation
Working capital*	Primarily protects buyer against a seller reducing working capital to decrease net debt
Capital expenditure*	Protects buyer against a seller slowing down capital expenditure to decrease net debt
Revenue expenditure*	Used, notably, in businesses where certain revenue expenditure, e.g., marketing, research and development, are key metrics. Protects buyer against a seller cutting expenditure to reduce net debt
Net assets/equity	Typically used instead of – sometimes as a 'floor' in addition to – a net debt adjustment. Far less prevalent in recent years
Enterprise value	Used in relatively rare cases where there is unusual uncertainty over enterprise value

*Used in combination with net debt adjustment.

Each of these adjustments is discussed briefly below. More detailed analysis, together with examples of disputes, is included in later chapters.

16. BGH 8 Sep. 2004 – XII ZR 194/01, NJW-RR 2005, p. 155.

Earn-outs should not be confused with purchase price adjustments which have a different purpose from addressing changes in the closing period. Earn-outs are deferred compensation, whereas purchase price adjustments are not deferred, only calculated at closing. Earn-outs are discussed in Chapter 8.

[B] Net Debt Adjustment

The net debt adjustment results in a valuation on a 'cash-free, debt-free' basis. Thus the buyer is compensated for the level of debt taken over at closing; similarly, the seller is compensated for any surplus cash (free cash) in the business at closing.

[C] Working Capital Adjustment

Since variations in cash and debt are, in part, directly attributable to changes in the level of working capital, a net debt adjustment typically requires a corresponding adjustment in respect of (net) working capital. Net working capital and net debt represent the most common combination of purchase price adjustments.

The basic purpose here is to protect the buyer from actions by the seller that maximise the cash - or minimise the net debt - position of the target business at closing by reducing net working capital. This is achieved as the buyer pays - on a dollar-for-dollar basis - for working capital in excess of a level that is agreed by both parties to be 'normal' (commonly referred to as the working capital 'reference value' or working capital 'target'). Correspondingly, the buyer receives a purchase price reduction for any shortfall against the reference value. If the completion mechanics work properly, every movement in net debt that has to do with working capital is offset by the working capital adjustment so that the net purchase price is unaffected.

[D] Capital Expenditure Adjustment

A seller may be motivated to slow down capital expenditure in order to maximise the cash position of the target business at closing. As a consequence, the buyer would obtain an 'underinvested' business with an artificially high cash position (which it would pay for as part of the net debt adjustment).

The rationale behind a capital expenditure adjustment is that it offsets this higher cash position by correcting for any shortfall in expenditure in the closing period compared with an agreed amount of aggregate capital expenditure (or reference level). The adjustment may be limited to a decrease in the purchase price, or go both ways and also increase the purchase price if capital expenditure is higher than the reference level. Adjustments in respect of expenditure incurred in excess of the agreed reference value are often subject to a ceiling in order to protect the buyer from expenditure it considers excessive. A capital expenditure adjustment also has the merit that it can be used in some cases to enable a buyer to exercise greater influence over what specific expenditure is incurred by the target business up to closing if specific expenditures are identified in the SPA.

[E] Revenue Expenditure Adjustment

Purchase price adjustments in connection with revenue expenditure feature relatively rarely in transactions. Similar to the working capital and capital expenditure adjustments, the rationale is to protect a buyer against a seller attempting to improve the target entity's net debt position. The difference is that revenue expenditure adjustments protect against other ways the net debt position could be influenced that are not already captured by either of those other adjustments. More common examples relate to marketing or research and development expenditure (against reference values) which is discretionary or can be delayed.

[F] Net Asset Adjustment

The net asset or equity adjustment (both terms are used interchangeably in this publication in the context of purchase price adjustments) calls for a price adjustment in respect of the difference between net assets and an agreed reference value at closing. A surplus over the reference value increases the purchase price; a deficit reduces it. The idea is to capture the net effect of changes between signing and closing in the book value of equity. This equates the change in commercial value of the equity, the owners' residual claim against the assets, with the change in book value.

Net asset adjustments used to be fairly widespread but have become rare in recent years.[17] This probably has to do with an increasingly sophisticated market that has exposed the problems associated with these adjustments.

One such problem is that many changes in the book values of assets have nothing to do with 'value' as understood in the context of a transaction and, consequently, should not lead to a purchase price adjustment. The book value of net assets is not the same as value transferred on closing. Consider a non-cash one-off write-down of goodwill or a change in accounting policies to capitalise internal costs (such as development expenditure). Both result in a change in net assets. Should a buyer, however, pay more (or less) because of these and other items that may have nothing to do with value[18]?

A practical problem has to do with the fact that, since equity represents total assets less total liabilities, it is impacted not only by how each *balance sheet* item is accounted for but also by accounting choices concerning the *income statement*. The SPA, therefore, must specify accounting rules not only for a limited number of net debt and working capital items, but for all balance sheet and income statement items. The SPA has, *inter alia*, to limit arbitrary accounting choices that underlie the determination of book values at closing; a simple reference to consistency or GAAP invariably

17. Transactions involving financial institutions, for which debt and net assets have a different significance from other firms, are an exception. For these, net asset adjustments are common.
18. One might argue that an impairment write down of goodwill reflects a change in expectations of the financial performance of an acquired business, and that this change can be of relevance to value. However, it is far from clear that this should lead to a dollar-for-dollar purchase price adjustment.

does not suffice. Further, the SPA has also to include a definition of normalised earnings in a manner that ensures that only components to which the parties agree should result in an adjustment to the price. In theory, this means the parties must be in a position to anticipate any and all items that could affect net income, so as to ensure they do not result in an adjustment; in a sense, they have to 'normalise' the net income of the closing period. In the author's experience, normalising unknown income - and expense - of a future period, is difficult, to say the least.

In practice, the more thoroughly the parties go about defining balance sheet items in the SPA to ensure that a net asset adjustment captures only those items that are relevant to value, the more closely those remaining will resemble net debt and working capital items. The result should, theoretically at least, be very similar: a mechanism that captures only items for which it is appropriate to have a dollar-for-dollar adjustment. The difference, however, is that the starting point for a net asset adjustment is *all* balance sheet captions, from which those not relevant to value have to be excluded, a process more complex (if done properly) than simply specifying a smaller population of items relevant for adjustment.

Due to these problems, net asset adjustments increase the scope for potential disagreements between the parties considerably.[19] Similar problems arise with warranties of net assets or minimum equity. Since net asset adjustments are rarely used today, they are considered here only in the context of specific disputes.

[G] Adjustments to Enterprise Value

The purpose of the purchase price adjustments outlined so far is either to derive an equity value from enterprise value or to take account of, say, a level of working capital at closing that does not correspond to underlying enterprise value assumptions. Occasionally a party to a transaction (usually the buyer) sees the need for a purchase price adjustment that changes what might be described as the 'intrinsic' enterprise value. This is rare for this kind of adjustment to be agreed to and almost never a good idea.

An enterprise value adjustment may be mooted when a valuation is based on the results of a period for which figures are considered critical to the valuation but are not yet available, for example when a financial year ends during the closing period (and is not, therefore, available at signing).

The problem with an adjustment to enterprise value is that it can make the final purchase price difficult to predict, and easy to disagree on, since minor changes to, say, EBITDA can translate into major changes to price (through the multiple). In one instance of this nature, the purchase price was subject to adjustment depending on the recalculation of the gross margins of certain contracts entered into by the target business prior to closing and its income for a defined period.[20]

19. For an example of an equity adjustment in a post-M&A disputes *see* ICC Case 11587 in the following section.
20. ICC Case 11587.

If a party is unable to come to a conclusion about the value of the business at the time the deal is signed, then the information it is waiting for arguably weighs too heavily in the valuation; as such, any adjustment overstates the importance of the information, which usually relates to a comparatively short period (relative to the many years of a going concern's future trading). Additional, apparently critical, information is still required to value the business. Conceivably, in these cases, signing is simply taking place too early.

[H] Acquisitions Carried Out in Steps

Some acquisitions are performed in steps whereby the buyer initially acquires less than 100% of the share capital (although often a majority interest) with an option to buy the balance of the shares in a subsequent step or series of steps.

In these cases, the purchase price adjustment should correspond to the percentage of the shares acquired in each step. It is usually necessary first to determine 100% of the purchase price adjustment and then to reduce it by the fraction not acquired. This generally applies to all types of purchase price adjustment. For example, if the initial acquisition is a 70% interest in the target entity, and a net working capital adjustment on a 100% basis is USD 10 million, then the purchase price adjustment at the time of the initial acquisition step is USD 7 million.

If the parties instead adjusted for 100% in a 70% acquisition, then the buyer would pay for the entire working capital surplus (in the example above), but would not be entitled to 100% of any future distributions from this excess working capital.

For subsequent steps in the acquisition process the parties should, theoretically, re-measure both the reference value and the working capital at the relevant date of these steps.

In practice, it may be unrealistic to renegotiate the working capital reference value or re-measure the working capital position in subsequent acquisition steps, especially when there are multiple steps involving only minor amounts. The parties may therefore agree at the outset fixed adjustments for all acquisition steps. In such cases the seller may consider protecting itself from any changes the buyer may effect to working capital after gaining control.

§2.03 THE LOCKED BOX: THE PRINCIPAL IDEA

The concept of the locked box first appeared in PE auctions in Europe in the early 2000s and has since come to be adopted in a wide range of transactions. It is a popular completion mechanism in Europe and the norm for many PE transactions. It continues to be less common in the US and Asian Pacific markets. [21] This has led to situations in the past in which US buyers who participated in an auction process in Europe were

21. A smarter way to get deals done, *International Survey: Identifying International Market Practice for Equity Value Adjustments and Sale and Purchase Agreements*, Grant Thornton, November 2017, p. 5.

asked to bid on a locked box basis with which they were unfamiliar. However, the use of the locked box is increasing in the US and Asia Pacific.[22]

The locked box is an alternative way of dealing with the uncertainties of the balance sheet at closing. The parties agree on a fixed price in the SPA with, usually, no subsequent adjustments. The fixed price is an equity price, calculated based on a balance sheet at a date before signing, frequently that of the last audited financial statements. This date is referred to as the 'effective date' or the 'locked box date'. The balance sheet at this date is the 'effective date balance sheet' or 'locked box balance sheet', and the period between the effective date and closing is the 'locked box period'. The purchase price is fixed on the basis of the effective date balance sheet and reflects the levels of cash, debt, and working capital at that date, after which the (acquisition target) 'box' is 'locked', so that no value may 'leak', other than in relation to matters specified in the SPA. There is no true-up at closing. The SPA has leakage protections.

The locked box has the following principal advantages:

- it is easier for a seller to assess bids in an auction process;
- it avoids the often time-consuming negotiations over defining in the SPA the bases of accounting to be applied to the completion accounts; and
- in addition, it avoids the actual preparation and review of the accounts and subsequent discussions, which result in (usually downwards) adjustments to the purchase price.

However, there are also potential downsides to a locked box approach. As the final purchase price is fixed and there is no true-up at closing, the due diligence on the reference date accounts is usually more important than in completion accounts processes where the buyer gets to review financial information as at closing. At the same time, strong sellers and competitive bidding processes - which make a locked box transaction more likely - tend to mean more restricted access to information during the due diligence phase.

Another disadvantage of locked boxes can be that the SPA naturally does not contain a collaborative resolution process similar to the completion accounts process for a purchase price adjustment (*see* Chapter 3). A collaborative resolution process provides the parties an opportunity to agree on a compromise before an independent expert makes a determination. Locked box SPA disputes, while less likely to occur, overall, are therefore more likely to head straight into litigation or arbitration.

Locked box agreements are economically, but not legally, backdated transactions. The retroactive transfer of economic interest means that the seller effectively manages the target company for the benefit of the buyer, and that profits generated by the target business between the effective dates and closing accrue to the purchaser. To compensate for this, the SPA usually specifies an interest rate (sometimes called a daily profit charge) to be applied to the fixed purchase price. The locked box interest charge is discussed in more detail in §7.04.

22. *Ibid.*

The locked box is often considered to be seller-friendly (even though there are circumstances in which it can be buyer-friendly).[23] This links its popularity to the relative strength and weakness of sellers and buyers during the M&A cycle: during cyclical peaks, in a seller's market, the locked box tends to be more popular than during downturns, when buyers are in stronger positions.

§2.04 HYBRID COMPLETION MECHANISMS

Some completion mechanisms incorporate aspects both of purchase price adjustments and the locked box. This happens, for example, when a fixed purchase price is agreed but there is nevertheless a reason or requirement to adjust for an item at closing (e.g., an intercompany balance), or when a purchase price adjustment is linked to a date when annual financial statements are prepared and closing takes place a few days later. This latter case might occur when, for example, closing is proposed in early January for a target business with a year end on 31 December, and the parties wish to use the year-end accounts as the basis for closing; this requires locked box type 'value leakage' protections for the period between 31 December and the closing date.[24]

23. For example in the rare case that the buyer knows the target management well.
24. Consider in this case that closing could occur before 31 December in which case it is the seller, not the buyer, who may require protecting itself against leakage.

CHAPTER 3

The Completion Accounts Process

§3.01 INTRODUCTION

While the transaction negotiations are in train, the subsequent preparation of completion accounts (alternatively called 'closing date accounts') can tend to be relegated to little more than a process not unlike the annual preparation of accounts for audit – a necessary but routine, indeed tedious formality, to be undertaken at a later date. The completion accounts process, up to final agreement between the parties, can be time-consuming, especially when it requires time to settle disagreements during which there continues to be uncertainty over the final purchase price. This is among the reasons for the growing use of the locked box transaction.

As the completion accounts are the basis of the purchase price adjustment and the calculation of the final purchase price, they have a central role in any transaction with a purchase price adjustment. This chapter covers the key aspects to consider in mitigating problems arising from completion accounts.

§3.02 OVERVIEW OF COMPLETION ACCOUNTS PROCESS

The arrangements for the preparation and finalisation of completion accounts are set out in the SPA and typically follow the process shown in Figure 3.1.

Figure 3.1 Completion Accounts Process Overview

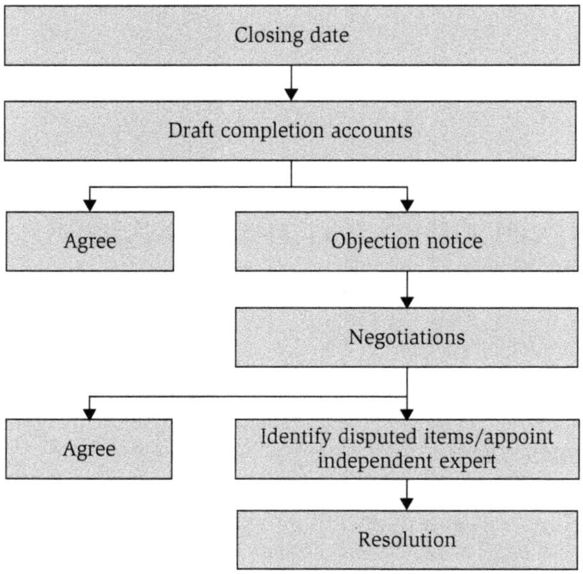

The completion accounts process starts when after closing one party (more often the buyer) prepares draft completion accounts and the resulting calculation of the purchase price. The SPA usually sets out a defined period during which the draft completion accounts must be delivered to the other party.[25] This period typically ranges somewhere between twenty business days from closing for a straightforward transaction to ninety days or more (often less in the minority of deals in which the seller prepares) for a complex transaction in which the preparation of the completion accounts requires the consolidation of single-entity accounts of (multiple, international) subsidiaries. An example of wording that may be used in SPAs is as follows:

> As soon as practicable, and in any event no later than thirty Business Days after the [Closing Date], the [Purchaser] shall procure that the Company prepares and delivers to the Seller, for its review, drafts of the Closing Accounts and the Final Purchase Price Statement drawn up in accordance with paragraph [].

Once the draft completion accounts and purchase price calculation have been delivered, the receiving party has the opportunity to review these. The review period is contractually predetermined and is usually shorter than the period for preparation of the completion accounts. If the reviewing party agrees with the draft accounts, then the final purchase price is determined on this basis, and the process is complete. If the

25. The SPA may specify interest for the period until the actual delivery or finalisation, which can be especially relevant in case the draft completion accounts are not delivered when required.

receiving party does not agree with all or part of the completion accounts, then the next step in the process is for the receiving party to prepare an objection notice (also called dispute notice or notice of disagreement) in which it details the areas of disagreement. Objection notices are written statements that can run into hundreds of pages when there are many areas of disagreement and many individual legal entity accounts on which the consolidated completion accounts are based.

The objection notice is followed by a period of negotiations - the resolution period - during which the parties attempt to reconcile their differences on the contentious items. The resolution period can be around fifteen business days for a straightforward completion process or significantly longer if more complex. The idea is that the parties negotiate in good faith to eliminate or narrow areas in dispute. If the parties reach agreement on all contentious points at the end of this period, then the final purchase price is determined and the process ends. If, on the other hand, they do not resolve all differences, then the disputed items are referred to an expert for determination of the final completion accounts and purchase price. The expert may be predetermined in the SPA, or the parties may agree in the SPA only the process by which the expert will be determined. If the parties agree to name a single expert in the SPA (a firm or an individual), they should ensure that the expert is not conflicted, and further consider that this can make the expert determination more expensive later on in the event it is required.

The SPA should set out, clearly and comprehensively, the mechanics for each step, including:

- Who prepares the accounts and in what time frame.
- The time available to the recipient for review and for arranging access to people involved in the preparation and to documents.
- The process for agreeing and not agreeing the accounts, including how objections are to be notified to the other side and the requisite time frame.
- The process for resolving disputes (again, with time frame).
- In the event of the parties failing to reach an agreement, the provisions for resolving any dispute(s) through the engagement of an independent third party, including how such a third party is to be selected, the nature of the role they are to play, and the extent of their involvement. This third-party process is often referred to as an 'expert determination'.[26]
- How the respective parties' costs are to be borne, including those of the independent experts.
- The deadline until which new information that comes to light can be considered. This is a point that is frequently not specified in which case it is easy to disagree over the use of hindsight.

An example of wording in the SPA for the review and objection process is as follows:

26. The expert determination is also sometimes referred to as 'arbitration'. However, in this book the term arbitration is used to mean a form of alternative dispute resolution after any expert determination.

No later than the last day of the Review Period, the Seller shall serve a written notice on the Purchaser stating whether or not it agrees with the Draft Documents. In the case of any disagreement, the notice (the 'Objection Notice') shall specify in reasonable detail each matter or item in dispute and, to the extent practicable, any adjustments which the Seller considers should be made to the Draft Documents.

During the Review Period, the Purchaser shall, upon reasonable notice and during normal business hours, allow the Seller (and its agents or advisers) to access and review the Company's working papers relating to the preparation of the Draft Documents and such books and records of the Company as the Seller (or its agents or advisers) may reasonably require for the purpose of reviewing the Draft Documents.

If, during the Review Period, the Seller:

(1) serves a written notice to the Purchaser confirming its agreement with the Draft Documents, they shall, with effect from the date of service of such notice, constitute the Closing Accounts and the Final Purchase Price Statement and shall be final and binding on the Parties; or
(2) fails to serve an Objection Notice, the Draft Documents shall, with effect from the expiry of the Review Period, constitute the Closing Accounts and the Final Purchase Price Statement and shall be final and binding on the Parties.

If the Seller serves an Objection Notice in accordance with paragraph [ ] of this Schedule, the Parties shall, during the period of fifteen Business Days commencing on the date of service of the Objection Notice (the 'Resolution Period'), seek in good faith to reach agreement on the disputed matters. If, before the Resolution Period expires, the disputed matters are:

(1) resolved by the Parties in writing, the Draft Documents (revised as necessary to reflect the Parties' agreement) shall constitute the Closing Accounts and the Final Purchase Price Statement, and shall be final and binding on the Parties with effect from the date of their agreement; or
(2) not resolved by the Parties in writing before the expiry of the Resolution Period, then the Parties shall require the disputed matters to be referred to the Expert for determination in accordance with paragraph [ ] of this Schedule.

§3.03 WHO PREPARES?

The issue of who prepares the completion accounts is not necessarily a given. In a majority of cases, the buyer is the natural choice as the buyer is in control of the business (including the accounting function) after closing. However, there can be a certain logic, usually put forward by the vendor, for their side preparing the accounts, on the grounds that their staff (at least up to completion) are familiar with the accounting policies and practices applied in the past. This logic may apply in particular to carve-out transactions where, prior to the transaction, accounting information was prepared by corporate headquarters. While the exception, in these situations there can be a reason for the vendor to prepare the completion accounts. In other situations, as the buyer will be unfamiliar with the target's accounting processes, it may be hesitant to enter into a potentially contentious process, under time pressure. In complex transactions, PE buyers may feel that they do not have the time or resources immediately after closing to prepare the completion accounts. However, these cases are exceptions, and it is more often the buyer who prepares.

In the course of most transactions staff will transfer from the ultimate employ of the seller to the buyer. Consequently, staff who in the past have prepared accounts for one party will be asked to do so for the other. Senior management should be aware of the concomitant sensitivities involved and should expect a shift in loyalty on the part of those individuals. The question of who prepares may therefore also involve considering the timing at which loyalties shift from seller to buyer.

There is a distinct 'first-mover' advantage to the preparer of the completion accounts. The party who prepares gets to bring its own evaluation of judgmental areas (e.g., allowances for doubtful debts or inventory) to the first draft of the accounts, and it is for the non-preparer to object (with an explanation of the basis for the objections). As in negotiations, the first explicit mention of a figure serves as an 'anchor' in the rest of the process, from which the other side needs to move away. In addition, the preparer is usually afforded more time to prepare the accounts than the non-preparer has to object. On the other hand, more time may mean more effort and cost involved in preparing which can be a disadvantage.

Another advantage to a buyer who prepares is that it helps ensure that the seller is kept out of business after closing to a greater extent than if the seller prepares.

The right to prepare can therefore be an important tactical advantage, and the question of who prepares can be a negotiating point when the SPA is drafted.

A disadvantage of preparing the completion accounts may be the difficulty of knowing or anticipating what approach the other side will adopt during the completion accounts process. For example, a preparer who takes a 'middle-of-the-road'-approach may be confronted with an overly aggressive stance taken by the other side unexpectedly (*see* below §3.08 [E]), and there is a risk that the outcome is different from one where both parties would have adopted either middle-of-the-road or extreme positions.

Whichever side cedes the preparation of the accounts should safeguard its interests by, as a minimum, ensuring that it and its advisers will have sufficient time to review the accounts, as well as satisfactory access to people and documents. Securing access rights requires specific wording in the SPA, such as whom the party may speak to (including the target's advisers), what records it has access to, and even whether it has the right to make photocopies, etc.

§3.04 BASIS OF PREPARATION OF THE COMPLETION ACCOUNTS

[A] The Accounting Hierarchy

It is sometimes proposed to simply use generally accepted accounting principles (International Financial Reporting Standards (IFRS), US Generally Accepted Accounting Principles (US GAAP), or local accounting rules) as the basis for the completion accounts. It may come as a surprise to non-accountants that two accountants given the task of preparing a set of accounts in accordance with 'generally accepted accounting principles' could come up with two entirely different results. Yet, as known from numerous high-profile corporate debacles, within the framework of accounting principles the preparer of accounts is afforded considerable scope for manoeuvre. Consequently, the basis on which completion accounts are to be prepared has to be laid down in (for some, excruciating) detail in the SPA.

The basis of preparation usually follows a hierarchy of accounting rules to the applied to the completion accounts as shown in Figure 3.2. The usual order, as shown here, is that specific rules prevail over past practice and past practice over generally accepted accounting policies. However, sometimes the order of past practice and GAAP is reversed (*see* section [B] below).

Figure 3.2 The Completion Accounts Hierarchy

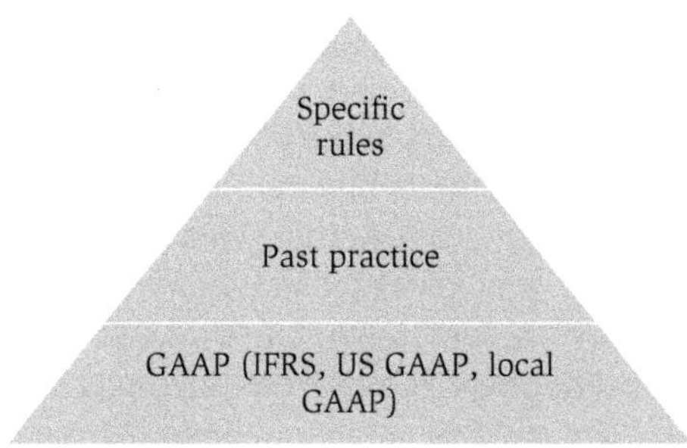

Specific measurement rules. These may have no regard for the way the target entity's accounts have been prepared in the past. For example, the rule for creating an allowance against doubtful debts may be that there will be an allowance against any account receivable which is unpaid within the period of credit granted, or where cash has not been received by a specified date after completion. This is regardless of how the target entity has hitherto computed the allowance. Another example of a specific measurement is the dollar amount deduction for a pension deficit (*see* below §4.04 [C]). Such rules aim to provide no room for judgment.

Consistency with past practice of the target entity or vendor group. Where no specific rule of measurement is laid down, then the respective accounts caption will be determined on a consistent basis as it has been in the past. The preparer of the completion accounts may not use a new set of accounting practices or measures different from those applied in the past (on which the target entity was valued). This is to protect against unexpected changes that would favour one party.

In accordance with *generally accepted accounting procedures* (e.g., IFRS, US GAAP, or local GAAP). This usually refers to the GAAP relevant to the target entity before the transaction which is also frequently the basis on which the buyer analysed and valued the target business.

As can be seen, the further down the hierarchy, the more scope the preparer generally has to apply their judgment. The application of the above hierarchy can be illustrated by a simple example using inventory allowances as shown in Table 3.1.

Table 3.1 Basis of Preparation: Hierarchy of Measurement – Inventory Allowances

Basis of Measurement	*Application*
Specific measurement rules	Allowance is made in full for items where the quantity on hand exceeds total movements in the last six months
Past practice	Past practice was that allowance was made in full for items where the quantity on hand exceeds total movements in the last twenty-four months
Generally accepted accounting principles	Inventory is stated at the lower of cost and net realisable value

In considering the appropriateness of past practice and stated accounting policies, it is advisable, where the target entity has been issued with an accounting manual (e.g., if it is part of a group of companies preparing accounts on a uniform basis), to ascertain whether the rules set out in the manual form an acceptable basis for the completion accounts and whether the target entity does indeed follow those rules. The accounting hierarchy can also reference the written accounting guidance of the target group

In addition to limiting the scope for judgment (and therefore dispute), the use of specific measurement rules can be helpful when staff are transferring from one owner to another and are being asked to adopt a different approach to preparing the completion accounts.

Furthermore, while in the example above it is referred under 'past practice' to allowances being computed in a mechanistic way, it is common for them to be determined based on management's judgment. While a seller will quite reasonably defend the preparation of completion accounts prepared on a similar basis as in the past, an aggressive buyer can, equally reasonably, be expected to seek adjustments which have a dollar-for-dollar impact on the final purchase price.

Lastly, it is often appropriate to specify that the accounting rules in force at the time of signing are relevant to the preparation of the completion accounts in order to avoid disagreement in the case of changes in GAAP.

Example Completion Accounts Dispute (High Court of England and Wales)

The case of *Mihail Tartsinis v. Navona Management Company*[27] (English Commercial Court) is a curious case which provides some lessons on how *not* to go about preparing completion accounts.

Briefly, the plaintiff and a fellow businessman sold to Navona shares in a company that owned a fleet of ships. The key issue in the transaction was the fleet and to what extent a decrease in its underlying value should lead to a purchase price adjustment. While the fleet was reported in the accounts of the target company at net book value, the parties apparently did not dispute, during the course of their negotiations, that this was considerably higher than the underlying market value (which had recently fallen). What amounted to completion accounts were issued by Navona showing (incorrectly, as it should have been written down) the fleet at an unadjusted net book value rather than the lower market value. As a consequence the seller claimed a price adjustment to reflect the higher net book value, which the buyer refused to accept, asserting that the value of the vessels relevant to the determination of the purchase price was the lower value that had been used to calculate the provisional purchase price under the SPA and which represented an assessment made by the parties of the vessels' market value. Legal proceedings ensued.

In the event, the court 'rectified' the contract. After considering the evidence, it concluded that there was pre-contractual agreement over the (lower) value of the fleet and substantially dismissed the plaintiff's claim. This dispute will be discussed further in §11.03 where standards of value are discussed.

While the case contains some interesting legal issues, from the narrow point of view of completion accounts and related matters, lessons include that it is important to reach an agreement between the parties about the basis on which the completion accounts are prepared, including the relationship between accounting numbers and the commercial value transferred.

Another important lesson is the broader point that those involved in a transaction should act in a 'joined up' manner so that there is clarity among the entire deal team, which in this context extends to whoever ultimately prepares the completion accounts on the matters involved, including:

- Clarity as to the basis on which the target entity's accounts have been drawn up in the past, any shortcomings, and the consequences for how the completion accounts are to be drawn up.
- Ensuring that the SPA (and more specifically, the purchase price adjustment mechanism) is drafted properly to reflect what is intended by the parties.
- Procedures to ensure that the completion accounts are reviewed before release.

27. *Mihail Tartsinis v. Navona Management Company* [2015] EWHC 57 (Comm).

[B] GAAP Override

A further issue that can arise is how to deal with items that are consistent with past practice yet are non-GAAP compliant. A target entity that draws up its accounts in accordance with local GAAP may not convert these to make them comply with say, IFRS, on the grounds of materiality. It may also be the case that the target has made an accounting error in the historical accounts that may or may not be corrected in the completion accounts.

The issue then relates to the order of items (2) and (3) in the hierarchy above. The hierarchy can be reversed, meaning the parties agree that generally accepted accounting policies prevail over consistency. This is called a 'GAAP override'. Whether or not to agree to a GAAP override can be a significant decision in a transaction, as it determines, for example, whether an accounting error in the accounts prior to closing must be corrected in the completion accounts if it is discovered during the completion accounts' preparation or review.

The reason one party (usually the buyer) may prefer a GAAP override is that it provides protection against unknown errors in the target's accounts, especially in situations where due diligence access was very limited or where there is already the suspicion on the part of the buyer that the seller's historical accounts may be incorrect; however, the buyer cannot determine this conclusively during the due diligence.

The disadvantage of a GAAP override is that the correction leads to a one-off effect that is (usually) unexpected and may result in a decrease or increase to the purchase price that has nothing to do with 'value'. This can lead to economically unjustified changes to the final purchase price.

A GAAP override is an exception, and the parties more often agree to the hierarchy as it is shown above (i.e., consistency prevails over GAAP). This means that accounting errors in the historical accounts (usually the last audited financial statements prior to closing) will be carried forward in the completion accounts.

Standard SPAs usually include some version of the accounting hierarchy. However, if a clear hierarchy is missing, then a dispute is more likely. These disputes continue to occur.

A hierarchy should be clear and unambiguous. An ambiguous clause led to a dispute in the following case.

Example of an Error Correction in the Completion Accounts (High Court of England and Wales)

In *Shafi v. Rutherford*,[28] the question arose whether an error in the historical financial statements should be corrected in the completion accounts. In 2007, the parties formed a company in order to establish a dental practice. Each party initially held 50% of the shares. The new company leased equipment for the practice. In 2009, the parties decided to part company, and one of the two owners, Ms Shafi, agreed to sell her 50%

28. *Ms Sofia Shafi v. Dr Alexandra Rutherford* [2014] EWCA Civ 1186.

interest to Ms. Rutherford. The SPA included a purchase price adjustment with the following provision:

> In the calculation of the Completion Liabilities, liabilities shall include any and all sums paid at or payable by reference to the period up to and including the Completion Date including but not limited to [certain specific matters].[29]

The parties agreed that operating leases were not included in Completion Liabilities under this definition, whereas finance lease liabilities were included to the extent that future payments due were payable by the reference to the period up to and including the Completion Date.

The SPA further contained the following hierarchy:

> 1.2 The draft completion accounts shall:
> 1.3 be prepared in accordance with the specific accounting policies and principles set out in Part III of this schedule so that, in the case of any conflict, such policies and principles shall override the provisions of paragraphs 1.4 and 1.5;
> 1.4 subject to paragraph 1.3, be prepared in accordance with the accounting policies, principles, practices and procedures adopted by the Company in the preparation of the Accounts, which include the policies set out in paragraphs 1, 2, 3 and 5 of Part III of Schedule 4, so that, in the case of any conflict, such policies, principles, practices and procedures shall override the provisions of paragraph 1.5;
> 1.5 where none of the accounting policies, principles, practices or procedures referred to in paragraphs 1.3 and 1.4 deal with the matter, be prepared in accordance with generally accepted accounting principles in the UK as applicable to small companies as at the Completion Date.[30]

In the company's 2008 annual accounts, the leases had been (incorrectly) accounted for as operating leases. The leases were also treated as operating leases in the draft completion accounts.

The parties could not agree on the completion accounts, and the matter was referred to expert determination. The expert determined that the 2008 accounts had not been prepared in accordance with relevant UK GAAP and that the leases should have been treated as finance leases all along. However, the expert found that there was no mechanism under the agreement for him to amend the 2008 accounts and decided that he could not take into account in the purchase price adjustment the finance lease liability which resulted from the correction the lease accounting.[31]

Legal proceedings ensued. The main issue concerned the proper construction of paragraph 1.4 (above), specifically whether the incorrect lease accounting treatment had to be carried over into the completion accounts, a question of hierarchy. The judge concluded that the completion accounts should have taken account of the proper treatment of the leases:

> given that they were to be prepared in accordance with the accounting policies, principles, practices and procedures adopted in the preparation of the accounts,

29. *Ibid.*, para. 13.
30. *Ibid.*, para. 11.
31. *Ibid.*, para. 22.

> such accounts having been expressly stated to have been prepared on the basis of [relevant GAAP].

and further:

> when clause 1.4 referred to 'the accounting policies, principles, practices and procedures adopted in the preparation of the Accounts', it was referring to the policies et cetera used by the profession generally on which those accounts are stated to be drawn up, not to the way in which the company has actually applied those policies.[32]

In other words, at issue was whether the hierarchy in paragraph 1.4 meant that the liabilities of the company should be computed by reference to correct accounting policy, supplemented if necessary by reference to practices adopted, or that they should be computed according to such policies except where contradicted by the actual treatment of those liabilities in the 2008 accounts, whether that treatment was right or wrong. The Court of Appeal found that the judge had been right to accept the first of those alternatives. The completion accounts were to provide the final adjustment between the parties of the consideration for the sale of the shares. The court saw no reason why in those circumstances the parties would have wished to carry forward erroneous accounting treatment of liabilities.[33]

§3.05 SUBSEQUENT EVENTS AND LIMITATIONS OF THE USE OF NEW INFORMATION

The measurement basis of the purchase price adjustments is, in concept, the commercial values of the individual items (referred to here as 'fair value', a term that will be further discussed in §11.03 [C]), not their book values, even if individual adjustments are based on accounting figures (*see* §4.02). On the one hand, one might argue that any additional information that becomes available over the completion accounts process removes uncertainty as to the fair values of individual adjustments (such as uncertainty over the collectability of receivables) and therefore improves the outcome. Consistent with this view, changes to the completion accounts due to new information do not necessarily mean that earlier drafts of the completion accounts were incorrect, only that better information has become available. On the other hand, accounting estimates are generally based on limited information that is available at the time. In a dispute, the question of what information can be taken into account in determining an adjustment can take centre stage and is often a legal matter.

The longer the completion accounts process, the more opportunity there is for new information to surface. If new information can be used up until the finalisation of the completion accounts process, this can mean a continuous change of the net purchase price adjustment (in extreme cases, until an expert's decision). A long period also generally favours the buyer, who has better access to information after closing. A buyer may argue that it is only fair to be able to use all information that becomes

32. *Ibid.*, para. 27.
33. *Ibid.*, para. 40.

available and reflect it in the final purchase price. A seller may counter that information asymmetry after closing means that the buyer can use information selectively, that only bad news may come to light and that the seller may be ambushed late in the process.

Accounting standards contain guidance on events after the reporting period that can be relevant, for example when GAAP is referenced in the accounting hierarchy (above §3.05 [A]). IAS 10.3 differentiates between adjusting and non-adjusting events:

- An adjusting event is an event after the reporting period that provides further evidence of conditions that existed at the end of the reporting period.
- A non-adjusting event is an event after the reporting period that is indicative of a condition that arose after the end of the reporting period.

IAS 10.8 requires an adjustment for an adjusting event and no adjustment for a non-adjusting event (even though a disclosure may be required (IAS 10.21)).[34]

It is usually appropriate to limit in the SPA the period for the consideration of subsequent events in the completion accounts (and to ensure that this takes precedence over subsequent events guidance in GAAP). A common date used to limit the period is the delivery of the first draft of the completion accounts by the buyer or seller.

An example of a dispute over subsequent events is below.

Example Dispute over Information to Surface after Closing (International Arbitration)

The target company had a receivable with a customer that related to a long-term construction contract for an infrastructure project in Eastern Europe. The receivable was part of working capital at closing. The seller had not recorded an allowance against the receivable and stated that it had expected the customer to pay in full. During the completion accounts process, the parties considered the receivable to be fully recoverable.

Approximately two months after closing, the relationship between the target management and the customer deteriorated. The customer claimed that there had not been sufficient progress on the project. Target company management accepted that the project was behind plan and agreed to discount the invoice – which was still unpaid – by 50%. It wrote down the receivable accordingly.

The buyer revisited the accounting treatment in the completion accounts as part of a dispute that had developed for other reasons and argued that the problems had already existed at closing, but that the seller had withheld relevant information during the due diligence phase. In the buyer's view, the carrying value of the receivable should have been reduced at the time of closing.

The seller argued that the project had not been behind plan at closing and that the partial write-down was, in essence, the result of the buyer's poor project management skills. In the seller's view, the receivable was fully recoverable at closing. The SPA did not include specific guidance on subsequent events. The dispute settled.

34. US GAAP differentiates between Type 1 and Type 2 events.

§3.06 TO AUDIT OR NOT TO AUDIT?

There is no requirement for completion accounts to be audited. However, it is sometimes proposed that – instead of agreeing in the SPA the process set out above in §3.02 – the completion accounts should simply be audited by a third party. The idea is that an independent external auditor will use an objective and fair approach to determine the purchase price adjustment, removing conflict, and that an audit might also provide a degree of comfort. Another idea sometimes advanced is that at the end of the completion accounts process described in §3.02, the final completion accounts should be audited.

While it is true that an audit might provide a degree of comfort, notably to the party who has not prepared the accounts, it is usually not the appropriate tool to resolve the completion accounts process. As the audit procedures must be separate from the preparation of the accounts, and the auditor must be different from the one who prepares the accounts, an audit still leaves open the question of which party prepares. Moreover, it is far from clear what criteria an independent auditor should apply to achieve a fair outcome. For example, if the party that prepares exercises all individual areas of judgment at the extreme end of a permissible range (under the accounting rules specified in the SPA) in order to maximise or minimise the purchase price adjustment, should the auditor accept all such accounting choices? Alternatively, on what basis should the external auditor reject them? An audit also raises practical questions: Who does the independent auditor talk to when auditing the accounts, and where are these individuals' loyalties placed?

An auditor will also work to a certain materiality level. This may make it difficult for the accounts to be contested and for dollar-for-dollar adjustments to be won.

Provided the basis of preparation has been satisfactorily nailed down and the non-preparer and their advisers have sufficient time and access to people and documents, then this should suffice.

§3.07 DISPUTE RESOLUTION

Occasionally, disagreements over completion accounts can be high profile disputes, as in *Chicago Bridge & Iron Co. v. Westinghouse Electric Co. LLC. LLC*, in which one party, Westinghouse, presented a net working capital calculation that amounted to over USD 2 billion less than the estimated pre-closing net working capital amount.[35] How these disputes are to be resolved is an area in which the lawyers advising on a transaction will typically lead. These are some of the principal areas to consider:

- Whether a third party is engaged as an expert or an arbitrator. As a general rule, a process involving an expert is less time-consuming than one involving an arbitrator and, hence, less costly. In cases involving completion accounts, because there is perhaps one or at least a limited number of specific issues to

35. Chicago *Bridge & Iron Co. v. Westinghouse Electric Co. LLC*, 2017 WL 2774563 (Del. 28 Jun. 2017).

be resolved and this falls readily within the capacity of the expert (usually a member of the relevant professional body), it is often appropriate to appoint an expert. Typically, submissions are made to the expert by either side over the course of the process, ordinarily with a right of reply, and a decision follows within a relatively short space of time.

- The SPA should specify that only the issue or issues being contested is to be considered (not, for example, the full completion accounts, which could potentially open up other issues not contested by the parties). The authority of the expert determiner should be limited. This was a lesson of *Chicago Bridge & Iron Co. v. Westinghouse Electric Co. LLC.*[36]
- The SPA should also specify that the expert determination cannot go beyond the positions of either party. That is, if one party claims that an item leads to an adjustment of USD 70 million, and the other party claims that it is only USD 40 million, then the expert determination should generally not fall outside of this range.

An in-depth discussion of the advantages and disadvantages of appointing an expert or an arbitrator and their respective roles is beyond the scope of this publication. Furthermore, there may be differences in the law of the country by which any agreement is to be governed and disputes dealt with.

§3.08 OTHER ASPECTS

[A] Accounting Input into SPA Draft

Those tasked with financial due diligence for the buyer should provide input into the basis of the completion accounts including the accounting definitions in the SPA. They should be instructed to analyse, during the due diligence phase, the basis on which the target company's historical accounts have been prepared, the basis on which they should have been prepared, and the basis on which the completion accounts should be prepared, as well as highlight any key discrepancies to the deal team. Otherwise, there is a risk that like will not be compared with like. Care should be taken when agreeing the terms of any purchase price adjustment mechanism to ensure that any input from the financial due diligence team is duly accounted for in the drafting of the SPA and the completion accounts mechanism. In particular, if any specific item is to be treated differently to the rest, this must be clearly stated.

[B] Preparation of a Full Balance Sheet

The completion accounts are schedules with cash, debt, working capital, capital expenditure and other items. They may be limited to the items that are part of the

36. *Ibid.*

purchase price adjustments as defined in the SPA, or alternatively represent a full balance sheet, including balance sheet items that do not lead to an adjustment. From the perspective of the recipient of the draft accounts it is generally preferable that the schedules amount to a complete balance sheet and not be limited to the items that lead to an adjustment. This serves primarily as protection of the party that does not prepare or has less access to information, as it is easier to identify items that should have been included in an adjustment but were omitted. For example, items may have been moved outside of the adjustments, and a full balance sheet with some detail will enable the other party to identify such items and to reconcile individual items into the trial balance.

[C] Materiality

A further factor to consider is materiality. Other than where specific measurement rules are applied that result in a definitive value being reached, the broader basis of measurement would typically involve consideration of materiality. An example would be where a target entity is a division of a group and the divisional accounts are drawn up to a higher level of materiality than those of an individual company (whose accounts are subject to an individual audit opinion).

A dollar-for-dollar purchase price adjustment may be appropriate even if it would not be material in the context of the group's or even the target's individual financial statements. Materiality thresholds can be agreed in the SPA. It is necessary to distinguish these from a collar amount around an adjustment (*see* §5.05).

[D] The Preliminary Purchase Price

Another aspect of the completion accounts relates to the preliminary purchase price (or estimated purchase price), the amount usually paid at closing. When the final purchase price is determined, only the difference to the preliminary price is paid (by whichever side owes it).

One consideration in setting the preliminary purchase price is that in the event it is determined by the seller's (good faith) estimate, the buyer may need to ensure that the estimate is within a pre-agreed range and does not exceed the available equity and debt financing. It is generally preferable to owe a final payment rather than to be a creditor. A buyer will usually attempt to agree a preliminary purchase price that is lower than the expected final price. This can be especially important if the other party is a special purpose vehicle or based abroad.

[E] Approaches to the Completion Accounts Process

Most strategic investors and PE sponsors do not take an overly aggressive approach during the completion accounts process as there are usually reputations and continuing relationships to consider. However, there is a small minority of investors who can be overly aggressive in their attempt to maximise or minimise the final 'cash event' in the acquisition process.

If a party asks its internal deal team or external advisers to look for ways to maximise or minimise a purchase price adjustment, it fair to assume that it will find something. The other side should then prepare for the next steps in the completion accounts process.

CHAPTER 4
Net Debt

§4.01 OVERVIEW

Net debt is deducted from (and, if applicable, net cash added to) enterprise value to arrive at equity value. There is no definition of net debt laid down in law or accounting standards; identifying what is, and is not, to be included in net debt in a transaction is a matter for the parties to negotiate and to document in the SPA.

In practice, many items may be considered to have the characteristics of debt, although the case for some is more clear-cut than for others.

To provide a flavour of what are concerned with, items listed below have been treated as net debt. They are ranked starting with what might be considered to be 'harder' (relatively uncontentious) items usually included in any definition of net debt, progressing to 'softer' items (those less commonly treated as such):

- Bank and other (explicitly) interest-bearing debt;
- Debt factoring and similar financing;
- Finance leases;
- Accrued interest;
- Derivative securities;
- Pension obligations; Supplier finance;
- Non-controlling (minority) interest;
- Employee loans;
- Intercompany balances;
- Break costs (e.g., of leases) and early debt repayment penalties;
- Cash that is working capital in nature, e.g., cash in tills (which would not form part of 'cash' within net debt) or cash that cannot be taken out of the business, i.e., trapped cash;
- Deferred revenue / prepaid amounts;
- Capital expenditure creditors;
- Restructuring costs;

- Effects of converting foreign currency debt at the spot rate;
- Dilapidation provisions;
- Accrued bonuses;
- Warranty provisions;
- Other customer-related claims, including unusual or excessive credit notes and unidentified receipts which may have to be repaid;
- Other contingent liabilities (to the extent not covered through indemnities);
- Current tax assets and liabilities;
- Operating leases (if flipping from operating to finance benefits one side);
- Early retirement provisions;
- Unrealised foreign exchange losses;
- Deferred tax assets and liabilities.

The merits or otherwise of these items can be debated (and frequently are), particularly those closer to the foot of the list. Whether they are ultimately included in net debt usually comes down to the respective negotiating positions of buyer and seller.

Before discussing individual adjustments at greater length, including those that commonly feature in legal disputes, it may first be helpful to consider some conceptual matters.

§4.02 CONCEPTUAL MATTERS

[A] Interest-Bearing Debt

It is sometimes suggested that a starting point for classifying items as net debt in a transaction is whether they are interest-bearing, and this definition of net debt is sometimes agreed in letters of intent. However, although explicitly interest-bearing debt (such as bank debt) is invariably treated as net debt, the use of the term 'interest-bearing' is not without problems. For example, is debt-factoring interest-bearing (there is a financing cost associated with factoring, but it is not necessarily reported in financial statements as interest)? On the other hand, a defined benefit pension obligation (commonly treated as debt) is not, strictly, interest-bearing (companies report an interest cost in their financial statements, but no cash interest is paid). Should it be considered 'interest-bearing'?

The term 'interest-bearing' is, therefore, not necessarily instructive in itself.

[B] Financing Versus Operating Items

Where there is usually consensus is that items relating to financing activities should be treated as net debt. It is therefore no surprise that they are among the 'hardest' items in the list in §4.01 above. However, net debt often also includes liabilities of an operating nature.

One might ask why, if items relate to operations, they should be deducted in the equity value bridge: are they not already reflected in enterprise value, the present value of net operating cash flows? The answer is: if the valuation model reflects these in enterprise value, then there are, indeed, no grounds on which to deduct them as net debt. In practice, however, that is often not the case as valuation models do not unfailingly capture the cash effects of operating items. Long-term obligations extending many years into the future are difficult to capture in a DCF model that usually extends out about five or seven years and then assumes a terminal value. Pension obligations are a case in point. In this case a net debt deduction transfers the economic burden of past commitments that have not, as at the transaction date, become 'cash-relevant' from the buyer to the seller (who incurred the cost, and the liability, but not the cash outflow). Incurring the non-cash cost generated benefits for the seller. Continuing with the example of unfunded defined benefit pension obligations, these represent pension promises to employees (instead of cash payments) in return for services they provided to, and which benefited, the seller. The work performed by and compensation to the employees are part of the operating activities of a business. The associated liability (the future payment of compensation for past service) is an operating liability. It is similar in nature to a liability for unpaid salaries or wages except that any cash-out may occur many years hence.

If the business is sold at the time the pension promise becomes 'cash-relevant' (albeit potentially many years after closing), the buyer will ultimately bear the economic burden of employees' work which benefited the seller. Unless the obligations have been funded involving assets that are not required in the normal operations, the buyer will service them with cash that would otherwise be available for distribution to the shareholder (the buyer) or other uses. A net debt deduction moves the present value of the future economic cash burden from buyer to seller.

Other examples of potential net debt items that arise from operating activities are discussed later in this chapter. While there are different accounting rules and valuation issues for each, the underlying rationale - moving the economic burden from buyer to seller by deducting the value from the purchase price - is the same.

[C] Accounting Choices and Value

Accounting is by fiat, that is to say, accounting rules are created by standard setters or lawmakers. Among other things, accounting rules specify how assets and liabilities should be valued in the accounts. Accounting measures of value are not necessarily the same as economic value. Take, for example, historical acquisition cost which often has nothing to do with commercial value.

The relationship between valuation and accounting figures, the 'value relevance of financial reporting', has been the subject of academic research, including on market efficiency. It has been said that the market 'sees through' the accounting[37] with the implication that accounting is not relevant to the value of a business (leaving aside secondary effects).

37. *See* the discussion in Penman, Accounting for Value, Columbia Business School Publishing, 2010, p. ix.

When the market 'sees through' the accounting, what it looks to is (presumably) future cash flows.[38] However, the market is not directly observing future cash in- and outflows, but rather information that allows their forecasting. This could be information about technological innovation, manufacturing capacities, intellectual property, the quality of management, or headcount numbers, to name a few. However, it is accounting information that produces a representation of these and other circumstances and events. Accounting is therefore usually a basis for understanding a business, and valuation is anchored in accounting. This will be discussed further in Chapter 11.

Returning to the equity value bridge, in concept, all of its components, including net debt, should be measured at fair value, even if they are derived from accounting figures. How these components are accounted for should theoretically not be relevant to the net purchase price adjustment and the final purchase price. Their carrying values in the balance sheet are only the starting point for the measurements at which they adjust the purchase price (albeit a convenient starting point because accounting figures are readily available).

Secondary effects of accounting choices can, however, have direct relevance to value and need to be considered separately, again at fair value. For example, tax payments are made on the basis of taxable income according to tax accounting rules. The financial accounts may be the basis for debt covenants. Secondary effects should therefore enter into the enterprise valuation or the purchase price adjustment so that they are reflected in the equity value. The discussion of deferred taxes in §4.04[I] is an example.

It is worth considering how the carrying values of items in a balance sheet are compared to their fair values:

- *Items whose book value typically equates to fair value at the reporting date.* These include cash and cash equivalents, short-term investments and marketable securities, trade creditors, and financial borrowings (though interest rates may fluctuate and, with them, the value of the liabilities); they are short-term and forever revolving.
- *Items whose book value does not equate to, but approximates, fair value.* These include receivables (subject to estimates for unrecoverable amounts), inventory (at the lower of cost and market), investments recorded under equity accounting, accruals, and provisions (which are subject to specific accounting rules, for example pension obligations, and management estimates).
- *Items whose book value often differs substantially from fair value.* These include long-term debt securities (investments held to maturity that are reported at historical cost) and some provisions. Other examples, albeit with less relevance for completion mechanisms, include tangible and intangible assets other than goodwill (recorded at historical acquisition cost less depreciation or amortisation, subject to impairment reviews), and goodwill (recorded at historical cost, subject to impairment reviews).

38. *Ibid.*

- *Items not recorded in the balance sheet at all.* Items with possible relevance for completion mechanisms include many types of off-balance sheet liabilities such as leases (if classified as operating), factoring (if the receivables are 'derecognised'), and commitments and contingent liabilities (e.g., if probability thresholds are not met or a loss cannot be reasonably estimated).

§4.03 INTERACTION WITH WORKING CAPITAL

For a purchase price adjustment mechanism to work properly, a seamless interaction between the individual adjustments is necessary. A basic interaction between the net debt adjustment and working capital is between cash and individual components of working capital. Most day-to-day transactions of a business affect both. For example, a consequence of the receipt of funds from customers is that cash increases (net debt decreases) and trade receivables decrease (working capital decreases). The effects offset each other. Cash payments to suppliers and trade payables interact similarly.

To the extent that a change in cash stems from a change in working capital, a properly functioning completion mechanism means that the working capital adjustment neutralises the change in cash (net debt) exactly so that there is no impact on the net purchase price. At closing, it does not matter whether a particular receivable has already been converted into cash, or if a particular trade payable has already been paid. Consequently, accelerating collections from customers, deferring settlement of trade payables, or liquidating inventories will not affect the net purchase price if the working capital and net debt adjustments interact properly (assuming, of course, that the working capital reference value is set at an appropriate level – more on this in Chapter 5).

When things go wrong in completion mechanisms, it is often here. A typical problem is that an item is captured twice, both as working capital and as net debt (e.g., a capital expenditure creditor). Alternatively, an item may not be captured at all (e.g., an accrual for outstanding supplier invoices), giving the seller an opportunity to manipulate the cash or the working capital position prior to closing – as a consequence of which the buyer overpays. A seamless interaction reduces the risk of a post-deal dispute.

Many items can be treated as alternatively net debt or working capital. The economic outcome is often not the same. For example, if deferred revenue is included in the definition of working capital, then only amounts above those included in the reference working capital lead to a reduction of net working capital at closing (and to the purchase price). This is a different outcome from a dollar-for-dollar net debt deduction (as long as any amount of deferred revenue is included in the reference value). If the parties agree to treat an item as working capital in the completion accounts but it is not included in the reference value (e.g., because it has never been reported in the past), then in theory this would achieve the same economic result as a net debt deduction. However, in practice, it may still not lead to the same outcome. A significant working capital adjustment resulting from such an item may cause the other party to look for offsetting items elsewhere in working capital during the completion accounts process – an option that is not readily available for a net debt deduction. From the perspective of a buyer, it is therefore generally preferable to include an item in the definition of net debt rather than working capital.

§4.04 INDIVIDUAL NET DEBT ADJUSTMENTS

[A] Factoring

[1] Introduction

Debt factoring is among the more complex issues encountered in completion mechanisms and one that can be difficult to think through conceptually. This is primarily because treating factoring appropriately (as debt) also has implications for the treatment of working capital.

Factoring is, in essence, the sale of receivables by a business to a third party (a factor) at a discount. The benefit to the business is that it converts its receivables into cash immediately. Factoring not only generates cash but also gives companies the ability to manage the balance sheet and cash flow at a specific reporting date or during a reporting period.

There are a number of different types of factoring arrangement and these need to be considered in determining the appropriate accounting treatment. The relevant accounting standards are:

- IFRS: IAS 39 and IFRS 9 (although these make no specific reference to factoring);
- US GAAP: FASB ASC 860-10.

The key issue is whether the factoring arrangement is recourse or non-recourse:

- Non-recourse: the factor bears the risk of uncollected invoices. In general, this is accounted for as a sale of the receivables, which are 'derecognised' (i.e., to say, removed from the balance sheet, as if the customer had paid). This is a common type of off-balance sheet financing.
- Recourse: the factor does not take the risk of uncollected invoices. Depending on the terms, the accounting treatment may be on- or off-balance sheet. Under IFRS, receivables are generally 'derecognised', meaning they are no longer recorded on the balance sheet if substantially all of the risks and rewards of ownership have been transferred, with control as a secondary test.[39] Factoring with recourse will more often fail the risks and rewards test than non-recourse factoring and is more often accounted for as a loan (i.e., on-balance sheet). Under US GAAP, the accounting treatment is determined by FASB Accounting Standards Codification (ASC) section 860-10-40.

39. James M. Wahlen, Jefferson P. Jones, Donald Pagach: *Intermediate Accounting: Reporting and Analysis*, 6.31.

[2] *Factoring in the Context of the Transaction*

If the company in receipt of the finance retains the receivables on its balance sheet and records a liability, the treatment in a transaction - specifically, the completion mechanism - is usually uncontroversial: the liability, readily visible in the balance sheet, is treated as net debt. There is no impact on working capital since the factored receivables have not been derecognised.

Disagreements over the treatment of factoring in the context of a transaction tend to arise when factored receivables are off-balance sheet - that is to say, when they are derecognised. The cause of such disagreements is possibly that the respective parties (and their advisers) find it difficult to consider such amounts as debt because they are not (by definition) visible in the balance sheet.

When a seller argues against a net debt deduction, they tend to use the following reasoning:

- The company has always factored, and the buyer can continue to factor, after closing if they so wish; factoring is 'part of the business'. However, the fallacy is easy to expose. The fact that a specific type of financing has been in place before closing and may continue to be in place afterwards is not relevant to whether it is debt. A company may have had bank debt for many years which may remain in place after closing. Such borrowings are not somehow less 'debt-like' simply because they have been there for a long time or will continue to be there.
- Considering balance sheet effects, factoring gives the same result as customers paying (albeit early, and ignoring any discount and other charges). It looks like an operating, not a financing transaction, a seller would argue. If that is the case, why treat it as debt? However, such an impression is given only by how the factoring is accounted for - and the accounting should not matter. It may look as if the customer has paid early, but they have not. Rather, the factoring arrangement has generated liquidity to make it look as if that were the case. The liquidity comes not from the customer, but from the factor (with an inherent financing cost), similar to a loan or other asset-backed financing; it just does not look that way in the balance sheet after the payment is made.

[3] *Factoring and the Completion Mechanism*

Factoring, then, is a financing transaction and the associated liability should be included in net debt. This offsets the increase in the cash position resulting from the factoring arrangement which the buyer pays for, dollar-for-dollar (since it reduces net debt).

However, the mechanics do not end there. A factoring arrangement under which the receivables have been derecognised results in lower working capital (all else being equal). If the target business has factored in the past, its historical working capital, as reported, will have been artificially low and will, as a consequence, understate its true working capital needs. To correct this, that is to reflect in the reference value the true working capital needs of the business, the factored receivables have to be added back to reported working capital on a pro forma basis in order to establish accurate working capital levels (including averages) as well as reference working capital.

It is sometimes argued that it is not necessary to add back factored receivables as described above, or to include factoring liabilities in net debt; and that allowing variations in factored receivables to resolve themselves through the working capital adjustment, without an adjustment to net debt, achieves the same economic outcome. That is not the case. This can be demonstrated by means of a simple example.

[4] Factoring Example

This considers the impact on the net debt and working capital adjustments of the following possible combinations:

- A working capital adjustment where factored receivables are added back (option 1) or not added back (option 2), both to the reference value and closing working capital.
- A net debt adjustment which includes factored receivables at closing (option 3) or excludes them (option 4).

Table 4.1 shows the working capital development of a target company. It is assumed that:

- the company factors 90% of its receivables at any time;
- these receivables are derecognised upon being factored;
- working capital consists only of trade receivables;
- there is no debt other than in relation to factoring;
- the average working capital is also the agreed reference working capital (i.e., the reference value).

Table 4.1 Factoring Example: Scenario

	Jan	*Feb*	*Mar*	*Apr*	*Average (mean)*	*Amount at Closing*
Gross trade receivables	100	90	80	70	85	100
Less: factored receivables	(90)	(81)	(72)	(63)	(76.5)	(90)
Net reported trade receivables	10	9	8	7	8.5	10
Cash in target company due to factoring	90	81	72	63	n/a	90

Table 4.2 shows the results of each of the four permutations set out above together with the consequences for the final purchase price.

Table 4.2 Factoring Example: Results

	Permutation	*Working Capital Adjustment*	*Factoring Debt*	*Cash Balance from Factoring*	*Net Impact on Purchase Price*
1.	Factored receivables included in working capital; factoring liability included in net debt	15.0	(90.0)	90.0	15.0
2.	Factored receivables NOT included in working capital; factoring liability included in net debt	1.5	(90.0)	90.0	1.5
3.	Factored receivables included in working capital; factoring liability NOT included in net debt	15.0	0	90.0	105.0
4.	Factored receivables NOT included in working capital; factoring liability NOT included in net debt	1.5	0	90.0	91.5

Each permutation results in a different net purchase price for each combination of adjustments. This shows that the deduction cannot be resolved through the working capital adjustment alone. The only clean solution is option 1, where an adjustment is made against a working capital reference value to which factored receivables are added back and which includes the amounts factored in factoring debt. It the same outcome as that if no factoring were in place, and this result is consistent with the purpose of a purchase price adjustment, which is to neutralise the effect of changes to the price from financing transactions before closing. It is therefore the only outcome that ensures the seller transfers the value the buyer pays for.

This treatment sometimes runs into the following objection: the buyer is being asked to pay for 15.0 of surplus working capital (against a reference value of 85.0 if factored receivables are added back) but receives only 1.5. The balance of 13.5 has already been sold (by way of factoring) and the buyer will not collect the 13.5 after closing, even though they pay for it. The adjustment of 15.0, however, seems to suggest that the buyer should expect to receive 15.0, not 1.5. Is the buyer therefore overpaying by 13.5?

The answer is no. It is true that the buyer obtains only 1.5 in working capital, despite paying for a working capital adjustment of 15.0. However, the buyer also obtains a higher cash balance at closing than would be the case without factoring. It is higher by exactly 13.5 (the difference in factored receivables at closing versus the reference amount, or 90% of 100 less 90% of 85.0) relative to the working capital level that would have come were there no factoring. Economically, while the buyer pays 15.0 for working capital even though they only obtain a surplus of 1.5 against the reference value, they obtain 13.5 more in cash. The buyer does not pay for this extra cash because of the net debt deduction.

Many times in transactions factoring is not dealt with appropriately, and in each case this means that someone overpays. It is safe to assume that this will often go unnoticed.

[5] Reverse Factoring

Reverse factoring is where a financing company (factor) pays a supplier's invoices in the first instance (net of agreed fees) before the debtor, often a large corporate, is required to. The factor recovers the financing from the corporate. Reverse factoring is depicted in Figure 4.1.

Figure 4.1 Reverse Factoring

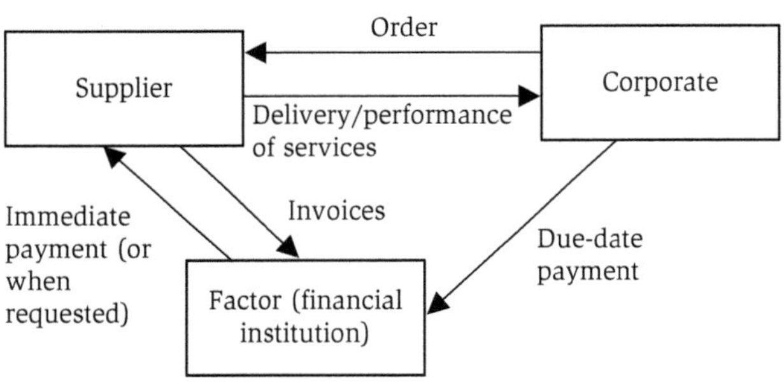

Reverse factoring is increasingly widespread. One purpose is to allow a group of smaller suppliers to benefit from the better credit rating of a corporate customer while generating cash in a financing transaction by accelerating receivable collections.

When entering into reverse factoring, suppliers' payment terms may be extended. The corporate then has additional time to pay the factor.

Just like the factoring transactions discussed above in §4.04 [A], reverse factoring is a financing transaction. From the perspective of the supplier, it removes trade receivables from the balance sheet as cash is received from the factor. From the perspective of the corporate, it replaces trade creditors with a liability to the factor. However, the corporate may not report these creditors as financial liabilities. This is what happened at UK construction and services group Carillion plc. The group collapsed under the burden of less-profitable-than-expected large contracts (many related to public-private-partnerships) and a GBP 1.5 billion debt pile and went into liquidation in early 2018.[40]

In a report after the collapse of the group, Moody's observed that Carillion's 2016 balance sheet and cash flows:

> failed to give a clear picture of the full scale of its liability to banks. While the balance sheet said the group's bank loans and overdrafts amounted to GBP 148 million, an additional amount – possibly as much as GBP 498 million – was owed to banks under the reverse factoring arrangement that started in 2013. This higher figure appears to have been reported within 'other creditors' and was consequently excluded from borrowings.
>
> Carillion reported group operating profit (excluding disposal gains) totalling GBP 501 million for the period from 2013 to 2016, an outcome seemingly corroborated by the cash flow statement, which showed cash generated from operations (before pension deficit recovery payments) of GBP 509 million over the same period.
>
> However, there was no disclosure that the cash inflow included bridging finance supplied by Carillion's banks under the reverse factoring arrangement. This would have contributed GBP 498 million (98%) of the GBP 509 million cash inflow if the facility had been fully utilised at the end of 2016.[41]

[B] Leasing

[1] Introduction

Sir David Tweedie, former head of the International Accounting Standards Board (IASB), once famously joked that one of his lifelong ambitions was to fly in an aircraft that was on the airline's balance sheet.[42] His comment reflected wider concerns over off-balance sheet financing around the time of the financial crisis. By 2016 the IASB estimated that companies using IFRS or US GAAP had approximately USD 2.9 trillion of lease commitments that were off balance sheet.[43] The recent fundamental changes to lease accounting can essentially be viewed as a reaction by standard setters to concerns over these off-balance sheet liabilities. These changes will bring almost all lease liabilities on balance sheet. Overall, these changes are among the most significant of the reforms introduced by the IASB since the financial crisis of 2007/2008.

Following a lengthy period of gestation, IFRS 16 'Leases' will apply to accounting periods commencing on or after 1 January 2019, although early adoption is permitted

---

40. Where Did It Go Wrong for Carillion?, BBC News, 15 Jan. 2018. https://www.bbc.co.uk/news/business-42666275.
41. Moody's Investor Service, Announcement: Moody's: Carillion's Collapse Exposes Flaws in the Accounting for Supply-Chain Finance Arrangements, 13 Mar. 2018, https://www.moodys.com/research/Moodys-Carillions-collapse-exposes-flaws-in-the-accounting-for-supply--PR_380769.
42. This section draws extensively on 'What Changes to Lease Accounting Mean for M&A Transactions' co-authored by Phil Hersey, Heiko Ziehms and Anna Hartley, World Accounting Report, October 2017, available at https://www.worldaccountingreport.com/accounting-issues/what-changes-to-lease-accounting-mean-for-ma-transactions-126889.htm.
43. http://www.ifrs.org/news-and-events/2016/01/iasb-shines-light-on-leases-by-bringing-them-onto-the-balance-sheet/.

if the entity has already implemented IFRS 15 'Revenue from Contracts with Customers'.

Leases play an important role in transactions given the interaction of the target entity's accounting for leases with valuation and the equity bridge, since lease liabilities are usually included in the definition of net debt. The abovementioned reforms give them even greater relevance.

Whichever airline Sir David chooses to travel within the future, it is very likely that the aircraft will be on the airline's balance sheet. Indeed, airlines will be among those businesses most affected by the new standard, along with travel and leisure companies and businesses where property expense represents a significant part of the cost base, such as retailers, financial services, legal services, and business consulting.

[2] IFRS 16 'Leases'

Under current IASs (IAS 17), leases are classified as either 'finance leases' or 'operating leases'. The vastly different accounting treatments for these two types of financing arrangement has meant that similar businesses operating in the same sector have not always been readily comparable. In some sectors leases are highly material and a key source of finance. Until now, businesses were often able to structure leases in a way that they remained off-balance sheet.

The new standard, IFRS 16, removes the distinction between operating and finance leases for lessees and introduces a single approach that effectively moves almost all operating leases onto the lessee's balance sheet. The objective of the new standard is to provide users of financial statements with a fuller picture of a company's leverage and aid the comparability of financial information across companies. The changes will also affect key deal metrics and will be pertinent to M&A disputes.

The effect of bringing an operating lease onto the balance sheet will mean that an entity will recognise an additional asset (termed 'right-of-use' asset) together with a corresponding lease liability, resulting in an increase in reported debt and gearing. In the income statement, there will be a reduction in operating expenses (the operating lease payments), which will be offset by increases in depreciation and interest.

In the cash flow statement, the repayment of the principal component of the lease instalment will be recorded as a financing activity, rather than a single operating cash flow (the lease payment); the interest element may, under IAS, be recorded as either a financing, operating, or an investing activity. When M&A practitioners use the cash flow statement to calculate free cash flow, it will be important for them to consider whether interest has been recorded as an operating or investing activity. Interest expense should, if necessary, be reassigned to financing activity in order to avoid incorrectly deducting interest from free cash flow.

[3] US GAAP

The changes to accounting for leases under US GAAP are not identical to those under IFRS. While the Financial Accounting Standards Board (FASB)'s new lease accounting standard ASU 2016-02 'Leases' (Topic 842) also brings most leases onto the balance sheet, the finance and operating lease distinction has been maintained. Accordingly, operating leases will continue to be recognised as a single operating expense in the income statement, on a straight-line basis over the life of the lease, and EBITDA will be unchanged relative to the current treatment. This means that, in the equity bridge referred to in §2.01 [B] above, there will be no upward effect on enterprise value as a result of 'converting' operating lease charges to depreciation and interest and thus an increased EBITDA, but there may nevertheless be an increase in debt if the definition in the SPA includes lease liabilities. Under an EBITDA-based valuation method, practitioners should thus be aware that with US GAAP financials any lease liability should already have reduced EBITDA. Deducting the lease liability would mean double counting the lease obligation.

The reform of lease accounting was an opportunity for closer convergence between US GAAP and IFRS standard setters. In the event, they chose not to seize this.

[4] Relevance to Transactions

[a] Effect on EBITDA-Based Valuations

The effects of the changes described above on the income statement and EBITDA-based valuations are shown in the example below (Figures 4.2 and 4.3). Under IFRS, bringing a lease onto the balance sheet effectively replaces the operating lease charge in the income statement with interest and depreciation expenses, which are below EBITDA. All else being equal (in particular the multiple used), this leads to a higher enterprise value.

Capitalising a lease also increases debt (by the amount of the lease liability), resulting in a higher net debt deduction in the equity bridge (again, if the definition of net debt in the SPA includes lease liabilities).

It would be a coincidence, however, if the two effects were to offset each other exactly, and in practice they usually do not. Consequently, capitalising a lease (all else being equal) may impact the purchase price for the equity.

Figure 4.2 Lease Accounting and Valuation of the Target Business

IAS 17 £ MM	2019
Revenue	100.0
CoS	30.0
Gross Profit	70.0
Operating expense	-50.0
Lease expense	-5.0
EBITDA	**15.0**
Depreciation	-3.0
EBIT	**12.0**
Interest	-0.5
EBT	**11.5**

IFRS 16 £ MM	2019
Revenue	100.0
CoS	30.0
Gross Profit	70.0
Operating expense	-50.0
Lease expense	0.0
EBITDA	**20.0**
Depreciation	-3.0
Depreciation (lease)	-4.5
EBIT	**12.5**
Interest	-0.5
Interest (lease)	-0.8
EBT	**11.2**

2019 Purchase Price Impact

IAS 17	
EBITDA 2019	15.0
EBITDA Multiple	8x
Enterprise Value	**120.0**
Net debt	25.0
Equity Value	**95.0**

IFRS 16	
EBITDA 2019	20.0
EBITDA Multiple	8x
Enterprise Value	**160.0**
Net debt	69.9
Equity Value	**90.1**

Figure 4.3 Effect of Lease Accounting Treatment on Equity Value

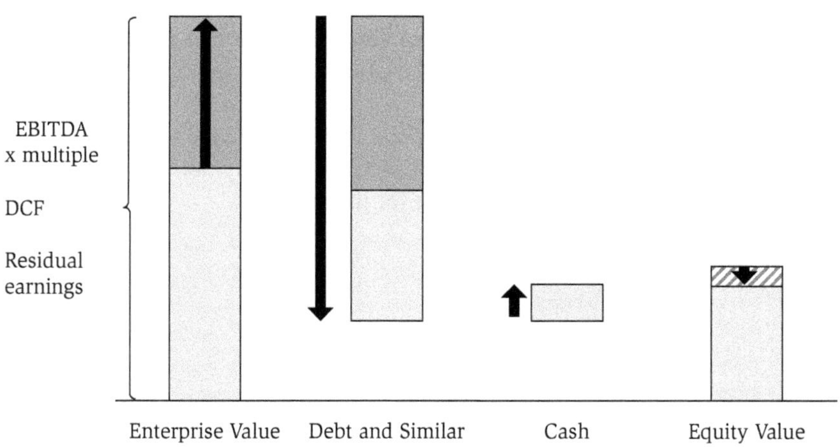

[b] *Valuation Multiples and Effect on Net Purchase Price*

One key determinant of whether the net purchase price will increase or decrease is the multiple used in the case of a multiple-based valuation. A higher multiple results in a correspondingly higher enterprise value, with a greater likelihood of its exceeding the revised debt amount (reflecting the change in lease debt).[44]

In theory, valuation multiples should adjust so that the effects of higher enterprise values and higher debt exactly offset each other and the only change to net purchase price reflects secondary effects (*see* below §4.04 [B] [5]). This logic is comparable to when observers of the stock market note that analysts are already 'pricing in' some factor or other in relation to leases regardless of the accounting.[45] In practice, such efficient price-setting in M&A transactions is far from being 'a given'. Consider that, when valuing a non-listed business the valuation multiple is often calculated with reference to comparable listed companies. As a result of the new standard, the comparable company multiples may also need to change. Even if the market priced leases correctly, historical multiples of the peer group would still reflect the previous off-balance sheet treatment and therefore need to be restated.

The higher the multiple, the greater the effect of effectively moving the period's expenses associated with the lease from above to below EBITDA on enterprise value. This means that for deals involving high-growth sectors with high multiples (say, technology), adopting IFRS 16 may put further upward pressure on valuations. Conversely, in respect of lower multiples, it would be more likely that any change in enterprise value would be below the associated change in debt. Thus, a significant downturn in the M&A market leading to lower valuations may in some cases be exacerbated by a net debt deduction for lease debt in excess of the benefit to enterprise value from a higher EBITDA.

Another determinant of the purchase price calculation can be the timing of the transaction. Whereas operating lease treatment means straight-line expensing over the lease term, capitalising the lease means interest expense is higher in early years and decreases as the liability decreases. IFRS 16 may therefore lead to higher lease expenses recognised in the early periods of a lease relative to later years. This effect is below EBITDA, and important to consider in multiple-based valuations that reference net earnings.

[c] Effect on Cash Flow-Based Valuations

The effects on a discounted cash flow (DCF) valuation are different from those of multiple-based valuations. As discussed above, the repayment of the principal component of the lease instalment will be recorded as a financing activity, below free cash flow; the interest element may, under IAS, be recorded as either a financing, operating, or an investing activity. In the first case it is below free cash flow, and in both alternatives above free cash flow. In free cash flow-based valuation, if no adjustment is made, the enterprise value has already been reduced by interest in both these alternatives. It is therefore important for M&A practitioners using DCF models to avoid

44. In the example, a 'break-even' EBITDA multiple, i.e., a multiple that would make equity values identical (using alternatively IAS 17 or IFRS 16), would be 8.98.
45. *See* 'Accounting's Big Shake-up to Bring More Transparency', Financial Times, 20 Jan. 2016, available at: https://www.ft.com/content/138fe994-bdd5-11e5-846f-79b0e3d20eaf.

deducting interest from free cash flow when there is also a deduction for lease debt – a potential 'double dip'.

The effects on cash flow-based valuations are, however, not limited to cash flows above or below the free cash flow subtotal. In practice, capitalising a lease may also change the weighted average cost of capital (WACC) – both the weights of debt and equity and the cost of debt – as well as gearing. While in theory there should be no effect on value, in reality complex valuation models will likely produce different outcomes.

[5] Secondary Effects

The changes to lease accounting may expose unpleasant truths about a target entity, for example high levels of leverage. Additional reported leverage could result in non-compliance with loan covenants, potentially triggering additional regulatory capital requirements for companies in the financial sector.

Certain profitability ratios, such as return on assets, may also fall as a result of the additional assets taken onto the balance sheet. As a consequence, transactions may be viewed as being riskier or less attractive. It is therefore important to consider these secondary effects in the valuation.

[6] Leases and Post-M&A Disputes

The dispute discussed above in §3.04 [B] related to an error in the accounting treatment of a finance lease that had been incorrectly treated as an operating lease in the historical accounts. The binary nature of the accounting treatment often makes disputes over the classification of a lease contract material. An error correction that brings new debt into the completion accounts is usually made at a time when there is no offsetting increase in enterprise value derived from higher EBITDA or free cash flow. This is a common issue with GAAP overrides (*see* above §3.04 [B]). With the new lease accounting standard, however, fewer of these disputes could be expected in the future.

This does not mean, however, that disputes over lease accounting will disappear. M&A-related disputes originate from ambiguous wording, or wording that does not anticipate developments after closing. Disputes also originate from judgmental areas of accounting. As with many accounting standards, IFRS 16 opens the door to these kinds of disputes.

Ambiguity can originate from SPAs concluded prior to the introduction of IFRS 16 and which did not foresee the consequences for financial statements. For example, earn-out clauses agreed some time ago that include earn-out consideration based on EBITDA might not have foreseen the increase of EBITDA resulting from replacing operating lease costs with depreciation and interest. Front-loading of interest may increase earn-outs calculated with reference to net income. A disagreement over the earn-out basis may ensue.

Another source of disputes may be a target entity's lending agreements referencing 'finance lease liabilities' that increase with higher lease debt. This may lead to unforeseen costs related to renegotiating with lenders.

Similarly, the introduction of IFRS 16 opens up judgmental accounting areas - and disputes - when one party, usually the preparer of financial information, exercises discretion in accounting choices that produce outcomes to their benefit. Under the new accounting standard, right-of-use assets and accompanying liabilities are valued using a set of assumptions for interest rates, the exercise of options, inflation, future reinstatement costs, or residual value guarantee payments, which can have an impact on the value of assets and liabilities. These are discussed below.

[a] Interest Rate Implicit in the Lease

The interest rate used to value the lease liability is the 'interest rate implicit in the lease' at its inception date. Where this cannot be established, the liability is estimated using the 'incremental cost of borrowing' for the lease. This will be the case for many leases. Determining the incremental cost of borrowing is highly judgmental (the rate that an entity would borrow at to acquire the right-to-use asset - that is to say, borrowing secured on that asset reflecting that entity's credit rating). The nature of NPV calculations used to value the liability is such that small changes in the discount rate can have a material impact on the valuation of the liability. In a corporate transaction, increasing the estimated incremental cost of borrowing would reduce net debt and, depending on the deal price mechanism, may increase the value of an entity - creating a potential area of dispute.

[b] The Lease Term

The lease term begins on the commencement date and comprises the non-cancellable period of the lease, together with:

- periods covered by an option to extend the lease if the lessee is reasonably certain to exercise that option; and
- periods covered by an option to terminate the lease if the lessee is reasonably certain not to exercise that option.[46]

Options to extend lease contracts are common features of many leases. IFRS 16 generally requires *re*assessment of the lease term after the initial determination only when the company takes actions that could have a significant effect on the lease term.

With a net debt deduction, the timing for the exercise of options can be critical. If the lessee (the target company) exercises options to extend leases during the closing period, additional lease liabilities may be created and included within the net debt deduction. However, there may be no offsetting increase in the enterprise value

46. IFRS 16:B34.

derived from the EBITDA multiple at this stage. It is therefore important to consider the consequences to net debt and limit the ability of management to extend a lease during the closing period.

[c] Intangible Assets

There remains an inconsistency between the leasing of physical assets and intangible assets (licensing). A lessee can elect to apply IFRS 16 to leases of intangible assets, other than those items listed in IFRS 16:3 (licences, rights under licence agreements, and others), which are excluded from the scope of IFRS 16. As such, many intangible assets will not be subject to the new leasing standard. For operating leases incorporating both physical assets and intellectual property, the allocation between the two elements is a potentially complex judgmental area. Whether a party has an incentive for a higher or lower share for physical assets will depend on the deal price mechanism, the age of the assets, and so on. However, this effect could be material.

[C] Deferred Compensation: Pension Benefits

[1] Introduction

A feature of many transactions, defined benefit pension plans can be highly problematic. Pension liabilities are very sensitive to changes in actuarial assumptions, in particular interest rates. In recent years, the size of pension deficits, magnified by a long period of falling bond yields, combined with the typical duration gap between assets and liabilities, has created a major headache for dealmakers. Despite the fact that many companies have taken action to address the problem by closing defined benefit plans to new entrants or amending scheme rules, many legacy schemes continue to exist. In some (occasionally high profile) cases, deals have foundered because purchasers have been unwilling to take on such large obligations. Alternatively, transactions have been structured so as to ring-fence pension liabilities.

The reasoning behind pension obligations being treated as part of net debt in transactions has already been explained in §4.02 above. This section starts with a brief description of the two main types of pension plans, as well as the accounting rules and key actuarial assumptions underlying the valuation of pension obligations, before moving on to discuss examples of post-M&A disputes.

There are other types of deferred compensation – notably health care, insurance, and early retirement benefits – that can resemble pension benefits. However, the focus here is on pensions.

[2] Types of Pension Plans and Their Accounting Basis

Some background and knowledge of accounting are necessary to understand the treatment of pension liabilities in transactions. The discussion here is necessarily limited and based primarily on IFRS (IAS 19). While broadly comparable to US GAAP

(ASC 715), there are important differences between the two, which are well documented elsewhere in accounting texts.

There are two principal ways an employer can sponsor retirement benefits for employees:

- Defined contribution plans: The employer and/or employee contributes a certain amount to a pension plan (often a fraction of an employee's salary), but without promising specific benefits on retirement. The pension the employee receives depends on the amounts contributed and the investment returns of the plan. 401(k) plans in the US are a type of defined contribution plan.
- Defined benefit plans: The employer promises specific benefits payable under certain conditions such as retirement, disability or death and a vesting period. These are often set as a fixed monthly amount or a fraction of an employee's average or final salary before retirement, weighted by the time of service (the formula can be complex). The employer can decide to set aside amounts to fund these pension promises fully, partially, or not at all.

Under IFRS, a plan is considered a defined contribution plan if an employer's legal or constructive obligation is limited to the amount it contributes to a separate entity. In principle, only the plan assets, namely the amount that has accumulated by the time the pension becomes payable, are available to the employee.

Let's turn to the net debt deduction in a transaction. The plans that play a key role here are, with few exceptions, defined benefit plans. The reason is that, with defined contribution plans, the sponsoring employer does not usually have a responsibility (beyond their share of the initial contributions while the employee was still working and the employer received the benefit of their work) to fund the obligations of the plan, including making good deficits. The liability of the defined contribution plan is equal to the plan assets.[47] When quantifying the employer's obligation, the net debt deduction should be independent of the accounting (*see* above §4.02 [C]). In transactions, pension liabilities should therefore, in concept, be valued on a commercial, or fair value, basis - that is to say, the net present value of the future cash flows required as funding of the defined benefit obligation, after deducting the value of any plan assets available for this purpose.[48]

The valuation process requires actuaries to make assumptions about financial and demographic variables, including:

- Discount rate (often determined by a yield curve and credit spread);

47. In fact, it can be more complicated. In some jurisdictions, certain plans may be classified, for accounting purposes, as defined contribution plans even though there can be a residual risk that the sponsoring employer may have, if not a legal, a constructive obligation to make good deficits. Some hybrid plans that combine features of both may be accounted for as defined benefit or alternatively defined contribution.
48. It may be appropriate to consider in a transaction context whether any of the plan assets include operating assets of the firm, and implications for the valuation. This is an exception but can be the case with some Collateralised Trust Agreements (CTAs).

- Salary increases (if salary is part of the pension promise);
- Pension indexation;
- Longevity.

Salary increases and pension indexation are usually linked to inflation. The yield curve, credit spread, and inflation usually have the main impact on the pension liability. Other assumptions may include employee turnover and vesting period of benefits.

The discount rate affects the balance sheet directly; inflation and longevity affect the cash flow of pension payments. As there is at least some degree of discretion in respect of most of these variables, actuaries can usually get to a range of acceptable values for the pension liability under IFRS, US GAAP or other accounting rules. In some cases, accounting rules require pension valuations that are outside of a range of commercial values, for example by requiring the use of a high discount rate or outdated mortality tables.

Agreeing the commercial value for a net debt deduction is what pension-related negotiations in M&A transactions are usually about.

[3] The Discount Rate

The discount rate is often the principal battleground in transactions, since pension obligations (and hence the net debt deduction) can be sensitive to even minor changes in this assumption. Under IAS 19, the discount rate used to value pension liabilities has to be determined by reference to the yield of 'high-quality' (often interpreted as AA-rated) corporate bonds.

To put things in perspective, consider that AA-rated bond yields for the Eurozone used by actuaries to value pension liabilities (assuming a duration that corresponds to a mixed population) under IAS 19 was approximately 3.6% on 31 December 2013, and moved to 1.2% on 30 September 2016 and 2.0% on 30 September 2018.[49]

Here are some examples of other recent developments in bond yields in large economies:

- US corporate twenty-year AA-rated bond yields decreased from over 6% in 2007–2009 to 3.5% in July 2016, while ten-year AA-rated bond yields (another frequently used duration) decreased from around 6% to 2.35% in approximately ten years to July 2016.[50]

49. AON Eurozone Yield Curve, Development of Discount Rates for Sample Populations – last updated 30 September 2018, available here: http://www.aon.com/getmedia/9ce63b16-a135-477c-be84-f7b166b3c831/Rechnungszinsinformation_Eurozone_EN.pdf.aspx.
50. *See* bondsonline.com.

- In 2014 alone, average discount rates used for pension accounting purposes decreased from 4.84% to 4.05% in the US, and from 2.24% to 1.21% in Switzerland (a more than 50% decrease).[51]

Pension liabilities have an inverse relationship to discount rates. The liability will increase when the discount rate decreases (and vice versa). Typical pension plans have a duration between fifteen and twenty and, as noted earlier, this makes pension liabilities very sensitive to changes in the drivers of the discount rates.

How sensitive? A rule of thumb is that for a typical term, a 0.25% change in the discount rate means a 3%--4% change in the defined benefit obligation. The author has found this to be a helpful rule of thumb to quickly and approximately understand sensitivities of discount rates in a transaction context. A recent analysis of DBOs shows that the change in the defined benefit obligation attributable solely to the change in bond yields amounted to: 31.7% for 2014; a decrease of 7.4% for 2015; and an increase of 26.7% for the nine months to 30 September 2016.[52]

Negotiations in M&A transactions often come down to where the parties are prepared to meet within an acceptable range of bond yields based on current market data (buyers argue for a value at the lower end of the range whereas sellers favour the upper end).

During this period of exceptionally low yields, market participants have responded with various tactics to soften the impact on transactions of high net debt deductions - essentially finding reasons to increase discount rates. These range from including lower (A-rated) bonds in addition to AA-rated bonds to simply adding a premium. The latter stance implies that prices in the bond market were arguably unsustainable (in fact, yields have recently started to rise). While it is true that bond yields have been extremely low, it is difficult to second-guess even bubbly market prices and to derive an 'appropriate' yield this way that is capable of being justified.

There are ways to hedge exposure to interest rate changes (and other risks) in defined benefit obligations. In some transactions, this can be a way to reduce what is otherwise often significant scope for disagreement over the measurement of the DBO.

[4] Other Actuarial Assumptions

Pension liabilities are sensitive to the following actuarial assumptions other than the discount rate:

- Longevity: A broad rule of thumb is that a three-year increase in life expectancy can increase the pension liability by 10% to 20%. Mortality tables used by actuaries typically lag behind the significant improvements in life expectancy (even though these have more recently been levelling off). As a result, in

---

51. AON Global Report: Global Survey of Retirement Plan Accounting Assumptions, June 2015, p. 5. As highlighted in this report, the changes to discount rate assumptions may, in part, be due to changes in inflationary expectations.
52. AON; the most recent AA-rated bond yields are available at http://www.aon.com/germany/downloads/aonhewitt/Rechnungszins_alternativ.pdf.

negotiations buyers occasionally propose adjustments to the tables to get to more realistic (higher) values (e.g., using life insurance data). More detailed longevity data can be available, in the UK down to individual postal codes. However, adjustments to mortality tables are comparatively rare in practice. An argument against them (in particular if a business is sold to PE with a finite holding period) is that, as tables tend to lag life expectancy, the buyer can expect, when in due course they sell the business, to use life expectancies that are also outdated. However, this only works if life expectancy continues to increase at steady rates which is not necessarily the case. Note that longevity risk is a cash flow risk that buyers face even if they deduct the pension deficit. This risk can be hedged.[53]

- Projected salary and pension increases: shrewd sellers who anticipate the dynamics of the negotiations in a disposal process may, when a target company draws up its accounts before a transaction, use assumptions that minimise the pension liability. Even if buyers see through this approach, this can anchor the negotiations in the seller's favour.

[5] Treatment in Transactions

Negotiations over the deduction of unfunded pension deficits are more often over their valuation than over the question of whether or not to deduct. In contrast to most other net debt items, pension liabilities tend not to be measured at closing but are agreed upon by the parties as a fixed value prior to signing (and specified as such in the SPA). Technically, a fixed amount deduction can be effected by defining it as a 'specific accounting rule' as referenced in the accounting hierarchy discussed above in §3.04. The reason the use of a fixed deduction is often appropriate is that the value of pension obligations tends to be less influenced by day-to-day changes in the business than shorter-term liabilities. [54] Measuring the deficit at closing opens up the determination of the final purchase price to (usually unnecessary) uncertainty. In addition, because measuring pension liabilities involves making significant assumptions and it affords the preparer of the completion accounts an element of discretion which may not be desired by the other party to the transaction. It can be more expedient (and safer) to agree the value of a pension liability before signing than to have to set out the assumptions in the SPA so meticulously as to avoid ambiguity later.

53. For example, Heineken, which acquired the UK business of Scottish & Newcastle in 2009, completed a longevity hedging and reinsurance transaction in 2015 in which it transferred GBP 2.4 billion of longevity risk related to around 19,000 pensioners in the defined benefit pension scheme of the Scottish & Newcastle Pension Plan. See Heineken in 2.4 billion pound longevity swap deal with Aviva, Reuters, available at: https://uk.reuters.com/article/uk-heineken-longevity-idUKKCN0RE0UD20150914.
54. An important qualification is when employees, or groups of employees with vested benefits leave before closing.

Example: Measurement of Deficit at Closing (International Arbitration)

The case relates to an acquisition in which the seller had agreed to compensate the buyer for the deficit in a defined benefit pension scheme over a period after closing. The SPA included the provision that the pension obligation was to be measured as at closing, using a methodology 'consistent with past practice'.

The actuaries for the target company had determined the discount rate by reference to AA-rated bonds (for the relevant term). This relationship in late June 2007, before signing, is shown in Figure 4.4. On the basis of this (or similar) data, the actuary had derived an appropriate discount rate for the relevant duration.

The financial crisis prompted significant volatility in bond yields. Yields at the end of November 2008 are shown in Figure 4.5. Based on similar data, the buyer's actuaries derived a discount rate after closing. The disagreement related to whether the discount rate determined by the buyer's actuaries was on a basis 'consistent' with past practice.

Figure 4.4 AA-Bond Yields June 2007

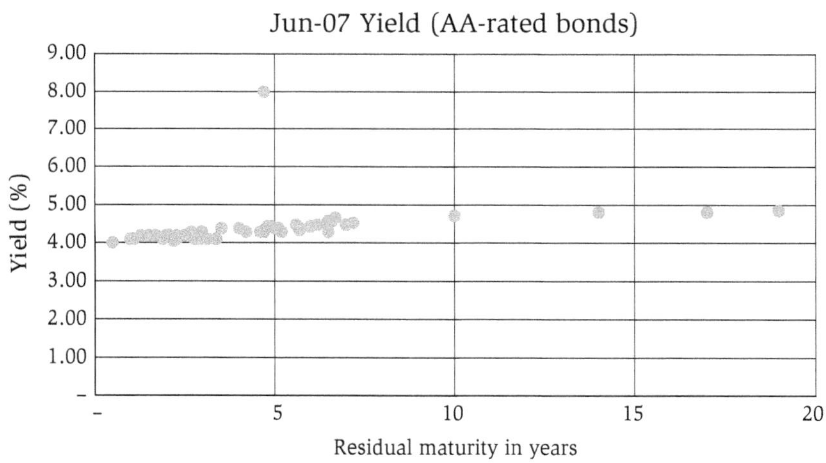

Figure 4.5 AA-Bond Yields November 2008

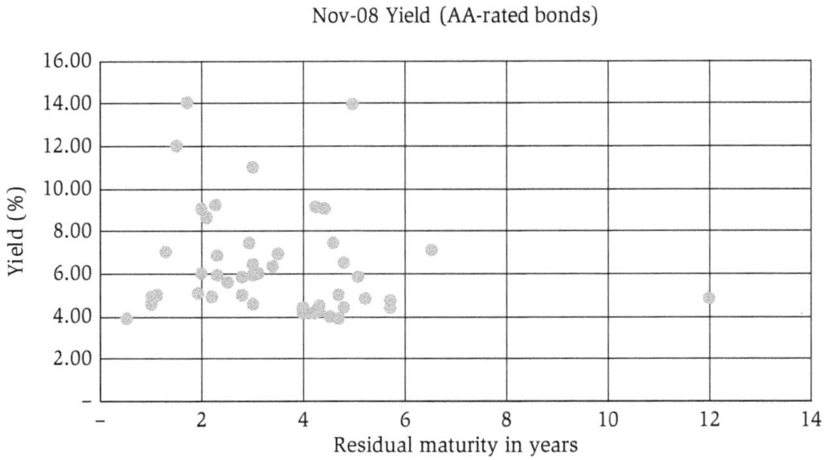

Had the turbulence in the credit markets been foreseeable, it could have been dealt with, for example by setting a fixed bond yield in the SPA. The difficulty was in anticipating it at the time.

Legacy Plans

Another issue is that a sponsoring employer may be unaware of so-called 'legacy' pension plans, perhaps because they were introduced years ago, may relate to relatively few employees and were subsequently closed – or a combination of these. Their existence may only come to light sometime after closing, when retirement benefits are claimed. In such cases a suitably worded warranty might provide a buyer with some protection (and encourage a prudent seller to take steps to satisfy themselves that they have uncovered all such plans).

Pensions in M&A-Related Disputes

Despite the importance of pension obligations in transactions and the complexity involved in their measurement, disputes in this area are not particularly common. This is likely because, as mentioned above, in many cases a fixed amount is agreed as a net debt deduction and as a result there is little scope for later disagreement. Having said that, when disputes do arise, the amounts involved can be significant relative to the size of the transaction.

The dispute discussed above in this section related to the measurement of the pension deficit. Another area where disputes can arise is over whether a particular obligation meets the SPA definition of net debt in the first place. One item in dispute in the sample of international arbitrations revolved around what the term 'defined benefit obligation' in an SPA encompassed a French *indemnité de fin de carrière* (a term used not only for pensions but for a variety of retirement benefits). The dispute could have been avoided had the definition of financial indebtedness covered the various types of deferred compensation.

[D] Provisions

[1] Introduction

A provision is defined by IASs as 'a liability of uncertain timing or amount' (IAS 37.10). It has to be recognised when:

(a) an entity has a present obligation (legal or constructive) as a result of a past event;
(b) it is probable that an outflow of resources embodying economic benefits will be required to settle the obligation (the word 'probable' is defined in IAS 37.23 as meaning 'more likely than not'); and
(c) a reliable estimate can be made of the amount of the obligation' (IAS 37.14).

If all three criteria are met, then the amount recognised as a provision should be the best estimate of the expenditure required to settle the present obligation at the balance sheet date (IAS 37.36). Provisions for one-off events (such as restructuring, environmental clean-up, settlement of a lawsuit) are measured at the most likely amount (IAS 37.40). Provisions for large populations of events (warranties, customer refunds) are measured at a probability-weighted expected value (IAS 37.39).

US GAAP knows an 'estimated loss accrued for a loss contingency' (i.e., a contingent loss that is recognised as a liability). In US GAAP, ASC 450 and ASC 460 are the primary sources of guidance. A contingency is defined as:

> An existing condition, situation, or set of circumstances involving uncertainty as to possible gain (gain contingency) or loss (loss contingency) to an entity that will ultimately be resolved when one or more future events occur or fail to occur.[55]

There are important differences between provisions in IFRS and loss contingencies in US GAAP in terms of both recognition and measurement. Under US GAAP, a loss must be accrued if information is available before the financial statements are issued that indicates that it is probable that an asset had been impaired or a liability had been incurred at the date of the financial statements, and the loss can be reasonably estimated. 'Probable' is defined as likely, which is a higher threshold than 'more likely than not' under IFRS. All else being equal, this means that more contingencies qualify for recognition as liabilities under IFRSs than under US GAAP.

For a range of possible outcomes, if no amount in the range is more likely than any other amount in the range, the *minimum* amount in the range is used to measure the amount to be accrued for a loss contingency under US GAAP. Under IFRS, if no

55. The Master Glossary of the FASB Accounting Standards Codification.

amount in the range is more likely than any other amount in the range, the *midpoint* of the range is used to measure the provision.[56]

[2] Treatment in Transactions

Many provisions, including pensions already discussed above in §4.04 [C], as well as warranties, litigation, and restructuring, relate to operating, not financing activities. While pension deficits are almost always treated as debt-like, for others, the treatment is less clear-cut.

The reason certain provisions can be treated as net debt even if they relate to operating activities was discussed above §4.02 [B]. It had to do with the timing difference between incurring an expense (and getting a benefit at this date) and the date of the cash outflow. If closing occurs between the two dates, then the buyer has the burden of a future cash outflow, but no longer the benefit. The net debt deduction moves the present value of the cash burden from buyer to seller who had the benefit at the time the (non-cash) expense was incurred.

If a provision is recurring and constantly revolving, so that by the time it becomes cash-relevant it will have already been replaced by another provision, then there is a case to treat it as working capital, not debt. Key considerations when negotiating whether or not to deduct a provision in a transaction therefore usually include the length of time involved before the liability converts into cash, and whether it is recurring. Long-term provisions (like pensions) or one-off provisions (like litigation and restructuring costs), are more often debt-like (unless already covered by indemnities). The case is less clear-cut where provisions relate to items that may or may not be considered 'a normal part of the business', for example many types of warranty obligations.

Another aspect to consider is the interaction between a provision and an indemnity. An indemnity is a promise made by the seller to reimburse the buyer dollar-for-dollar for a specific liability if it arises.[57] The outcome of litigation or environmental clean-up costs may, for example, be better covered by an indemnity rather than a net debt deduction if amounts are difficult to estimate: Indemnifying the buyer does not require an estimate to be agreed at closing (that can turn out to be incorrect later). In the case the seller has indemnified in full, there should not also be a net debt deduction for the same item.

Lastly, provisions that are treated as net debt in a transaction but are part of reported working capital in the monthly management accounts should not only be excluded from the definition of working capital at closing, but also from historical working capital when the reference value is determined.

---

56. RSM, *US. GAAP v. IFRS: Contingencies And Provisions At-A-Glance*, August 2014, p. 2, available at https://rsmus.com/content/dam/mcgladrey/pdf/contingencies-provisions-at-a-glance.pdf.
57. Below 12.01 [C].

[3] Provisions in Post-M&A Disputes

It is, perhaps, inevitable that provisions are often the subject of disputes since estimates involve a high degree of subjectivity and accounting rules give considerable discretion to the preparer of financial information. The sample of post-M&A disputes includes a number of different types of related disputes.

One type of dispute arises when one party claims that a particular item does or does not fall under the definition of net debt. A case in the sample of disputes is an International Chamber of Commerce (ICC) arbitration which related to an acquisition of a professional French sports team. The SPA definition of 'debt' included provisions for 'long- and medium-term bonus claims of players', but not short-term obligations. However, the SPA did not define precisely which obligations were short-, medium- or long-term. The dispute arose over whether bonus provisions that related to a player were correctly classified as 'medium-term'.

Another area of disagreement is the requirement to record a provision. As noted in the introduction to this section, IAS 37 requires the recognition of a provision if an outflow of resources is 'more likely than not' to occur (IAS 37.15). This means a probability of greater than 50%. Whether or not to record a provision is a matter of the assessment of probabilities. This links into the question of what information can be taken into account. As discussed above, a way to reduce the risk of a dispute in this regard is to limit in the SPA the period of time after closing for which new information can be taken into account (*see* §3.05).

Many disputes also arise over the measurement of provisions, namely which costs should be included. IAS requires the most likely outcome to be used as the provisioning amount (in case of a range of outcomes, the mid-point of that range). There is however limited guidance in the accounting standards as to which costs should be included in a provision. Not surprisingly, companies apply different practices. One dispute in the sample was over the inclusion of costs in a provision of an onerous contract. IAS 37.10 defines an onerous contract as:

> A contract in which the unavoidable costs of meeting the obligations under the contract exceed the economic benefits expected to be received under it.

IAS 37 requires a provision to be recorded for an onerous contract based on the unavoidable costs of meeting the entity's obligations under the contract. Unavoidable costs reflect the lower of the cost of fulfilling a contract and any compensation or penalties arising from failure to fulfil it (IAS 37.68). The dispute related to which costs were considered unavoidable and therefore included in the provision.

There can be a similar disagreements over the measurement of restructuring provisions. Costs of restructuring are deducted from the purchase price when the target is sold as a restructured business, but the restructuring measures have yet to be completed. With a net debt deduction, the parties intend to move the cash cost of these measures from the buyer (who pays for a restructured business) to the seller.

IAS 37 contains specific guidance for restructuring provisions. A provision is to be recognised when there is:

(a) a detailed, formal plan identifying the main aspects of the restructuring (IAS 37.72); and
(b) a valid expectation in those affected that the entity will carry out the restructuring by starting to implement the plan or by announcing its main features to those affected (IAS 37.10).

A restructuring provision should include only direct expenditures caused by the restructuring, not costs that associated with the ongoing activities of the entity. As their measurement requires considerable judgment. It is not surprising that restructuring provisions have been used as a way to manipulate earnings. An example is 'big bath' accounting, a manipulation that reduces a period's income significantly (often the first period under new management) by deliberately overestimating restructuring costs, only to 'bleed' those costs back to income and report earnings improvements in subsequent periods. There can be similar dynamics at work in a sales process. It is for the quality of earnings analysis to identify these manipulations.

A way to reduce the risk of a dispute is to agree a fixed amount as a net debt deduction for restructuring measures before signing. This amount may be determined independently of the accounting and should be consistent with the business plan on which the bid is based.

[E] Derivate Securities

[1] Introduction

So far in this section debt-like items that represent direct obligations to third parties such as financial institutions (banks, lessors, factors, institutional investors, etc.), former employees (deferred compensation), or government agencies (taxes) have been discussed. Companies can also enter into commitments that derive their value indirectly (from underlying assets). Such arrangements are derivatives. Common types of derivatives are options, futures, forwards, and swaps. For example, the price of a call or put option on a stock depends, among other factors, on the stock price to which it bears a (no-arbitrage) relation. Derivatives can be structured to depend on the prices of a variety of underlying variables, including share prices, commodity prices, debt securities, indices, weather events, emissions, electricity prices, and many others.[58]

The principal use of derivatives is to shift risk among investors. In the case of an interest rate swap, for example, a company may have borrowed at a variable interest rate and uses a swap to effectively convert variable into fixed interest rate payments. As a result, the borrower has effectively removed its exposure to interest rate volatility.

Derivatives can relate to financing or operating activities. An interest rate swap that swaps variable against fixed interest payments can be considered an extension of the underlying loan agreement, and therefore a financing activity. On the other hand, a forward sale is a common way of selling commodities and can be viewed as an

58. John C. Hull, *Options, Futures and Other Derivatives*, (6th ed., Pearson 2006), p. 552.

operating activity. The cost associated with derivatives used for hedging (whether or not charged to the income statement) is essentially the cost of removing exposure to volatility from everyday business activities, bringing the business to a less volatile state. Again, this cost could be an operating cost or a financing cost, depending on the underlying security or variable.

Accounting for derivative instruments, or hedge accounting, saw a significant reform with the recent introduction of IFRS 9, the new financial instruments standard that replaced IAS 39. The reform can be viewed in part as a response by the standard setter to accounting issues that were highlighted by the global financial crisis.

This section discusses the most common derivatives and then turns to their treatment in a transaction.

Financial Options

Options give their holder the right, but not the obligation, to buy or sell a fixed quantity of an asset either at some future date or during a specified time period in the future, and at a specific price. There are two basic types of options: 'call options' give the right to buy an asset at a certain price, and 'put options' the right to sell an asset at a certain price. The most common type of financial options are stock options.

An option is considered a derivative security as its price depends on the price of the underlying share. The price at which an option can be exercised is called the 'exercise price' or 'strike price'. When the exercise price of a stock option is equal to the current price of the share, then the option is *at-the-money*. A call option with an exercise price below the current share price is *in-the-money*. The same is true for a put option with a strike price above the current share price. A call option with a strike price above the current share price and a put option with a strike price below the current share price are all *out-of-the-money*.[59]

Futures Contracts

A futures contract is an agreement to buy or sell an asset in a specified quantity, at a certain time in the future, and for an agreed price. It is a derivative instrument as its value depends on the price of an underlying asset. Futures contracts are usually standardised instruments and traded on exchanges at a publicly observable price, allowing the parties to buy or sell them at any time when the markets are open.

Forward Contracts

Like a futures contract, a forward contract is a contract that requires the holder to buy or sell an asset for a specified price at a specified future time. The difference between the two types of derivatives is that forward contracts are not normally traded on an exchange but in the over-the-counter market. Forward contracts are often used to hedge foreign exchange exposure.

59. *Ibid.*, n. 28, p. 657.

Swaps

A swap is an agreement to exchange cash flows in the future at a certain formula. For example, an interest rate swap may exchange floating interest payments for fixed payments. At the inception of the swap, the total value of fixed interest rate cash flows over the life of the swap is typically equal to the expected value of floating interest rate cash flows. The swap is *at-the-money*. After some time, as the floating rate changes, the swap moves *in-the-money* or *out-of-the-money*. For a corporate, the purpose of a swap is usually to reduce or eliminate risk posed by interest rate volatility.

[2] Treatment in Transactions

It is sometimes suggested in negotiations that all out-of-the money-derivatives should be treated as debt-like. This makes sense when their holder has an obligation to make a payment to a counterparty. This is the case, for example, for an interest rate swap where (from the target entity perspective of a fixed-rate payer) the fixed rate exceeds the variable rate. Such an obligation represents an economic burden at closing which a buyer acquires and which – if not already reflected in the carrying value of the loan – can be moved to the seller as a net debt deduction.

If a target company that is not a financial institution has entered into a currency swap which, for example, requires it to make up the difference in value of a weakening pound against US dollar, then it can also be argued that this commitment should be treated as debt.

However, out-of-the-money derivative securities do not necessarily represent an obligation to transfer value to a third party. For example, a call option that has a strike price above the share price is out-of-the-money (from the perspective of the option holder). Similarly, a put option on a share with a strike price below the spot price is also out-of-the-money. These out-of-the-money derivative instruments represent only a right, not an obligation, to transfer value to a third party. If they remain out-of-the-money, the option will not be exercised and their value will be zero at the time of expiration. However, before they expire, given the possibility that the share price moves above the strike price and the options move into-the-money, even out-of-the-money options have a positive value. (While the intrinsic value of the option is zero, the time value is not zero.) There is therefore usually no reason to deduct an out-of-the-money option in these cases.

For most businesses that are not financial institutions, call or put options are not a necessary part of operating the business. Acquirers should therefore value them separately and (even if out-of-the-money) their fair value may be added to the enterprise value. This essentially treats them like cash (or other non-operating assets), reducing net debt.

Another case is the acquisition of a company that has issued share options (e.g., as employee remuneration). IFRS 2 requires a company to measure and recognise share-based payment awards (to employees or other parties) in its financial statements at the fair value of the goods and services received. They are expensed as vesting conditions are satisfied.[60] Expensing share options has been required since IFRS 2 was issued in 2004. US GAAP has similar provisions in ASC Topic 718, Compensation--Stock Compensation and in ASC Subtopic 505-50, Equity - Equity-Based Payments to Non Employees.[61]

In general, once the awards have vested, they represent a reward for work already performed, similar to other kinds of deferred compensation.[62] At the time a share-based award is expensed, it reduces EBITDA; however, until an option is exercised, it has not yet diluted the existing shareholders (if equity-settled), or become cash-relevant (if cash-settled).

The treatment of stock options in an acquisition depends on whether or not outstanding options survive the transaction. The buyer may assume or substitute the target company's options; the options may alternatively be cashed out or cancelled. In some countries, an acquirer is required to make an appropriate offer for convertible securities in acquisitions (under certain circumstances).[63] A discussion of these alternatives is beyond the scope of this book. As a general rule, however, any cost of a target company's outstanding options to the shareholders of the acquiring company should be reflected in the purchase price at fair value. In the (small) fraction of private M&A acquisitions in which options are assumed by the acquirer, a net debt deduction can be appropriate to reflect the cost of dilution to existing shareholders.

[F] Deferred Revenue

[1] Introduction

Deferred revenue is revenue that has not been earned although cash has been collected from customers in the form of a prepayment. It is usually (though not necessarily) reported in a company's balance sheet in current liabilities. Deferred revenue is one aspect of revenue recognition that can directly affect net debt (for a discussion of revenue recognition, *see* Chapter 9).

[2] Treatment in Transactions

Whether deferred revenue should be treated as debt or as working capital in a transaction is a frequent source of debate and negotiation.

The case for treating deferred revenue as debt (usually advanced by the buyer) is as follows: the target company has received cash from customers that is recorded in the balance sheet at closing. If there is no deduction in this respect, the buyer pays for the cash by way of a dollar-for-dollar increase in the purchase price. However, it is the

60. Applying IFRS, Accounting for share-based payments under IFRS 2 - the essential guide, EY, April 2015, p. 2.
61. Expensing stock options was part of the reforms after the dot-com bubble of the late 1990s. The resistance to expensing stock options from lobbyists was significant.
62. *See* §4.02.
63. For example, The UK Takeover Code, Section D, Rule 15.

buyer who will incur the cost associated with earning the deferred revenue, and this cost will be incurred after closing. The receipt of cash (in the form of customer prepayments) and the disbursement of cash (to suppliers or employees to fulfil the contract) do not match. A net debt deduction moves the economic burden of servicing the contract to the seller.

The counterargument for treating deferred revenue as working capital (usually advanced by the seller) is this: receiving prepayments from customers is a recurring part of operations, and a constantly revolving level of prepayments exists at any given time. The target company will be able to fund the cash outflows to fulfil the contract out of future prepayments that will have been received by the time the costs become cash-relevant.

As can be seen, the treatment of deferred revenue is by no means clear-cut and depends to a large extent on the nature of the target company's business and/or the prepayment. To illustrate, consider the following two extremes.

Example 1: Businesses Engaged in Large-Scale Construction

Two (almost) identical target companies are engaged in the construction of large power plants. They are about to commence the construction of one such plant. On the day before closing, Company A receives a prepayment from a customer of 30% of the contract value. It defers revenue. Company B receives a similar payment, but a day *after* closing.
At closing, should a buyer pay the same amount to acquire the shares of the two companies?

It seems clear that the amount of deferred revenue at closing (assuming no construction work takes place on the two dates in question) should be the difference in price. This suggests a net debt deduction is appropriate. If the seller insisted on customer prepayments falling into the definition of working capital, it would be reasonable for the buyer to argue that reference working capital should not include any such prepayments, so that, on closing, any prepayments over and above reference working capital are effectively treated as reductions to working capital and, hence, to the purchase price. This would achieve the same economic result as a net debt deduction. Nevertheless, as discussed above (*see* §4.03), a buyer may still prefer a net debt deduction.

Example 2: Business Engaged in High-Volume, Individually Low-Value Transactions

A newspaper publisher routinely receives payments on (prepaid) subscriptions from a large number of subscribers. The aggregate prepayments vary from day to day and may spike during the holiday season, but individual amounts are small and it makes little if any difference when they are received. Whether any particular prepayment is received the day before or after closing is not material; there is always a level of prepayments in deferred revenue on any day of a month.

In this case, the prepayments meet the criteria of working capital: operating nature, short-term conversion into cash, constantly revolving (*see* §5.03) and the deferred item is more likely working capital.

The criteria that are touched upon in Chapters 2 and 5 when considering the treatment as debt or alternatively working capital generally apply here. When considering the treatment of deferred revenue, a question to ask is whether either the buyer or seller should be concerned about the exact closing (or locked box) date. If a party has reason to be concerned about the timing of a particular prepayment (as in example 1 above), then there is a case for a net debt adjustment. The more important the timing of payments, the stronger the case to treat as debt. If, on the other hand, the timing is not important (as in example 2), then deferred revenue (if recurring) is more likely working capital. It is the cases in between these two extremes that are often controversial in negotiations.

An approach that is occasionally advocated is a net debt adjustment only for the *future cost* of fulfilling the contract to which the prepayment relates, not the entire prepayment received. The result is that, economically, the seller retains the profit margin on the contract while the buyer recovers the future cost of fulfilling their obligations under the contract, the reasoning being that the seller originated the contract and should therefore obtain the reward. There are two arguments against this approach. First, it is not clear why the seller should retain the economic rewards relating to a particular contract only because cash has already been collected (as there would be no reallocation of the contract margin if cash had not been received). Second, agreeing an expected profit margin can be complex: The extent to which a seller should be entitled to retain profits by moving certain costs to the buyer is not at all clear, not even in concept.

[3] Deferred Revenue in Post-M&A Disputes

One reason deferred revenue is comparatively uncommon in disputes is that the amount of cash received and deferred at closing leaves relatively little discretion on the part of preparers of accounts.

The sample includes a dispute in which the parties had agreed on a net debt deduction for the costs of fulfilling a contract for which the target company had received a prepayment. When the completion accounts were drafted, the parties disagreed on the allocation of overheads into the contract. This shows that, if the method of measuring profit is not adequately defined in the SPA, the risk of a dispute is heightened. But even if it is defined, estimating costs to completion can be far from straightforward. Consequently, if the parties to a transaction wish to adopt this approach, it may be preferable to use a fixed percentage margin to avoid problems after closing.

[G] Capital Expenditure Creditors

[1] Introduction

Capital expenditure creditors are usually reported in a company's balance sheet in current liabilities within an aggregate figure for creditors, and not separately disclosed. Hence they tend to be regarded, prima facie, as part of working capital.

A net debt deduction for capital expenditure creditors is different from the capital expenditure purchase price adjustment discussed in §2.02[D]. The purpose of the latter is to protect a buyer from a seller delaying capital spend in order to maximise the cash position at closing, and it acheives this by measuring actual (cumulative) capital spending against a target level, adjusting for any deficit. Spending that was deferred during the closing period would not necessarily be captured by a net debt deduction for capital expenditure creditors *at closing*.

[2] Treatment in Transactions

The reasons to treat capital expenditure creditors as either working capital or net debt are similar to those discussed for deferred revenue earlier in this chapter. To the extent that the creditors relate to routine expenditure in the ordinary course of business, they would normally be included in working capital and taken into account in the computation of reference working capital. Exceptions to this would be:

- Where the target business is capital intensive and property, plant and equipment additions involve large sums which make it difficult to calculate accurately a reference working capital position at any given time (including the closing date);
- The target business incurs individual sums of capital expenditure from time to time which could result in actual working capital at closing not bearing comparison with reference working capital.

As mentioned elsewhere in this publication it is important to ensure that balances are not double counted, for example capital expenditure creditors included in working capital *and* as a net debt adjustment.

[H] Non-controlling Interest (Or Minority Interest)

[1] Introduction

A non-controlling interest (called 'minority interest' before IFRS 3 was introduced; in this publication both terms are used interchangeably) is the interest in a subsidiary company not attributable to the parent that owns a controlling interest. This is depicted in Figure 4.6.

Figure 4.6 Example Group Structure Showing Non-controlling Interest in Subsidiary

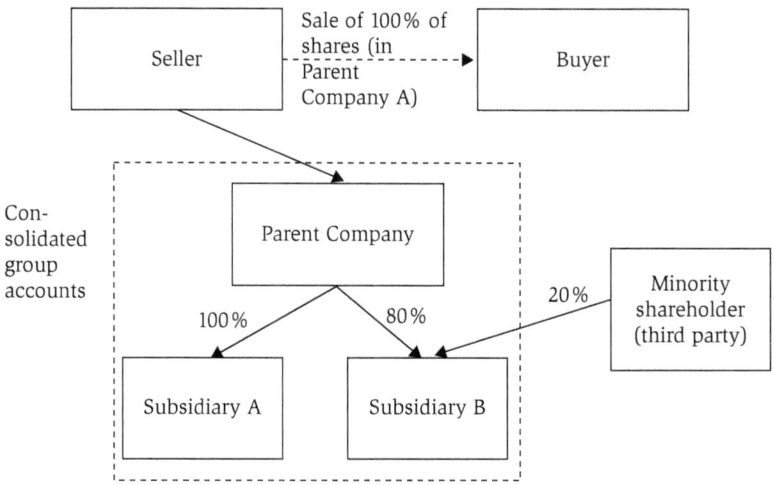

If Parent Company holds an 80% interest and an unrelated third party holds a 20% interest in Subsidiary B, the 20% interest is the minority – or non-controlling – interest. The minority interest may have come about for different reasons. For example, it may be held by the founder of a business who previously sold the majority stake, or perhaps by management as a form of incentive.

In the consolidated financial statements, Parent Company presents non-controlling interest within equity, separately from the equity of the owners (IFRS 10.22).

[2] Treatment in Transactions

[a] Overview

Continuing with the example above, let us assume that Seller intends to dispose of 100% of the share capital in Parent Company. Buyer values the enterprise using both a DCF (on a free cash flow basis) and a multiple method, in each case based on consolidated financial information (which includes 100% of the results of Subsidiary B).

Subsidiary B's value is then included in full in the enterprise value attributed to the group. The enterprise value for the group as a whole does not reflect the fact that a minority owner is entitled to a share in the surpluses that Subsidiary B will generate in the future. If dividend payments correspond to the ownership proportions, the acquisition of 100% of the shares of Parent Company entitles Buyer to only 80% of Subsidiary B's dividends.

Without adjusting the valuation, the buyer overpays. The purchase price for the common equity of Parent Company should, therefore, be reduced by the fair value of the minority interest in Subsidiary B. One way to achieve this in a DCF model is to remove expected dividend payments to the minority shareholder. However, it may be impractical to project cash flows for the subsidiary separately, especially if it is of minor importance. The DCF model is often prepared on the basis of consolidated group figures (i.e., 100% of the minority-owned subsidiary figures are entered) and not on the basis of the individual entities' respective projected cash flows. An alternative approach used more frequently is therefore to value the minority interest separately and deduct it from enterprise value as a debt-like item.

[b] Valuation Considerations

Valuing a minority interest, often a relatively small amount in the overall context of a transaction, can be unduly time-consuming. Because the fair value of a minority interest often differs from its book value, it is not necessarily appropriate to deduct the book value, unless the amounts involved are immaterial.

Buyers should also consider whether it is appropriate to apply the overall transaction multiple of the target group when valuing the subsidiary, since (among other things) the latter may operate in a different market or in a niche of the target group's market. For example, the subsidiary of a US Group that is fast-growing and that operates in an emerging market may be more adequately valued using a higher multiple.

The fair value of a minority interest is often different from the pro-rata value of the equity of the subsidiary in question, due to the value of control. On the one hand, valuation practitioners typically associate control with a higher price, known as a 'control premium'. On the other hand, it can be important to consider that some minority owners have veto or other rights that may increase the value of the non-controlling interest.

Valuing a minority interest can be time-consuming and cumbersome.[64] In view of the limited significance of the amounts in question, in many instances a detailed valuation of the non-controlling interest is not merited. Instead, simple approximations can be used and this, in fact, is most frequently done in practice.

64. Stephen H. Penman, *Financial Statement Analysis and Security Valuation* (4th ed., McGraw-Hill Education 2009), p. 370.

[c] Approaches in Practice

Fixed-Price Deduction

A common approach is for a minority that is not immaterial to be valued separately from the rest of the target group, with a multiple- or a DCF-based valuation method (or a combination of the two), and a net debt / net working capital deduction based on the subsidiary's balance sheet at some date before the transaction, around the time of the valuation. This value represents an equity value, which is then specified in the SPA as a (fixed value) net debt deduction. There is no further adjustment for the minority interest after closing.

Purchase price adjustments at group level are usually made on a 100% basis. This means that these adjustments include 100% of the minority-owned subsidiary's net debt and working capital items. As the minority-owned subsidiary's net debt and working capital positions will have changed to closing, whereas the net debt deduction for the subsidiary may be fixed, this could result in a discrepancy at closing. However, this is rarely a concern in practice. Otherwise, the parties can agree a separate net debt adjustment for the minority, or a correction to the overall group net debt adjustment as part of the true-up at closing.

Buyout Value

The minority interest is also sometimes determined as the (hypothetical) cost of buying out the minority owner. This is often a higher amount than a multiple- or DCF-based valuation of the subsidiary would suggest.

Valuation at Closing

Another approach is to specify in the SPA that a valuation using a multiple is to be performed at closing, along with a multiple to be used.[65] However, this can easily lead to disagreement over reported EBITDA of the subsidiary (if an EBITDA-multiple is used). Protecting against this risk would require the SPA to identify all those components of EBITDA that should be excluded from the basis to which the multiple is applied, similar in this aspect to protections in earn-outs (*see* §8.03). This is often not a workable approach. As is the case with many other valuation matters in a transaction, the time to fix the amount of a deduction for a minority interest is generally before signing.

65. *See* Kiem, *Kaufpreisregelungen beim Unternehmenskauf* (2nd ed., C.H. Beck, 2018), p. 220.

Book Value

It is sometimes proposed to deduct the minority share at book value. Generally speaking, the book value is not an appropriate basis for what should be the commercial valuation of a net debt deduction, unless it corresponds to the fair value, (just as the book value of the group is usually the basis of the purchase price for the shares in the target business).

However, if the minority interest is not material, or if a book value for the minority is identical to or close to its fair value, then this may be a straightforward alternative. The book value should then be fixed in the SPA at the time of signing, as measuring it at completion would mean unnecessary complexity and expose the parties to unforeseen changes to the book value of equity at closing similar to those discussed above at §2.02 [F].

[I] Deferred Taxes

[1] Introduction

Deferred taxes are hardly the first item to come to mind as a net debt deduction in a transaction. Indeed, such treatment is comparatively rare. However, there is a rationale for deducting deferred tax liabilities or adding deferred tax assets in certain circumstances.

Under IFRS, deferred tax liabilities are recorded for 'income taxes payable in future periods in respect of taxable temporary differences' (IAS 12.5). Deferred tax assets relate to income taxes recoverable in future periods in respect of deductible temporary differences but also to the carry forward of unused tax losses and of unused tax credits.[66] Temporary differences give rise to deferred taxes.[67]

Let's turn now to the treatment in transactions. Consider the following example.

Example: Deferred Tax

Two businesses are for sale. They are identical, the sole difference being the tax treatment of a particular operating asset. Both report the same carrying value for the asset in their financial accounts (both depreciating the asset over the same useful life). Their balance sheets are identical (except for a deferred tax item and equity). Company A, in the financial year prior to being sold, depreciated the asset in full in its tax accounts, reducing its taxable income for that year. Company B, on the other hand,

66. 'Taxable' and 'deductible' temporary differences are differences that, respectively, result in taxable amounts, or are deductible, in determining taxable profits of future periods when the carrying amount of an asset or liability is recovered or settled (IAS 12.5).
67. However, not all temporary differences result in deferred taxes. An exception is the initial recognition of goodwill – *see* IAS 12.15(a).

elected to depreciate the asset over five years in its tax accounts, the same period that it applies for financial accounts purposes. It therefore reports the asset at the same carrying value in its financial and its tax accounts.

Company B will benefit from lower taxes in the future. A reader of the companies' financial accounts alone might think each company has the same 'tax shield' (i.e., the same future depreciation expense). But a tax shield actually only exists for Company B. Do the two companies have the same value?

Clearly the difference in value is the present value of the difference in future taxes that the two companies will pay (all else being equal). Undiscounted, this difference is the deferred tax liability in respect of the asset recorded in Company A's balance sheet (provided the deferred tax liability is valued correctly). As such, this should result in a difference in value.

If the difference in future tax payments of the two companies is built into the valuation model, no deduction for net debt is required. In practice, however, this is not always the case (see below [2][a]). In Company A's valuation, therefore, there is a case for a net debt deduction; the buyer of Company A would otherwise overpay.

A possible objection to a net debt deduction might be where the temporary differences relate to short-lived balance sheet items that constantly renew themselves, so that they can be considered recurring. An example might be development expenditure - capitalised and amortised over a short period in the financial accounts but expensed immediately in the tax accounts. The deferred tax liabilities could meet the criteria for working capital.

[2] Interaction with the Valuation of the Target

[a] Income Approach

The income approach is discussed below usually in §11.04 [B]. The DCF method is the most commonly used form. A DCF model usually includes projections of future income tax payments. Many investors will model future income taxes of the target business separately. However, some use models that project income taxes on the basis of projected net *financial* (instead of *taxable*) income, thereby, in a first step at least, ignoring differences between the financial and tax accounts. If these differences are temporary and are not captured in the tax calculation in the DCF model, then they are effectively omitted from the model.[68] Since taxes on operating income are operating cash outflows (and therefore part of free cash flow), this, in turn, will result in an incorrect enterprise value. Setting aside discounting, the valuation error is the same amount as the deferred tax asset or liability.[69] So an adjustment for the deferred tax asset or liability effectively corrects for using the financial income as the basis of calculating taxes instead of taxable income.

68. The same applies if these differences relate to tax-loss carry forwards available to be set against future taxable profits subject to meeting the criteria of IAS 12.
69. International Accounting Standards do not permit the discounting of deferred tax assets or liabilities (IAS 12.53).

[b] Market Approach

This approach is discussed below in §11.04 [C]. It includes multiple-based valuations that often relate price to pre-tax earnings (e.g., EBIT or EBITDA). Such an approach effectively ignores income taxes in the earnings measure. Tax effects are instead incorporated in the valuation multiple (at least in concept). What does this mean for deferred taxes in transactions? It might be assumed that a normal level of deferred taxes is implicit in the multiple, and further that the target company's future tax burden will ultimately revert to the mean of the peer group of comparator companies. However, this assumption is not necessarily correct. Taxes can be managed (similar to other operating expenses that are also not generally expected in valuations to revert to the mean).

[c] Deferred Tax Assets

Treating a deferred tax asset as net debt would mean adding the carrying value to the purchase price, similar to a cash equivalent. One case where this is frequently done relates to pension deficits where the tax base can be substantially lower than the financial accounts figure. As for deferred tax assets related to tax loss carryforwards, the key question is usually whether the losses will be available to a buyer after a transaction; as such they are often considered and priced separately, and the deferred tax asset is then not added to the purchase price.

[3] Deferred Taxes in Post-M&A Disputes

Most disputes that relate to deferred taxes are not over the deferred tax asset or liability in the first place, but over an underlying asset or liability that has given rise to the deferred tax. A change to the underlying asset or liability therefore impacts the deferred tax. This can become relevant for example, in accounting warranty breaches. There can also be disagreement over the valuation allowance against deferred tax assets.

[J] Overdue Trade Payables

A business may be unable or unwilling to pay off its trade payables when they become due. There may be an explicit or tacit understanding with a supplier that payables can remain outstanding in order to avoid insolvency. Trade payables between related parties are sometimes settled only at the end of a reporting period, and, from a group perspective, it may not matter that they are overdue. In these instances, trade payables may lose their normal, short-term, revolving, operating characteristics which usually make them working capital. There is a case to be made that these kinds of payables become financing balances. Of course, things are not always clear-cut, and not every overdue trade payable is a financing item and therefore net debt.

[K] Cash and Cash Equivalents

As indicated in the equity bridge in §2.01, cash and cash equivalents increase the equity value. The idea is that the buyer can extract the cash after closing and should therefore pay for it dollar-for-dollar. This assumes of course that the buyer can extract such cash, that is, the cash is 'free'.

'Free' cash is cash that is not needed to operate the business; this means there are no legal, regulatory, or other restrictions preventing it from being extracted in full. Cash and cash equivalents that are not free should not form part of cash for purposes of the net debt definition. On close examination, most (though by no means all) businesses require a certain minimum level of cash for day-to-day operations; this cash is, effectively, working capital. It is sometimes referred to as 'working cash'. Examples are cash floats in tills at retailers or intra-month cash needs (to the extent they are not already reflected in the working capital reference value).

Other than cash needs for the day-to-day operations of a business, it may not be possible to extract cash due to exchange controls or capitalisation requirements for financial institutions; further, cash may be held in entities with negative net assets, and dividends may be restricted. (It is important when reviewing these cases to consider net assets under local GAAP as it is this which may restrict dividends).

In practice, there is often no net debt deduction for these types of 'trapped cash'. This is perhaps because the question of precisely which component of cash is free can be difficult to answer.

There are numerous reasons why firms hold more cash and cash equivalents than they need in their operations: the cash may be intended for payout as a dividend, or for future investments, or it may be held simply as a precaution. Further, the repatriation of earnings of foreign corporate subsidiaries may trigger taxes that could have been deferred, leading to large amounts of untaxed offshore earnings (not all of which are however cash).[70]

One approach some buyers take is to propose that the seller take all cash out of the target business before closing, so that the business is transferred, ostensibly, cash-free. This is the safest way for the buyer to obtain certainty that he or she is not paying for trapped cash, and the best test of whether it is, in fact, cash that can be taken out of the business at will because it is not needed for operating the business. However, in complex transactions with multiple subsidiaries, each with its own cash position, it is cumbersome to extract all cash, and rarely if ever done.

Another aspect to consider is the definition of cash and cash equivalents. The term 'cash at bank' may not be sufficiently precise, as it may not encompass items within the bank reconciliation which may reduce cash, such as deposits in transit or

70. According to an estimate by the US Congress Joint Committee on Taxation, in September 2016, US companies had USD 2.6 trillion in untaxed offshore earnings. *See* Untaxed offshore earnings of US companies rises to USD 2.6 trillion, The Washington Examiner, 29 Sep. 2016.

outstanding (or bounced) checks. Cash and equivalents may also include items that are really receivables (such as credit card receivables) and which the external auditors may have considered to be immaterial.

Which part of the cash balance is considered to be 'free' and which is subject to restrictions or required in the operations of the business should be defined in the SPA, either as a fixed amount or by specifying a measurement method (such as percentage of total cash or a percentage of sales).

CHAPTER 5
Working Capital

§5.01 INTRODUCTION

Working capital is the part of the balance sheet where many types of volatile 'real world' events often most prominently find their way into transactions. It was within working capital that the financial crisis of 2008 and 2009 left some of its most visible traces in many balance sheets – impaired trade receivables, unsellable inventories, or stretched payables. Given the areas of subjectivity in accounting for working capital, and the estimates required, it is perhaps no surprise that this is the balance sheet category where the largest number of disputes originate.

As discussed in Chapter 2, indicative offers at the early stages of a transaction often refer to a 'headline' or 'cash- and debt-free' price. This refers to enterprise value, the present value of the target's operating activities. Enterprise value is determined on the basis that *all* the assets and liabilities needed by the target business in order to operate are transferred to the buyer as part of the transaction, including an appropriate level of working capital. A shortfall in working capital at closing means that the target business is not transferred with all assets and liabilities that are normally needed to operate the business and that are intrinsic to the determination of the headline price. The seller transfers a deficit in value to the buyer. Conversely, a surplus of working capital means that the seller transfers more value than is assumed in the valuation.

Most businesses require a certain positive level of working capital as part of their normal operations. Much like a car requires at least some petrol in its tank, and that petrol ties up cash that the owner could use for other purposes, working capital (if positive) ties up cash that would otherwise be available for alternative uses. Why do businesses require working capital? Sales do not convert into cash immediately, resulting in trade receivables; many companies need inventories of raw materials and finished goods which can be viewed as an investment in current assets. Both are examples of positive working capital. Other components of working capital are negative: suppliers are not usually paid immediately upon delivery of goods or services, hence companies record trade payables.

For some businesses, overall net working capital is negative. Rather than tying up liquidity, negative working capital generates it (from operating activities). This is the case when a company takes credit from suppliers, turns inventory very quickly and is paid by its customers with cash. For example, Amazon reports negative working capital.[71]

It is very common for non-binding offer letters to specify that the headline price presupposes that the target business will be transferred with an 'appropriate', 'normal', or 'adequate' level of working capital without quantifying at this stage what the appropriate level is. The buyer expects the seller to run the business properly and, in particular, that there will be no deficiency of working capital as a result of the seller being overzealous in his or her desire to reduce net debt (by maximising the cash position). Such wording paves the way for a working capital adjustment in transactions involving completion accounts as well as locked boxes. In the latter case, it is (or should be) understood that the same rationale entails a normal level of working capital at the date of economic transfer, and any deficit or surplus is reflected in the fixed purchase price.

A normal level of working capital – 'the reference value' – is specified in the SPA as part of the working capital price adjustment mechanism, along with the basis of measurement. The actual level of working capital is subsequently measured at closing. If closing working capital exceeds the reference value, this means an upward (usually dollar-for-dollar) adjustment to the purchase price. Conversely, a deficit results in a reduction in the purchase price.

The rationale is that, if at closing the business has more working capital than it needs to operate, then the buyer pays for the excess dollar-for-dollar as the buyer could extract the surplus working capital from the business. If, on the other hand, there is a working capital deficit, the purchase price is correspondingly reduced because the buyer will have to bring working capital back up to a 'normal' level, requiring additional funding (which is deducted from the purchase price).

§5.02 INTERACTION WITH NET DEBT

For the working capital adjustment to work properly, a clean interaction with the definition of net debt is essential. This means that no item should be captured by both definitions (working capital and net debt), and no relevant item omitted. If the ultimate purchase price does not properly reflect the actual value of the net assets that are transferred, this can be a cause of discontent for whichever side overpaid, and can lead to disputes.

---

71. In the year ended 31 Dec. 2017, Amazon reported average Days Sales Outstanding (DSO) of 22.1, average Days Inventory Outstanding (DIO) of 44.8, average Days Payable Outstanding (DPO) of 93.9, and an average cash conversion cycle of minus 26.9 days (*Source*: CapitalIQ, difference due to rounding).

To understand this interaction, consider the way in which the cash (and cash equivalents) position interacts with individual components of working capital as demonstrated by simple day-to-day transactions: the receipt of funds from customers means that the cash position increases and trade receivables decrease. The effects offset each other: net debt decreases (as cash increases) and working capital decreases (as receivables decrease). Conversely, when a company pays a supplier, net debt increases (as cash decreases) and net working capital increases (trade payables decrease).

Every increase in net debt leads to a dollar-for-dollar reduction in the net purchase price. Every increase in working capital results in a dollar-for-dollar increase in the net purchase price (as long as the working capital adjustment is measured against the reference value). If the net debt and the working capital mechanisms interact as they should, then there is an exactly offsetting effect. It does not matter if a particular receivable has been turned into cash or a creditor has been paid on a particular date, because the effects on the purchase price of the changes in net debt and working capital offset each other. Accelerating collections from customers, deferring payment of creditors, liquidating inventories prematurely: none of these will have an impact on the net purchase price if the working capital and net debt adjustments interact correctly.

If the interaction functions properly, and an appropriate working capital reference value is agreed, the parties should, in terms of the purchase price alone, be indifferent to the precise level of working capital and cash (or debt) at closing. In this regard, working capital in excess of the reference value counts just like cash in the determination of the final purchase price, which makes sense as long as all of its components are genuinely as good as cash. This is a matter of clarity as to what working capital encompasses and the approach to its measurement. Both should be specified in the SPA. They are discussed in the following sections.

§5.03 DEFINING WORKING CAPITAL

There is no standard definition of working capital in the transaction context. What is treated as working capital and how it is measured (i.e., the precise basis of accounting) needs to be agreed between the parties and set out clearly in the SPA.

A convention is that, at a minimum, working capital includes trade receivables, trade payables, and inventory. This is often called 'core' or 'trade' working capital. However, these three components usually do not capture all items that are working capital in nature, and the definition of core working capital in SPAs therefore almost always needs to encompass other items in order to ensure a clean interaction with net debt.

As to which other items to include, there are no hard-and-fast rules. When considering whether a balance sheet item should be part of working capital, the following criteria usually must be met in order for an asset or liability to be working capital:

- working capital consists of operating assets or liabilities;

- they convert into cash in a short period of time; and
- they are constantly revolving.

They are discussed below. If all three are met, then there is usually a good case to treat the item as working capital for completion mechanism purposes.

[A] Operating Nature

As discussed in Chapter 2, enterprise value is the present value of future returns of the operations. It includes only *operating* assets and liabilities (as opposed to *financing* assets and liabilities).

Operating assets and liabilities arise from *operating activities*, i.e., activities connected with the production of goods or services which are the object of the enterprise. Making sales to customers who do not pay immediately, owing money to suppliers of goods or services needed for production, or managing stocks to be able to react to customer orders - these are all operating activities usually directly associated with the core purpose of the business. They give rise to trade receivables, trade payables and inventory, respectively, all operating assets or liabilities, and core components of working capital.

Financing activities, on the other hand, have to do with the distribution of surpluses generated by the operations (e.g., paying dividends or servicing debt) or perhaps, funding operating cash shortfalls (e.g., raising liquidity in the capital markets). When considering whether a balance sheet item should be treated as working capital, the first question is therefore whether the item relates to an operating activity or a financing activity.

While being part of operations is usually a necessary condition in order to be categorised as working capital, it is not the only condition: many assets and liabilities, while operating in nature, are not working capital, including, for example, fixed assets or pension liabilities.

[B] Conversion to Cash in the Short Term

Working capital converts into cash in the short term: Trade receivables are settled by customers, suppliers are paid and inventory is sold, normally within a few days, weeks, or months. This timing aspect brings working capital close to cash.

According to accounting convention, balance sheet items are classified as current if they convert to cash in no more than one year.[72] The treatment in transactions usually follows this convention since financial accounts readily provide the requisite information. However, in some cases, buyers may consider a year to be comparatively long for current assets to convert into cash in the context of the analysis of working capital (which they pay for dollar-for-dollar): a trade receivable that is almost a year

72. Strictly speaking IAS 1.66 sets out criteria that do not necessarily require cash conversion within one year.

old, or slow-moving inventory, may give rise to concerns over recoverability. Allowances and write-downs that reflect such concerns require judgment on the part of the preparer of financial information. However, the issue with current assets is more often their net carrying value rather than the classification as working capital or something else. On the other hand, for creditors, questions over the classification as working capital are not uncommon, for example for stretched trade payables which can turn into financing items (*see* §4.04 [J]).

[C] Constantly Revolving / Recurring Nature

Being of an operating and short-term nature is not necessarily sufficient to be working capital. A further criterion is that working capital items are constantly revolving. As they convert into cash, they are replaced by new short-term assets and liabilities (though not necessarily at the same time and by the same amount). At any given point in time, a business has a certain level of short-term operating assets and liabilities. The net position changes constantly and may follow cycles, seasons, or long-term trends (such as a growth or inflation).

If working capital never changed, it would be straightforward to agree a reference value against which closing working capital is to be measured. Indeed, if the level never changed, no working capital adjustment would be necessary. In reality, working capital changes constantly, and this is what presents the challenge - especially when significant swings are involved - when setting a reference value against which closing working capital is to be measured.

[D] 'Core' and 'Wider' Working Capital

There are numerous potential balance sheet items that meet these criteria beyond the three included in the definition of 'core' or 'trade' working capital. In order to help the reader with the problem of how to deal with specific working capital items, below is a list of balance sheet items and an explanation of how they may be handled (Figure 5.1).

Figure 5.1 Components of Working Capital

- Trade receivables - Inventory - Trade Payables	Core/trade working capital
- Prepaid expenses - Goods received not invoiced; - Short-term personnel-related accruals; - Employee withholding taxes - Value added or sales taxes - Other short-term tax assets or liabilities;	Other items often treated as working capital
- Prepayments received/deferred revenue - Provisions (different types) (*see* above §4.[D]) - Deferred tax (*see* above in §4.[I]) - Rent deposits - Insurance claim receivable (typically not part of ordinary activities)	Items that may be classified as working capital or net debt

The last category in the list in Figure 5.1 includes items which can be either working capital or net debt. For further discussion, please refer to Chapter 4.

It is important to review each element of the target business's balance sheet during the financial due diligence and to consider whether it should be treated as working capital or net debt. A technique that is sometimes used is to allocate each item of the balance sheet into one of four categories: working capital, net debt, infrastructure (that may indicate the need for a capital expenditure adjustment) and 'other' (for which adjustment is required). This type of analysis is sometimes called the 'bucket approach' or the preparation of a 'functional balance sheet'. Its purpose is to ensure that no balance sheet item is omitted from SPA definitions unless it has been considered and found not to require an adjustment. To be useful, the balance sheet analysis must be sufficiently granular to identify subcategories of line items that in themselves could be working capital or net debt.

An example of an omission in the definition of working capital is the line item 'goods received not invoiced'. Unless it is included in the definition of working capital, the seller could theoretically increase working capital at closing by requesting a key supplier to withhold invoices just before closing.

An example of a functional balance sheet analysis is in Table 5.1 (note that the allocation into buckets could have been performed differently, depending on the circumstances).

Table 5.1 Example Balance Sheet as of 31 May 2018

	Working Capital	*Net Debt*	*Infrastructure*	*Other*	*Total*
USD thousand					
ASSETS					
Cash And Equivalents (gross)		3,091			3,091
Restricted Cash		-210			-210
Short Term Investments		2,111			2,111
Total Cash & ST Investments	**0**	**4,992**	**0**	**0**	**4,992**
Accounts Receivable	2,397				2,397
Accounts Receivable – related parties	14				14
Other Receivables – taxes	79				79
Other Receivables – VAT	83				83
Other Receivables – Insurance claim				42	42
Other receivables – employees		7			7
Total Receivables	**2,573**	**7**	**0**	**42**	**2,622**
Inventory	4,981				4,981
Restricted Cash	210				210
Other Current Assets – Deferred tax					-
Other Current Assets – Deposits	17				17
Other	9				9
Total Other Current Assets	**5,217**	**0**	**0**	**0**	**5,217**

	Working Capital	*Net Debt*	*Infrastructure*	*Other*	*Total*
Gross Property, Plant & Equipment			1,720		1,720
Accumulated Depreciation			-761		-761
Net Property, Plant & Equipment	**0**	**0**	**959**	**0**	**959**
Long-term Investments – fair value of warrants		36			36
Goodwill				2,121	2,121
Other Intangibles				237	237
Other Long-Term Assets				339	339
Total Other Non-Current Assets	**0**	**36**	**0**	**2,697**	**2,733**
Total Assets	**7,790**	**5,035**	**959**	**2,739**	**16,523**
LIABILITIES					
Accounts Payable	2,532				2,532
Accrued Exp.	465				465
Curr. Port. of LT Debt		12			12
Curr. Port. of Cap. Leases		87			87
Unearned Revenue, Current	355				355
Other Current Liabilities – Deferred Tax (Current)				8	8
Other Current Liabilities – VAT	21				21
Other Current Liabilities – Tax Audit		12			12

	Working Capital	*Net Debt*	*Infrastructure*	*Other*	*Total*
Other Current Liabilities	82				82
Total Current Liabilities		111	0	8	3,574
Long-Term Debt – Unsecured Senior Notes		717			717
Capital Leases		831			831
Unearned Revenue, Non-Current		445			445
Def. Tax Liability, Non-Curr.				190	190
Construction liabilities				451	451
Pensions		1,229			1,229
Employee Loans		503			503
Other Non-Current Liabilities				856	856
Total Non-Current Liabilities	0	3725	0	1497	5222
Total Liabilities	3,455	3,836	0	1,505	**8,796**
Common Stock				5	5
Additional Paid In Capital				292	292
Retained Earnings				7,553	7,553
Treasury Stock				-97	-97
Accumulated Currency Loss				-19	-19
Other Comprehensive Income		-7			-7
Total Common Equity	**0**	**-7**	**0**	**7,734**	**7,727**

	Working Capital	*Net Debt*	*Infrastructure*	*Other*	*Total*
Total Liabilities and Equity	**3,455**	**3,829**	**0**	**9,239**	**16,523**
Net Working Capital	**4,335**				
Net Debt		**1,206.00**			
Net Infrastructure Assets			**959**		
Other				**-6,500.00**	

§5.04 THE REFERENCE VALUE

[A] Introduction

As working capital constantly changes, often significantly, determining an appropriate reference value is usually not straightforward. M&A practitioners typically develop an average value by examining month-by-month figures for the target business for twelve, twenty-four or (less often) thirty-six months, covering at least one full seasonal cycle. According to a recent survey, the most commonly used reference is the average reported working capital of the last twelve months.[73]

Determining the reference value using historical averages is the most common approach. An alternative is to use the working capital ratios (such as DSO, DIO, and DPO) of a peer group, and to apply these ratios to revenues and cost of sales, respectively, of the target business, in order to determine a normal working capital level. This approach can be relevant when the working capital development of the target has been significantly affected by non-recurring events (such as events during the financial crisis) that mean that the average is not representative of the target business's 'true' working capital needs going forward. However, these cases are less common.

All else being equal, a buyer inevitably seeks a high reference value against which actual working capital is measured: the higher the reference value, the greater any deficit (or lower any surplus) when actual working capital at closing is measured against it. A seller, on the other hand, argues for a low reference value. It is a zero sum game, the outcome of which typically depends to some extent on the relative strengths of the parties' negotiating positions.

73. Grant Thornton, A Smarter Way to Get Deals Done, International Survey: Identifying international market practice for equity value adjustments and Sale and Purchase Agreements, November 2017, p. 10. According to this survey, 63% of respondents reported that the 'Last 12 Months' (LTM) period before the completion date was the typical reference period for assessing the working capital target.

A similar dynamic applies in locked box transactions, the difference being that working capital is measured at the locked box date rather than at closing. The difference between actual working capital and the reference value at the locked box date is then included in the fixed purchase (or at least it should be). The conflicting incentives for buyer and seller are the same as in a purchase price adjustment. Actual working capital at closing is, of course, irrelevant in a locked box transaction in this context.

Factors which commonly influence the determination of an appropriate reference value are discussed below.

[B] Seasonality

[1] Non-seasonal Businesses

Developing a reference working capital figure for a business not affected by seasonality is relatively straightforward. Figure 5.2 shows the monthly working capital profile of such a business over twelve months.

Figure 5.2 Working Capital Profile: Non-seasonal Business

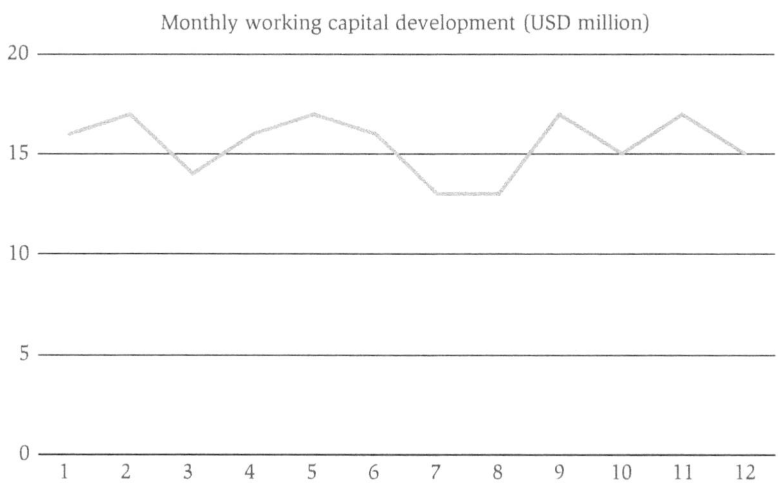

Assuming these twelve months are representative of the business at closing and of its overall working capital needs, including intra-month levels, then simply averaging the twelve months would form a reasonable basis for a reference value.

[2] Seasonal Businesses and the Notion of Different Reference Dates Depending on the Closing Date

In Figure 5.3, working capital fluctuates significantly: It is over three times higher during the summer months than in the seasonally lowest months. Prima facie, no single level of working capital could be considered to be representative of the overall working capital needs of the business.

Figure 5.3 Working Capital Profile: Seasonal Business

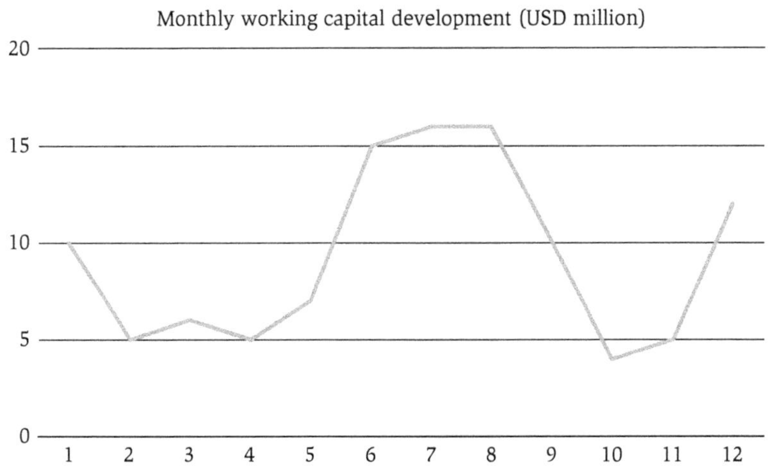

For such a business, some argue that a simple average over twelve months (or a longer period) is not appropriate, and that the working capital reference value should depend on whether working capital is at a seasonal high or low: In this example, if closing is expected during one of the summer months, or at the end of the year, the argument goes, the reference value should be based not on an average of the twelve months but on an average across the seasonally strongest months only. Equally, for a closing in a period of less activity a correspondingly lower value would come into play. Does this make sense?

It should be pointed out here that, because of its interaction with the cash position, working capital should not be viewed in isolation: a peak in working capital typically mirrors a trough in the cash position. A peak in working capital may be explained, for example, by high sales and, hence, receivables (before sales turn into cash), or an inventory build-up. Conversely, a low level of working capital typically signifies a higher cash balance.

The example below sets out the two alternative approaches. Closing is on either 30 April or 31 August of the year. The business has significant seasonality, with net working capital in August at over three times the level in April. Table 5.2 shows the net working capital position at month ends and net debt (reflecting the change in the cash position due to the working capital change). The average net working capital over the twelve-month period is 9. Net working capital on 30 April is 5, and on 31 August 16.

Table 5.2 Monthly Working Capital

	Jan	*Feb*	*Mar*	*Apr*	*May*	*Jun*	*Jul*	*Aug*	*Sep*	*Oct*	*Nov*	*Dec*	*Avg. (Twelve Months)*
Working capital	8	5	6	5	7	15	16	16	10	4	5	11	9.00
Net debt	500	500	497	498	497	499	507	508	508	502	496	497	
Cash change from WC	n/a	-3	1	-1	2	8	1	0	-6	-6	1	6	
Net debt	500	497	498	497	499	507	508	508	502	496	497	503	

Scenarios A and B show two alternative approaches to the reference value: in scenario A, the parties have agreed a reference value, 9, against which actual working capital is measured at any closing date in the year. In scenario B, there are two different reference values, depending on the closing date. Arguments in Scenario B are set out below, provided by seller and buyer, respectively, for an adjusted reference value.

For closing on 30 April: Reference value of 5 (the level of working capital in April)	Seller argues that working capital reflects seasonality and buyer is assuming less debt, hence equity price is higher
For closing on 31 August: Reference value of 16 (the level of working capital in August)	Buyer argues that working capital reflects seasonality (i.e., if seller does not provide that level working capital buyer is being shortchanged), hence buyer pays a lower equity price

It has been assumed in this example that actual working capital (at closing) is the same as in the period over which the reference value was computed. Tables 5.3 and 5.4 set out the calculation of the purchase price adjustments and equity value in each of the two scenarios.

Table 5.3 Scenario A: Constant Reference Value

Closing Date	*30 Apr*	*31 Aug*
Reference value	9	9
EV	1,000	1,000

Closing Date	*30 Apr*	*31 Aug*
Less net debt	-497	-508
Actual WC less Ref WC	-4	7
Equity value	499	499

Table 5.4 Scenario B: Reference Value Adjusted to Reflect Seasonality

Closing Date	*30 Apr*	*31 Aug*
Reference value	5	16
EV	1,000	1,000
Less net debt	-497	-508
Actual WC less Ref WC (5 (low) and 16 (high))	–	–
Equity value	503	492

A constant reference value (scenario A) results in the same equity value, independent of the closing date. Different reference values (scenario B) result in different equity values, depending on the closing date, whereas, under the assumptions given above, the value transferred from seller to buyer is unchanged.

In the example above, with seasonality, liquidity was simply moved between net debt and working capital and never left the two categories. The system was 'closed'. In reality, the cash position does not always move in step with changes in working capital. A perfect link between working capital and cash may apply in real life only for a very short period during which it is true that day-to-day working capital movements can be linked directly to cash (every dollar collected from a customer leads to a dollar increase in cash). Another way to look at this is to plot a cash position against the working capital line in Figure 5.3. While cash and working capital are directly linked at the moment when working capital converts into cash, this relationship would not necessarily be visible in an imaginary cash line in the figure. The reason is that, once received, cash can be spent on things that are accounted for outside the definitions of working capital or net debt. When a company acquires fixed assets, for example, cash disappears from the categories working capital and net debt. However, spending cash does not usually mean that value disappears – it is merely put to other uses or converted into other assets or reduce liabilities. These assets and liabilities may be outside the definition of working capital or debt. It does not matter where precisely the cash goes, it is not replaced with nothing.[74]

The fair approach (which results in a constant equity value) is to agree on a single reference value regardless of the closing date if the business is not growing (or shrinking). After all, all other things being equal, the underlying value of the business has not changed.

74. Unless it was wasted.

[C] High-Growth Businesses

High-growth businesses present a different challenge. Figure 5.4 depicts the working capital profile of a rapidly expanding company that requires an increasing level of working capital to support its growth. What should the reference value be in this case?

Figure 5.4 Working Capital Profile: High-Growth Business

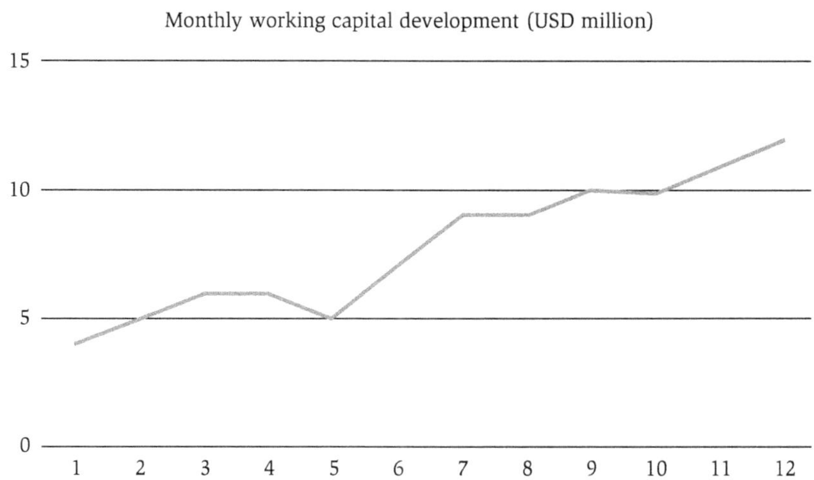

As indicated above, the reference value should represent a normal working capital level *at closing*. An average across historical working capital figures *before closing* would understate the working capital of the business requires at closing when it will have outgrown its past average levels.

One issue when determining a normal working capital value for a high-growth business is that the exact closing date is usually not known ahead of time. If the uncertainty covers a significant time period, it will require critical estimates in respect of when the closing date is due to fall. And, if closing were delayed for some reason, it might be necessary to revisit the reference value that had been originally agreed for an earlier closing date.

One approach, usually favoured by the buyer, is to use projected working capital, or a combination of historical and projected figures, to determine the working capital reference value. According to a recent survey, 24% of respondents used some combination of historical and forecast results or an entirely forecast period.[75]

For a growth company, the working capital level after closing will be higher than in the pre-closing period. A reference value that is solely based on a post-closing

75. Grant Thornton, A Smarter Way to Get Deals Done, International Survey: Identifying international market practice for equity value adjustments and Sale and Purchase Agreements, November 2017, p. 10.

projection of working capital would usually overstate the working capital needs of the business *at closing*. In effect, such a reference value would mean that the seller is being asked - by way of the working capital adjustment - to fund working capital growth *after* closing. This approach is not consistent with the notion that the buyer, not the seller, should fund the growth of the business it has acquired.

[D] High Growth and Seasonality

Figure 5.5 depicts the working capital development of a business that is not only rapidly expanding but also subject to seasonal influences.

Figure 5.5 Working Capital Profile: High-Growth Seasonal Business

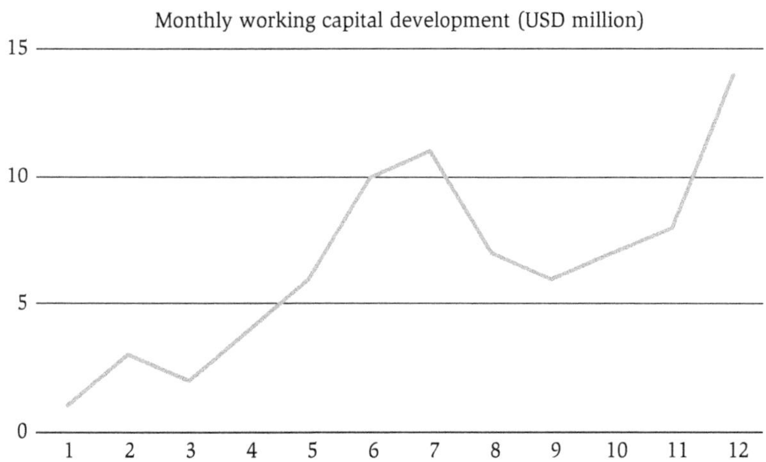

In this situation, it is necessary to separate the growth aspects from the seasonality. One approach is to (a) project working capital at the planned closing date using the business plan on which the valuation is based, and (b) analyse historical seasonality and, by overlaying those data, adjust the projected working capital for any seasonal influence. In these circumstances the suggested approach is to project an agreed reference working capital for a series of possible closing dates.

[E] Intra-Monthly Movements

The discussion of monthly working capital figures above concerned end-of-month balances. However, working capital may be subject to significant swings during the month, and a discussion of working capital would be incomplete without considering these intra-monthly movements. For example, a company may pay a major supplier on the second day of each month, which means that at month-ends, trade payables are close to their peak and, as a result, net working capital near its lowest point.

Intra-monthly working capital levels are much higher in this example than an analysis limited to month-end data would suggest.

Alternatively, a company may have significant creditor payment runs on the last days of each month, so that net working capital is at its peak at month-ends. This development is depicted in Figure 5.6.

Figure 5.6 Intra-Month Working Capital Profile

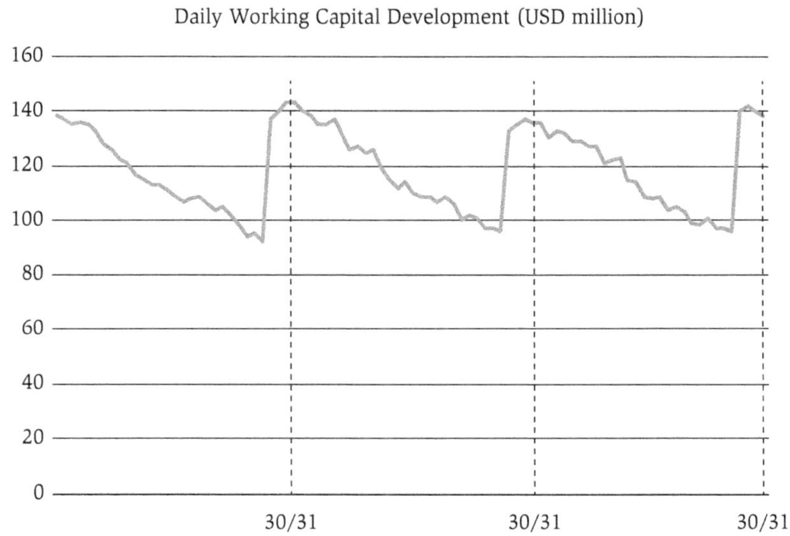

Further, many companies manage their cash and working capital positions at specific reporting dates, for example to meet covenants in credit agreements, or for interim or annual reporting purposes. In addition, significant cash outflows may occur on the same day of each month, making working capital 'lumpy' during the month.

As a result, month-, quarter- or year-end working capital figures may not be representative for the everyday working capital position of a business. In fact, they can be the *least* representative dates from which to gain an understanding of the true working capital needs of the business.

It is often necessary, therefore, to consider using averages not only at month-ends but also to use other data points, such as weekly or even daily figures.

[F] Switching Between a Completion Accounts Process and a Locked Box

In some negotiations, the parties switch from a purchase price adjustment to a locked box or vice versa. For example, an indicative offer may include a completion accounts process, and subsequently during the negotiations the parties agree on a fixed purchase price.

As discussed above, the reference value should represent the normal working capital position at closing (for a working capital adjustment) or at the locked box date (for a locked box transaction). For a fast growing business, the level of normal working capital will change between these two dates (*see* §5.04 [C]). In case of a switch during the negotiations from a locked box to a purchase price adjustment (or vice versa), the parties should therefore revisit what the normal level of working capital at the relevant date is.

[G] Normalising Working Capital

Historical working capital often includes one-off or non-recurring assets or liabilities. It is necessary to eliminate these from the reported figures in order to obtain an average that is representative of the business's underlying working capital requirements. Normalising working capital can be a complex process that requires access to trial balances and detailed explanations of the movements of individual assets or liabilities and whether they are recurring. This can be time-consuming, especially for items outside the definition of core working capital. A similar problem arises when the definition of working capital references assets or liabilities that include items that should be excluded from working capital at closing (even though they may not be considered exceptional). These items should then be eliminated from the historical figures as well.

The following are examples of items that might be normalised:

- Non-recurring receivables, for example from an insurance claim/awards related to legal action.
- Capital expenditure creditors (frequently recorded in trade payables).
- Movements in foreign exchange rates that have had an impact on figures denominated in a company's functional currency (even though the underlying foreign currency-denominated balances were unchanged).
- Short-term payables for financial leases (§4.04 [B]).
- Balances owed to financial institutions in reverse factoring (*see* the example under §4.04 [A] [5]).
- Intercompany items that may continue albeit move to a third party or to arm's length terms with the vendor.
- Accrued interest reported within trade payables.

In addition to these adjustments, it may be appropriate to eliminate the effect of commodity price movements on historical working capital figures that are the basis of the reference value, that is, to restate these figures, on a pro-forma basis, using (for example) spot prices at the time of the analysis. Otherwise, part of the purchase price adjustment would be due to differences between historical commodity price levels and the spot price which may make no commercial sense. In economies with high inflation, a similar pro-forma restatement may be useful to eliminate the effect of general price increases.

Pro-forma adjustments may also be necessary for one-off events during the historical period that lead to a sustained change in the level of working capital the target business needs going forward. For example, in case of a (permanent) change in payment terms with a key customer or supplier during the historical period, the historical working capital figures should be restated as if the new policy had been in place throughout the historical period over which the average is derived.

Lastly (although not primarily a matter of normalising working capital), buyers should also consider whether they need to protect against sellers pushing sales before closing (whether by discounting or other means) in order to increase trade receivables at closing.

[H] Accounting Choices and Changes in Estimates

Additional aspects of determining a working capital reference value are the consistent application of accounting policies and practices, as well as the reliability of estimates throughout the historical period from which the reference value is derived. The following are (by no means exhaustive) examples of items to be considered in this regard:

- Changes in the bad debt allowance. The effect of any changes (in particular arbitrary ones) in the method of calculating the allowance should be eliminated where possible in order to arrive at accurate figures that reflect bad debt experience consistently. In order to protect against bias in accounting estimates it may be appropriate to replace management judgment with a formula-driven accounting policy for the bad debt allowance in the completion accounts.
- Long-term contracting balances, including receivables recognised under the percentage of completion (POC) method. Estimates of the stage of completion and costs to complete as well as provisions for losses directly affect the carrying value of these items are discussed further in Chapter 9.
- Factored receivables that have been derecognised. This understates working capital, as discussed in §4.04 [A] (relative to the underlying working capital needs of the business). Factored receivables (and the associated debt) should be grossed up for purposes of a working capital reference value.
- Inventory valuation - cost capitalisation. It should be ensured that the capitalisation of costs, including the level of overhead absorption, has been done consistently. This is one of the most difficult accounting areas to address in the SPA and requires careful consideration of any discretion available to the preparer of the completion accounts. If there is an increase at closing, buyers should be clear on whether they are willing to pay dollar-for-dollar for an increase in capitalised internal costs of the target entity.
- Inventory valuation - net realisable value. Net realisable value brings market prices into the completion mechanism. In volatile markets where prices can be difficult to establish, there may be ambiguity or uncertainty, for example over which sources to use for market prices. This figures in post-deal disputes for

example in fast moving markets such as renewable energy. It may be appropriate to use a formula-based approach to inventory valuation in the completion accounts in these cases.

[I] Adjusting the Average to Reflect Different Rates for Borrowing and Lending

The discussion in §5.04 [B] above considered seasonality and it was concluded that, even for seasonal (no growth) businesses, it is appropriate to use an average reference working capital figure, derived over a historical period. Another facet in this regard concerns the cost of capital connected with variances in working capital from the average figure in either direction.

Seasonally strong months tie up more liquidity in working capital. This liquidity has to come from somewhere, and this is associated with a cost. A company uses cash (or a working capital facility) to fund the additional working capital needs during periods when these exceed the average. Conversely, in periods when working capital is below the average, the additional freed-up liquidity can be used to another end and may generate a return.

Treating these funding surpluses and deficits in the same way would be appropriate if the cost of capital for short-term investments and short-term funding needs of the business were the same. But, they are usually not. The spread in funding costs for positive and negative working capital movements against an average is relevant regardless of whether the target business cash or a working capital or revolving credit facility.

If the working capital reference value is determined as the simple arithmetic mean across historical net working capital figures, then the difference between borrowing costs and investment returns is not reflected. To rectify this, in some deals parties propose that the average should be weighted by the difference in the cost of capital.

As discussed, the working capital reference value should be set in a way that will not cause the parties concern if the closing date shifts. In concept, for the parties to be indifferent, an incremental cost of funding working capital deficits should be added to the average, and the reference value should therefore be slightly higher than the average.

While this somewhat arcane principle gets an occasional airing, it has become very rare in recent years, possibly because interest rates have decreased and borrowing rates and short-term returns alike are still very low.

[J] Intercompany Balances

Intercompany balances should be categorised according to whether they are working capital, debt, or to be settled before or at closing:

- Working capital balances with related parties may move to a third party after closing, or remain but at arm's length terms.
- It is not uncommon for intercompany items reported within working capital to be unpaid for longer terms than between third parties. Consider that these balances may have a financing nature. See 4.04 [J].
- It is often appropriate to agree to settle intercompany balances before closing in order to avoid credit risk with the other party after the transaction where possible, and the possibility that the counterparty may offset amounts owed post-closing.

§5.05 THE COLLAR APPROACH

One fairly common approach to working capital adjustments is that an adjustment is made only if the difference between actual and reference working capital (in either or only one direction) exceeds a *de minimis* amount. This is known as a 'collar'. No adjustment is made if actual working capital is within the collar, i.e., the *de minimis* amount is not exceeded. In case the *de minimis* amount is exceeded, the adjustment may be limited to the excess (the amount outside the collar) or it may be for the entire amount including the collar. This needs to be clearly set out in the SPA.

The collar is invariably a comparatively low amount. One of its purposes is to remove potential disagreements over small amounts that are, in aggregate, clearly within the collar: if an individual item over which there could be disagreement between the parties does not cause the aggregate to exceed the collar amount, this may reduce the probability of a dispute over such small items.

It is also sometimes argued that it saves time not to have to calculate exact amounts. However, this is true only if it is certain that the difference between actual and reference working capital is within the collar without having performed calculations; more typically, in order to establish whether the collar is exceeded, it is necessary to perform the same analysis as without a collar.

The potential drawbacks or risks of using a collar are often clearer than the advantages. While a collar is relatively common for the working capital reference value, the same approach is very rarely (if ever) used in relation to the net debt adjustment. However, the working capital adjustment should complement the net debt adjustment: A collar around one but not the other means the interaction between the two adjustments is no longer seamless. It is easy to leave money on the table here from the perspective of the buyer who is exposed to the seller's desire to manage down working capital (but to remain within the collar) and maximise the cash position. In the presence of a sophisticated, aggressive seller this represents a real risk, even if limited to the collar amount. It should be avoided where possible.

CHAPTER 6
Capital Expenditure in Completion Mechanisms

§6.01 OVERVIEW CAPITAL EXPENDITURE ADJUSTMENT

A capital expenditure is the use of funds to acquire or improve a long-term asset. As the use of funds can be either a cash outflow or involve taking on additional debt, the level of capital expenditure before closing influences the level of net debt at closing. With a net debt adjustment, a seller who slows down capital expenditure prior to closing increases the cash position at closing. The buyer not only pays for an inflated cash position (as part of net debt), but also obtains a business with a capital expenditure backlog.[76]

The principal idea behind the capital expenditure adjustment is to protect the buyer from this type of seller manipulation. It does this by reducing the purchase price for a shortfall against a target value in the cumulative level of capital expenditures in the closing period. The adjustment effectively offsets a cash position that, at closing, is higher than it should be only because capital investments were delayed or cancelled.

Capital expenditure adjustments may be one- or two-sided. A one-sided adjustment can only lead to a reduction in the purchase price. A two-sided adjustment means that the purchase price can also increase if cumulative capital expenditure between signing and closing is higher than the agreed level. In effect, the two-sided adjustment reimburses the seller for the target spending more than planned on capital goods during the period up to closing (which means that it has less cash than otherwise). Adjustments for higher-than-planned capital expenditures should in general be capped so that

76. For maintenance spending (one type of capital expenditures), it has been argued that prevention is cheaper than cure. *See* https://www.ft.com/content/cf700fad-6e87-3b32-867c-8686853c76f1. 'Catching up' an investment backlog can therefore require greater expenditures than what was originally deferred. This means that a capital expenditure adjustment may be better at removing the incentive from a seller to slow down capital spending than it is at putting the buyer in the same position as if the seller had spent as planned.

the buyer is not responsible for excessive, possibly useless, long-term investments. The SPA may also require approval from the buyer for individual capital expenditure items above certain agreed thresholds.

Another, less common function of the capital expenditure adjustment is that it can be used to allow the buyer to influence specific investment decisions between signing and closing: The parties can specify investments in the SPA. However, they should then ensure that these types of provisions do not represent 'gun jumping' (i.e. that the buyer does not already effectively control or influence the target's strategic business decisions before closing). However, these are legal considerations outside the scope of this book.

To work properly, the capital expenditure adjustment must be based on a planned level of spending over a period of time up to the expected closing date (and beyond if there is a risk that the transaction closes later than expected). The target level of capital expenditure over this period should be consistent with the business plan on which the business was valued. Similar to the working capital reference value, which represents a 'normal' working capital level of the business, the capital expenditure target often assumes the continuation of a 'normal' level of capital expenditure over time. The difference between the two is that a working capital adjustment is measured against a single reference value, whereas the capital expenditure adjustment is measured against an accumulating reference level that increases over the length of the closing period and therefore depends on the closing date.

As the capital expenditure adjustment requires a continuously growing reference level over the (expected) closing period, annual or quarterly capital expenditure budgets may need to be phased into monthly, weekly, or even daily target value. Whether to plan on a monthly, weekly, or daily basis essentially depends on how 'lumpy' capital spending is. For a large group whose capital expenditures are comprised of a large number of comparatively small individual items that, predictably, are evenly distributed across the working days of a month, monthly targets may be sufficient. If individual purchases of fixed asset are significant relative to the overall level of spend (i.e., expenditures are 'lumpy') then planning the capital expenditures can involve detailed weekly or even daily forecasts.

Another area of complexity is the definition of capital expenditure for the purpose of the adjustment in the SPA. This definition may or may not follow GAAP. A particular concern arises when capital expenditure, following GAAP accounting, includes internal costs. A buyer could thus effectively pay for capitalised internal overheads that are part of the business anyway. Their inclusion in an adjustment is usually not warranted as they do not offset a lower cash position at closing if they relate to internal costs that would have become cash-relevant in any event.

An example is the treatment of development costs that can be capitalised under IAS 38.57 under certain conditions (whereas research costs must be expensed). The accounting standard provides criteria that have to be met for development costs to be capitalised, including technical feasibility of completing the asset, the ability to use or sell the asset, that the asset will generate probable future economic benefits, and others. These criteria require judgment on the part of the preparer of the financial statement that can be open to bias. Further, it can be comparatively easy for a company to influence the allocation of staff time from research to development as the same employees often perform both functions. It is therefore generally preferable to limit the adjustment to capitalised external expenditure.

Example Dispute over Capitalised Expenditures (International Arbitration)

Capitalising expenditure can be used to move expenditure that would otherwise have been an operating expense in a period into depreciation in future periods (below EBITDA).

An example in a recent arbitration was the acquisition of a European automotive supplier, a capital intensive industry, by a US corporate. The SPA contained a capital expenditure adjustment that set out capital expenditure targets up to the expected closing date. The buyer alleged subsequently that research and development costs had been incorrectly capitalised during the closing period and included expenditures that should have been expensed as they related to research activities; the buyer further alleged that capital expenditure included indirect costs that, under the relevant local GAAP, should not have been capitalised. (The parties settled).

CHAPTER 7

Specific Aspects of Locked Box Transactions

§7.01 OVERVIEW

As discussed in §2.03, in a locked box transaction, the fixed price reflects the levels of cash, debt, and working capital at a historical reference date, the locked box date. The timeline for this type of transaction is shown in Figure 7.1.

Figure 7.1 The Locked Box Timeline

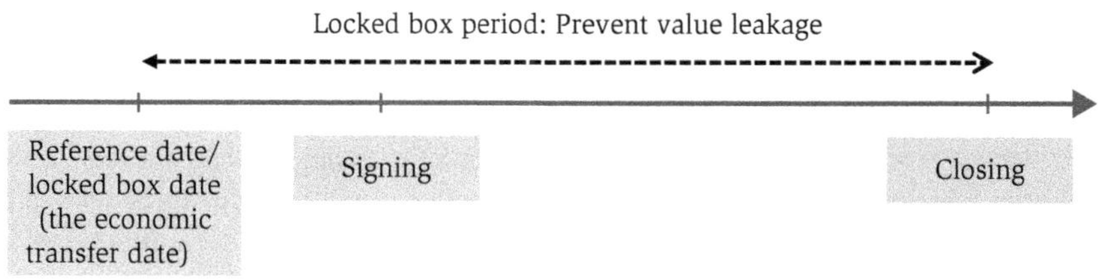

As discussed above, a locked box transaction is economically (though not legally) backdated to a reference date, the locked box date. The time between the locked box date and closing, the 'locked box period', consists of the period from the historical reference date to signing and the closing period. At signing, the length of the first period is known, whereas the closing period is often unknown, and the mechanism must therefore deal with uncertainty in respect of the length of the closing period.

The locked box is considered a seller-friendly mechanism, even though this is not necessarily always true. Its popularity is generally linked to the relative strengths and weaknesses of sellers and buyers during the M&A cycle: during strong M&A markets, sellers are these more often able to negotiate a locked box, (along with other seller-friendly terms). In these sellers' markets, the locked box therefore tends to be more popular than during downturns when buyers can more easily influence the terms of the acquisition, including the completion mechanism.

This chapter deals first with the reference date and length of the locked box period. It goes on to discuss how to prevent the leakage of value to ensure that, the value transferred at closing is consistent with the (fixed) purchase price. Value leakage protections serve to protect a buyer against value being extracted during the locked box period. This is a locked box-specific concern of the buyer, as there are no adjustments at closing that would adjust the purchase price accordingly to offset any value that has been extracted.

Lastly, the chapter covers the interest charge for the locked box period. Profits generated by the target business during the locked box period accrue to the benefit of the buyer. To compensate for the time that passes between the economic transfer and the payment of the purchase price, during which time the seller effectively manages the business on behalf of the buyer, the SPA usually sets out an interest change to be applied to the fixed purchase price. There is no consensus among professionals working on transactions on the conceptual basis on which this charge should be calculated.[77]

§7.02 THE REFERENCE DATE AND THE LOCKED BOX PERIOD

The historical reference date is often the target business's last financial year end and therefore the date of the last audited financial statements. As many companies use the calendar year end, the most frequently used locked box date is 31 December. However, if too much time has passed since that date, the parties can alternatively agree on a more recent locked box date, for example a half-year or quarter-end date. The balance sheet is then often part of unaudited half yearly, quarterly, or monthly management reporting.

However, it should generally have been subject to some level of external review beyond buy-side due diligence. For the buyer, financial due diligence on the locked box balance sheet is considered even more important than on the historical financials in a transaction with completion accounts as there is no true up at closing.

It is important, in general, for the locked box period to be comparatively short. The more time has passed between the date of the economic acquisition and closing, the more opportunity there is for the business to change and for value to be extracted. It becomes more difficult to avoid value leakage – to keep the box 'locked'. Consider (as a thought experiment) a locked box period of twenty years, and the difficulty of ensuring that no value leaks over this period. Most locked box periods do not exceed

---

77. Grant Thornton, A smarter way to get deals done International Survey: Identifying international market practice for equity value adjustments and Sale and Purchase Agreements November 2017, p. 7.

a few weeks or months. As 31 December is the most common locked box date, this explains that more locked box transactions are signed during the earlier months of the year than during the last quarter.

§7.03 VALUE LEAKAGE

It is a central concern for the buyer that no value is extracted from the target entity during the locked box period prior to closing, other than what the buyer has agreed to ('permitted leakage'). To ensure this, the SPA contains 'no leakage' provisions. Leakage that a buyer is concerned about often relates to transactions between the target entity and the seller (or parties related to the seller). The most straightforward example of leakage is a dividend payment by the target company just prior to closing. However, potential leakage is not limited to transactions between the target business and the seller.

Below is a list of mechanisms by which value can be extracted before closing:

- Dividend payments by the target to the seller.
- Share buybacks by the target from the seller.
- The accelerated repayment of shareholder loans.
- Transactions between the target and the seller or related parties that are not at arm's length, for example through transfer pricing.
- Intercompany charges between the target and the seller or related parties.
- Advisor fees in connection with the transactions.
- Waivers by the target of claims against the seller or related parties.
- Management compensation in excess of normal payments.
- Capital expenditure in excess of predetermined levels.
- Disposals of subsidiaries or ownership interests in other companies in excess of predetermined values.
- Loan guarantees and any other securities issued by the target on behalf of the seller or related parties.
- Out-of-court settlements of disputes.

This list is not exhaustive, and buyers and their advisors should consider other possible ways by which value could be extracted from a target entity during the locked box period.

The parties usually identify specific types of value leakage in the SPA (in addition to an 'ordinary course of business' covenant). As there is no purchase price adjustment at closing, there is no interaction between the leakage provisions and a net debt adjustment: The definition of leakage should therefore capture leakage whether or not it has already been paid at closing or is still payable.

Payments that the parties have agreed can be made prior to closing are specified in the SPA as 'permitted leakage'. Examples of permitted leakage are agreed dividend payments, bonuses, or the repayment of a shareholder loan. Permitted leakage is deducted from the purchase price before it is fixed.

Value leakage may be difficult to identify for a buyer if it is not recorded in the appropriate account. For example, if an intercompany charge incurred before closing is not recorded correctly, finding it can turn into a forensic exercise which a buyer may not initiate unless it suspects leakage has occurred.

§7.04 LOCKED BOX-RELATED DISPUTES

Locked box transactions are, overall, less likely to end in a legal dispute than completion accounts transactions. A type of dispute that is specific to locked box transactions is disagreement over whether leakage has occurred.

Below is another example of a dispute that related to a locked box transaction in which the locked box mechanism itself was among the key aspects of the dispute.

Example Dispute over Locked Box (High Court of England and Wales)[78]

An example of a complex dispute over a locked box transaction is the recent case of the National Bank of Greece which was sued in the UK over its EUR 2.7 billion Finansbank share sale.

The Claimants were senior executives of QNB Finansbank AS ('Finansbank'), a large bank in Turkey. The case concerned the claimants' entitlement to a fee (the 'Fee') which they contended became payable by the Defendant, National Bank of Greece SA ('NBG') under 'Incentive Fee Agreements' (the 'IFAs'). The purpose of the IFAs had been to incentivise the executives to sell NBG's interest in the Finansbank Group by providing them an opportunity to earn an incentive fee in the event of the disposal by NBG of more than 5% of its shares in Finansbank (defined as an 'Exit Event'). On 21 December 2015, NBG entered into an SPA under which it agreed to sell its shares in Finansbank to Qatar National Bank SAQ ('QNB'). The transaction closed on 15 June 2016, and QNB paid EUR 2.711 billion to NBG.

The subsequent dispute related to a number of matters, including when precisely the 'Exit Event' had taken place (either at signing (21 December 2015) or at closing (15 June 2016)). The date of the Exit Event was relevant to the determination of the last equity book value before the exit which, in turn, was the basis of the calculation of the Fees. The equity book values were significantly different on 30 March 2016 than on 30 September 2015 (the date of the locked box accounts), the two-quarter ends preceding closing and signing, respectively.

The court held that the Exit Event date was signing when the fixed price was agreed with QNB (subject only to 'Leakage') and that, the relevant equity book value was therefore that at 30 September 2015. This value had been available to the parties when they negotiated the (fixed) purchase price. After the SPA was signed, the Claimants were in no position to influence the achievement of a higher 'Exit Value'. The court recognised that the purchase price based on the locked box date (30

78. *Aras & Others v. National Bank of Greece S.A.* [2018] EWHC.

September 2015) was fixed and that any additional value or losses would effectively accrue to the acquirer, QNB. The relevant equity book value to be used in the formula for the calculation of the Fees was therefore that of 30 September 2015, the last quarter-end preceding signing.

§7.05 THE INTEREST (OR DAILY PROFIT) CHARGE IN LOCKED BOX TRANSACTIONS

[A] Introduction

As discussed above, the profits of the target business during the locked box period accrue to the benefit of the buyer. The target entity's balance sheet at closing reflects these profits (provided no value leaked) in a higher net asset position, and it is this net asset position that is transferred to the buyer at closing. As the business is, or should be, valued as at the locked box date (the backdated economic transfer date), the profits expected for the locked box period at a time before signing are part of enterprise value.

A backdated transaction means that the payment of the fixed purchase price at closing is made after the economic transfer date. To compensate the seller for the time difference between the date of economic transfer and payment, locked box SPAs often specify an interest charge. Other terms used for this interest charge are 'value accrual', 'daily profit charge', or 'ticker adjustment'. The locked box interest is calculated on the fixed purchase price and usually covers the entire locked box period. However, it can also apply to a shorter period, starting only at a date after the locked box date (e.g., an expected closing date). In that case, the primary purpose is to provide an incentive to the buyer not to delay closing and to compensate the seller only in the event of any such delay.

There is no consensus among professionals as to what the locked box interest charge should be, and this has led to a variety of different approaches being used in practice, often reflecting one party's strength in the negotiations rather than considerations such as risk and return, or the time value of money. Locked box interest can amount to a significant fraction of the overall purchase price, and should not, in general, be dismissed as immaterial.

[B] Conceptual Approaches to Locked Box Interest

[1] Overview

The locked box interest charge can be summed up as compensation paid by the buyer to the seller for the latter passing on the rewards of ownership in the target entity from the locked box date and not being paid until closing. The charge compensates the seller for the lost opportunity that would have been available to him or her had the payment been made at the locked box date.

A way to view the interest charge is in the context of the return the buyer could have earned on an asset of comparable risk. In a locked box transaction, the question arises what asset the interest charge relates to. The following alternatives might be considered:

- the fixed purchase price;
- the target company's equity;
- the target company itself.

These alternatives are incorporated in the different approaches to locked box interest discussed below.

There are two assumptions made in the analysis that follows: (1) buyer and seller have access to liquid capital markets; and (2) the purchase price is payable in full at closing.

A general observation in the context of assessing risk is that in case the transaction does not close (for whatever reason), the buyer will not pay the purchase price. The setup resembles in this respect a secured lending transaction in which the lender (the seller) is entitled to repossess the collateral (the target business) in the event of the default of the borrower (the buyer).

[2] Seller's Return on Capital Employed

One way to approach to the locked box interest is to use the rate of return on total capital employed of the seller's business during the locked box period. By deferring the receipt of the purchase consideration until closing, the seller argues that it is deprived of the opportunity to invest the proceeds in its own business during the locked box period. Had this opportunity been available, the seller would have made a return corresponding, in percentage terms, to that generated by all other activities.

This approach, however, runs into the following objection: a seller who believes that it was deprived of an opportunity to generate a return during the locked box period could have raised finance in the capital markets to take advantage of such opportunities *ad infinitum*. If the seller is convinced that it would have achieved returns in excess of its cost of capital, it could have done so. The fact that it chose not to suggests that it should not be compensated for the costs associated with the missed opportunity.

The seller's return on capital employed is, therefore, difficult to justify in theory and in practice at the upper end of a range of locked box interest rates that some sellers propose.

[3] Seller's Weighted Average Cost of Capital

Another approach is to use the seller's WACC. The reasoning is that this is the cost to the seller of replacing the liquidity that was unavailable during the locked box period because the purchase consideration was not yet paid.

This approach assumes that the seller could have obtained additional liquidity at its existing WACC, i.e., that the incremental cost of equity and debt financing would be the same as the existing, and that there would be no variation in the proportion of equity and debt finance.

A buyer may also put the argument that the interest rate charged should depend not on the capital profile of the seller but on that of the asset in question, i.e., the target entity. Should the seller suffer from an unduly high cost of capital, for example, the buyer would be unjustly penalised.

[4] Buyer's Incremental Cost of Borrowing

Another approach is to view the outstanding purchase consideration as a loan from seller to buyer. The price of the loan (the interest rate) would be the buyer's incremental cost of secured borrowing. Since the purchase consideration is payable in full at closing, the transaction does not close if the buyer defaults. In substance, the arrangement is therefore similar to a secured loan (*see* above §7.04 [B] [1]).

This approach can be difficult to implement. First, the seller is unlikely to know the cost to the buyer of a specific secured debt instrument (the buyer itself may not know). Lengthy analysis might be required which may not be worth the effort. Second, the approach means a different locked box interest rate, and hence a different final purchase price for each bidder, even where each bidder placed an underlying identical value on the target entity. This would make locked box transactions more expensive the riskier the bidder is, a disadvantage, for example, for young high growth companies, companies that are more highly leveraged, or emerging markets investors. Differences in total purchase price by bidder would also make it more difficult for the seller to compare bids in auction processes.

[5] The Risk-Free Rate

The use of a risk-free rate is based on the idea that, as the buyer takes on the (economic) risks and rewards of the target entity from the locked box date, the target entity's returns (which accrue to the benefit of the buyer) can be viewed as compensation for taking on this risk. Since the buyer assumes this risk, and it is compensated for it, it follows that the seller cannot also be entitled to compensation for the same risk. The seller can therefore only be entitled to a risk-free interest rate. In addition, at signing, the period between the locked box date and signing is already in the past and no longer subject to risk (at least in respect of known developments up to that point). What may have been considered a risk has already materialised (or not), except that the buyer may not be aware.

Further, not all risks associated with the target entity transfer to the buyer at the locked box date. For example, a material adverse change (MAC) clause in the SPA may specify that, if certain adverse events (however defined) arise, the transaction will not close. In this case, at least some (significant) risks remain with the seller.

Which party bears the risk in relation to the target entity's trading depends on the specific circumstances of the transaction and the SPA. It is fair to say that, generally, the locked box period is not entirely risk-free for a seller.

[6] Daily Profit Charge

Among the more common approaches to locked box interest is to use the (expected) profits of the target entity during the locked box period. From these, an (average) daily profit can be derived and added to the purchase price for each day until the closing date. This gives the name to the 'daily profit charge' or 'daily profit rate'.

A rationale behind the use of daily profits is to reimburse the seller for the returns that accrue to the benefit of the buyer over the locked box period, as opposed to a transaction with completion accounts in which the seller is entitled to these returns. Backdating the transaction, the argument goes, should not leave the seller worse off than in a locked box transaction. By anchoring the determination of the purchase price in a hard balance sheet, the locked box ensures a 'clean' closing mechanism while avoiding the uncertainty of a completion accounts process but with otherwise similar results.

However, this may overlook a difference between transactions using the locked box approach and a traditional completion accounts process. For the former, the profits of the locked box period are included in enterprise value, at least in concept: The valuation date for a locked box is the locked box date. For a purchase price adjustment, the valuation date is the closing date. Theoretically, a daily profit charge that reimburses a seller for lost profits in a locked box transaction means that he or she receives them *on top of* the consideration that already includes them. This would be double counting. While in practice this is a well-worn means of solving the problem of compensating the seller, it is difficult to justify in theory to the extent the profits are, in fact, already priced into enterprise value.

Another question in this context is the appropriate profit metric: Should 'profit' mean net earnings, EBIT, or EBITDA, cash flow, or something else? As locked box interest relates to the purchase price for the *equity* interest, not *enterprise* value, the daily profit charge should, therefore, correspond to the earnings to which the shareholders are entitled, i.e., net profits after interest, taxes, and any other expenses that reduce the return on the target's equity. Earnings measures such as EBITDA or EBIT overstate the return on equity. They are used as a basis of enterprise value rather than equity value.

Further, since the purpose of the daily profit charge is to represent the economic value created during the (finite) locked box period, it is usually not appropriate to use cash flows instead of earnings as a basis for measuring this value (contrary to what is sometimes proposed). There is no reason to omit value that has not yet turned into cash at closing from the daily profit rate.

Another aspect arises in case that the target entity records or expects a loss during the locked box period. The daily profit charge should then be negative: The seller effectively compensates the buyer for each day of losses that accrue to the buyer. Negative daily profit rates are however rarely if ever applied.

Lastly, a practical problem with the determination of the daily profit charge is that sellers typically have significantly more information than buyers about the target entity and its immediate prospects during the locked box period. Due to this information asymmetry, a daily profit charge is often set at the higher end of a range of profits that can be reasonably expected during the locked period. This underlines the general seller-friendliness of the locked box. The buyer needs to ensure, at a minimum, that the prospective financial information on which the profitability during the locked box period is based is consistent with the early period in the business plan that it used to value the business and on which it has based its bid.

§7.06 SUMMARY OF LOCKED BOX INTEREST RATES

Table 7.1 Summary Overview

	Explanation	*Comment*
Seller's Return on Capital Employed	The seller argues that it was deprived of the opportunity to invest the proceeds in its own business during the locked box period. Had this opportunity been available, the seller would have generated a return corresponding to that generated by all other activities.	If the seller is convinced that it would have achieved returns in excess of its cost of capital, it could have done so. The fact that it chose not to do so suggests that it should not be compensated for the costs associated with the missed opportunity. This approach is therefore difficult to justify in theory.
Seller's WACC	The average cost to the seller of obtaining the finance that was unavailable to them during the locked box period because the purchase consideration was not yet paid.	Sellers perceived as risky (volatile businesses, young growth companies) would be associated with more-expensive locked box transactions. The buyer would be 'punished' for a seller's high cost of capital.
Risk-free rate	The earnings during the locked box period that accrue to the benefit of the buyer, who (it is assumed) bears the risks and rewards of ownership in the locked box period.	In most locked box transactions, it is not the case that all risk is in fact transferred to the buyer effective at the reference date. For example, a MAC clause may mean that significant risks remain with the seller.

	Explanation	*Comment*
	If the buyer is rewarded for taking on this risk, then the seller cannot also be entitled to compensation for it and is only entitled to a risk-free compensation for the time value of money.	
Daily profit rate: target's net earnings between reference date and closing	The daily profit charge is meant to compensate the seller for lost earnings of the target company between the locked box date and closing as a result of backdating the transaction.	The profits during the locked box period should already be reflected in enterprise value for e valuation effective at the economic date of the acquisition, the locked box date. Adding a daily profit charge means double counting. Further, information asymmetries between the parties can result in high estimates of profits in the locked box period.

CHAPTER 8

Earn-Outs

§8.01 OVERVIEW

An earn-out is an arrangement under which the seller of a business receives payouts, in addition to the basic purchase price, that are contingent upon the achievement of agreed performance targets over a period of time after closing (known as the 'earn-out period'). Earn-out targets can be financial or non-financial.

An earn-out mechanism is often used when the price expectations of buyer and seller are significantly apart and can provide an effective means of bridging the gap. However, earn-outs can be problematic: what was an inability to agree on the target entity's value before signing can all too easily turn into a dispute - in other words, the can is merely kicked down the road.

This aspect of earn-outs was expressed by the Delaware Court of Chancery, which, commenting on the characteristics of earn-outs, noted that they typically reflect:

> disagreement over the value of the business that is bridged when the seller trades the certainty of less cash at closing for the prospect of more cash over time ... But since value is frequently debatable and the causes of underperformance equally so, an earn-out often converts today's disagreement over price into tomorrow's litigation over the outcome ... .[79]

Similarly, in *Starbev GP Ltd v. Interbrew Central European Holdings BV*, the judge, commenting on the issues that gave rise to the dispute, noted:

> The parties had clinched their deal, and the question as to how the deferred consideration would work in practice was pushed off into the indefinite future.[80]

---

79. *Airborne Health, Inc. v. Squid Soap, LP*, 984 A.2d 126, 132 (Del. Ch. 2009), quoted in Kevin R. Shannon and Michael K. Reilly, *Post-Closing Earnouts in M&A Transactions: Avoiding Common Disputes*, 2011.
80. *Starbev GP Ltd v. Interbrew Central European Holdings BV* [2014] EWHC 1311 (Comm), para. 57.

This dispute is discussed in §8.03.

At the heart of many earn-out-related disputes lies disagreement over the basis on which the earn-out is calculated. At a basic level, the issue is the (necessarily imperfect) connection between the metric used and the value it is supposed to measure. This connection can only ever be an approximation. The buyer, who is in control of the business during the earn-out period, can have an incentive to manage the earn-out basis (downwards), excercising judgement when preparing the accounts to minimise the earn-out payment or to just miss earn-out targets. Further, the earnings measures on which earn-outs are based often include one-off or non-recurring elements. All of these factors make earn-outs a prominent source of disagreement. Section §8.03 discusses typical disputes.

§8.02 PURPOSE AND ROLE OF EARN-OUTS

While the principal purpose of an earn-out is to bridge the price expectation gap between buyer and seller, there are some other important features.

[A] Bridging the Price Expectation Gap

An earn-out represents part of the target entity's value that is dependent upon one or more unknown future events. It is always the case that events occurring after closing cannot be known with absolute certainty. On the one hand, DCF valuations deal with uncertainty in the discount rate. However, if the expectations of buyer and seller as to uncertain future events are significantly apart and cannot be reconciled, the resultant price expectation gap may only be capable of being bridged by means of an earn-out.

An example of uncertainty that can be difficult to deal with in valuation is a binary outcome such as the FDA approval of a new drug that, if successful, is expected to turn into an important driver of future profits. The parties may disagree over the probability of such approval. An earn-out that is linked to FDA approval is a mechanism to measure that value subsequently when the uncertainty is resolved. Whatever trigger or measure is used for an earn-out, it should therefore be closely associated with 'value'.

[B] Allocation of Risk

With an earn-out the allocation of risk is moved from buyer to seller (to some degree). A DCF valuation requires estimates of future returns which (as already noted) are almost always subject to uncertainty.

An earn-out means that the buyer bears less risk: if the target's performance subsequently falls short of agreed targets, then the buyer will pay a lower or no earn-out. If actual developments exceed expectations, then the buyer will pay more, but will also have received a business that is worth more. The effect on the valuation of the target business of exceeding or falling short of projected trading is moved to the seller to some degree.

[C] Incentivisation of the Seller

Earn-outs are often used as a mechanism to incentivise an owner-manager or entrepreneur who is selling a majority stake in his or her business but will stay on managing or otherwise contributing to its performance after closing. The earn-out creates an incentive to maximise their efforts as they continue to share in the rewards after closing.

[D] Source of Acquisition Financing

An earn-out is also a source of acquisition financing. This is because the earn-out component of the purchase price that is based on a profit measure like EBITDA is effectively (or should be) paid out of the target entity's profits after closing only if these profits are actually achieved. The earn-out component of the consideration is deferred until it is clear that earn-out targets have been met. This part of the consideration therefore does not need to be financed by the buyer. This assumes that the earn-out targets are linked to cash flows that can be used for the earn-out payout.

This aspect of earn-outs was particularly relevant after the financial crisis when acquisition finance was difficult to obtain and significant parts of the total consideration in some deals were deferred into the earn-out period. An example of an earn-out during around this time, when the financial crisis inhibited bank financing for prospective purchasers, is *Starbev GP Ltd v. Interbrew Central European Holdings BV*, where an earn-out helped bridge a gap in a PE sponsor's acquisition financing.[81] This dispute is discussed in the following section.

§8.03 THE EARN-OUT BASIS

[A] Earn-Out Metrics

Earn-outs can be linked to financial or non-financial metrics, or a combination of the two. Each type is discussed below.

[1] Financial Metrics

Financial metrics typically relate to sales, sales growth, or measures of profit such as EBITDA, EBIT, or net profit. Occasionally they relate to other metrics, such as prices charged by a particular supplier in respect of certain products.

It is essential that the SPA defines precisely the basis on which the relevant performance measure underlying the earn-out is to be calculated. In the case of an earn-out linked to measures of profits (however defined), the SPA should, among other things, ensure that the target entity's accounts are drawn up on a basis consistent with that

81. *Ibid.*, para. 16.

applied before closing. By way of illustration, items to be specifically addressed here might include changes in accounting policies and practices (e.g., adopting a more conservative revenue recognition policy), one-off asset write-downs, changes as a result of new intercompany arrangements (e.g., where the buyer's group begins to supply certain products or services at higher prices than hitherto), or the charging of management and similar fees by the new owner. A single recharge of a group service, for example, could extinguish profits that would have otherwise triggered a significant earn-out payment. Equally, the parties will often limit the scope for discretion in the preparation of the earn-out statement and attempt to ensure that profits of the earn-out period are not affected by items that have nothing to do with value. Profits should usually be recurring and cash-relevant.

Capturing all possible adjustments to future income *ex ante* when the earn-out is agreed can seem similar to attempting to normalise future periods' earnings, (when it is difficult enough to normalise historical earnings). Even where an SPA contains comprehensive rules governing the calculation of earn-out profits, these can prove to be impractical or difficult to implement. Despite apparent (hard-fought) agreement before signing, there can be scope for disputes over interpretation later and wording that requires the exclusion of 'one-off' or 'non-recurring' items can easily be subject to disagreement. This is what happened in *Comet Systems, Inc. Shareholders' Agent v. MIVA, Inc.* which is discussed further below in this section.

The earn-out calculation should be based on financial information that is validated by an external party where possible, ideally audited financial statements. The following example highlights this.

Example Dispute: *Treatt plc v. Barratt and others* (England and Wales Court of Appeal)[82]

This dispute related to an earn-out that was based on audited accounts for certain calendar years ending 31 December. The buyer's own year-end was 30 September. After the acquisition, the buyer changed the year ends of the companies it had acquired to 30 September, so as to bring them in line with its own accounting year end and thereby facilitate the preparation of consolidated group accounts. The buyer did not, in addition, provide audited accounts with 31 December year-ends.

As a result, when the time came for the buyer to prepare an earn-out notice, it had no audited accounts of the acquired companies for the calendar year with which to do so. Instead, the buyer prepared the earn-out notice by reference to the audited consolidated accounts for the buyer's group (ending 30 September 2010), subtracting management account figures for the preceding three-months (1 October 2009 to 31 December 2009) and then adding figures (taken from other management accounts) for the three-month period following 30 September (1 October to 31 December).[83] The

82. *Treatt plc v. Barratt and others* [2015] EWCA *Civ 116*. There was an unsuccessful appeal: *[2015] EWCA Civ 116 (18 February 2015).*
83. *Barratt and others v. Treatt plc* [2013] EWHC 3561 (Ch), para. 45.

dispute was over whether the notice provided by the buyer on this basis was a valid earn-out notice pursuant to the relevant clause in the SPA.

The requirement in the SPA for the parties to use the audited accounts rather than management accounts was considered by the judge to be an important safeguard and designed to improve the reliability of the figures in the accounts.[84] The notice that was based on the management accounts was not considered a valid earn-out notice. This meant that the dispute as to the amount of the earn-out had to be referred to an independent expert determination in accordance with a process set out in the SPA. As indicated earlier, wording in relation to the earn-out basis that requires the exclusion of 'one-off' or 'non-recurring' items can easily be subject to disagreement. This is what happened in the following case in which the parties disagreed over whether a change-of-control bonus paid to the employees of the target corporation prior to closing was a 'one-time, non-recurring expense', in which case it would have been excluded from the earn-out basis.

Example Dispute over Non-recurring Elements in Earn-Out Basis (US Court of Chancery of Delaware)[85]

The earn-out in *Comet Systems, Inc. Shareholders' Agent v. MIVA, Inc.* consisted of a combination of two financial and one non-financial earn-out targets of Comet (the acquisition target), a connected desktop software company: a Revenue Goal, a Cost Goal, and a Specified Software User Base Goal. As a threshold condition to any payout on the Revenue Goal, the revenue per user had to exceed the cost per user in the relevant year (defined in the merger agreement as operating costs excluding amortisation and one-time, non-recurring expenses). As a threshold condition to any payout on the Cost Goal, the profit per user had to be at least a certain amount.

A central issue was whether a change-of-control bonus paid to the employees of the target company was a 'one-time, non-recurring expense' that should be excluded from the cost basis when calculating the earn-out.

MIVA, the buyer, prepared the earn-out calculation. Its calculation showed that an earn-out for the year 2004 resulted entirely from achieving the 2004 User Base Goal. For the 2004 revenue and cost goals, MIVA's calculation showed profit per user below the thresholds. In calculating the cost per user in the profit per user threshold calculations for both the revenue and cost goals, MIVA had included a USD 800,000 bonus to Comet's employees under the merger bonus plan.

In Comet's view, the bonus payment should have been excluded from the cost per user calculation because it was a 'one-time, non-recurring expense', whereas MIVA argued that 'one-time, non-recurring expenses' should not be read to encompass the bonus payment which it viewed as an ordinary cost of business as acquisition bonuses

84. *Ibid.*
85. *Comet Systems, Inc. Shareholders' Agent v. MIVA, Inc.* C.A. No. 2793-VCL Court of Chancery of Delaware. Decided 22 Oct. 2008.

contribute to employee retention during the sale process and thus revenue generation. Further, MIVA argued that Comet had paid out bonuses in the past, had treated prior bonuses as normal operating costs, and that bonuses were common in the technology industry.

The court found that the merger bonus was a one-time, non-recurring expense to be excluded from the earn-out basis.[86]

The following case relates to a PE investor who expected to hold the target company for a comparatively short time and agreed to share with the seller parts of an excess return in an on-sale. This is one type of earn-out.

Example Dispute over Excess Return Payments (High Court of England and Wales)[87]

The dispute between the Dutch subsidiary of brewer Anheuser Busch and an acquisition vehicle of CVC Capital Partners (CVC), the PE firm, related to CVC's acquisition of the Central and Eastern European brewing businesses from Anheuser Busch for EUR 1.5 billion in 2009, a multiple of 6.7 times EBITDA. Part of the consideration was deferred. The earn-out clause in the SPA stipulated that Anheuser Bush would receive a share of 40% of CVC's return above certain threshold levels on the future on-sale of the business. The thresholds were to apply in step changes over time, with increases over a four-year period after the sale. As the excess return payment, a type of earn-out, depended on the return upon a re-sale of the business, both the (initial) investment amount and the on-sale price were relevant to its calculation.

It is interesting to note how far apart the parties' perception of the value of the deferred part of the compensation were: The buyer considered the earn-out to be a 'low-value give', whereas the seller's investment bankers valued it at between USD 200 million and USD 400 million.[88]

Soon after closing, CVC started investigating potential exit opportunities. These efforts bore fruit when at the end of 2011, another North American brewer approached CVC with an indicative bid for the business of 11 times 2011 EBITDA, and CVC was looking at a successful exit opportunity. The transaction with the North American bidder closed in June 2012. The price was reported to be EUR 2.65 billion. Part of the overall consideration in this second transaction was a convertible note of EUR 500 million.

86. *Comet Systems, Inc. Shareholders' Agent v. MIVA, Inc.*, http://caselaw.findlaw.com/de-court-of-chancery/1267797.html.
87. *Starbev GP Limited v. Interbrew Central European Holdings BV* [2014] EWHC 1311 (Comm).
88. *Ibid.*, paras 23 and 24.

Shortly after closing, CVC notified Anheuser Busch that the investment threshold (a multiple times the invested amount, where the multiple depended on the divestment date) had not been surpassed, and no excess return payment triggered. This led to a swift response on the part of the seller, which had thought it would be in for a windfall. It appointed independent accountants to verify and report on the PE firm's calculations and shortly thereafter asserted that the investment amount as stated by CVC was not correct.

In August 2013, CVC exercised its option under the convertible note and received additional consideration of EUR 500 million (less certain deductions), and paid an amount of EUR 32 million of deferred consideration. In the seller's view, however, it was owed a total deferred consideration of about EUR 200 million.[89] One of the issues was whether the convertible note was structured in a way so that the earn-out payment would be reduced (as certain thresholds would not be reached). The Court of Appeal confirmed that the dominant purpose of the convertible note transaction was to reduce the payments due to the seller.

The following example of an earn-out dispute has to do with foreign currency conversion. It would seem that at least the exchange rate aspect of the dispute discussed below could have been avoided if the parties had specified in the SPA at which date the exchange rate should be determined and which rate to use.

Example Earn-Out Dispute over Foreign Exchange Conversion (ICC Arbitration)[90]

Two US companies and two Brazilian companies (purchasers) acquired shares in a Brazilian subsidiary from two Brazilian companies and a German company (the sellers). Part of the consideration was deferred. An amount of USD 7 million was paid by the purchasers as an advance on an earn-out. A post-deal dispute included several claims and counterclaims.

One of the counterclaims related to the exchange rates to be used to convert the USD 7 million into Brazilian reals, the currency in which the earn-out was payable. The buyers argued that the exchange rate at closing should be used, whereas the sellers argued that the exchange rate should be the rate at the time the earn-out was paid (two years after the advance payment when it had moved). The tribunal found that the appropriate exchange rate was the one at time the earn-out payment became due, not at the time of the payment of the advance.[91]

89. *Ibid.*, para. 54.
90. ICC Case 14691 Final Award, in: ICC International Court of Arbitration Bulletin Vol 24/Number 1 - 2013, p. 132. ICC 14691.
91. *Ibid.*, p. 132.

[2] Non-financial Metrics

Earn-outs can also be linked to non-financial metrics such as market share, regulatory approvals, clicks on a website, product launches, units sold, product/project development milestones, customer retention, or the receipt of subsidies, to name only a few. These can also be combined with financial metrics.

As with financial metrics, it is important to base a non-financial earn-out on metrics that cannot be easily manipulated. For example, once in control of the target company, a buyer may be able to influence the timing of some regulatory approvals, thereby influencing an earn-out that is linked to such approvals. Likewise, sales volumes (units) might be distorted through 'channel stuffing' (the practice of inflating sales by supplying retailers in one period with more products than they can sell, at the expense of volumes in a future period which is relevant to an earn-out).

The following example relates to the development of a project that was relocated after closing.

Example: *Deere & Company v. Exelon Generation Acquisitions* (US Superior Court of Delaware)

In 2010, Deere sold its wind energy business to Exelon for USD 860 million.[92] The assets sold included both operating wind farms and wind farms in development. The SPA included total potential earn-out payments of USD 40 million, contingent upon the successful completion of certain milestones on three new projects, among them the Blissfield Wind Project, which involved a USD 14 million earn-out provision.

The Blissfield Wind Project was originally intended to be developed in Lenawee County, Michigan. However, Exelon subsequently determined that, due to regulatory changes in the township, it would not be possible to develop it there. After exploring alternative sites, Exelon negotiated the relocation of the project from Lenawee County to Gratiot County, Michigan, where it successfully developed the Beebe Wind Farm.

Exelon argued that the project in Gratiot County was a new project. It argued that the SPA did not provide for relocation of the project and that the Blissfield Wind Project had been abandoned because it could not be completed in Lenawee County. Deere argued that the Blissfield Wind Project had been relocated, that it had not been required to be built in a specific location, and that the milestones under the SPA had been met, triggering an earn-out payment.

The court found that the project had been relocated, not abandoned, and that Deere was entitled to the earn-out payment.

92. *Deere & Company v. Exelon Generation Acquisitions, LLC,* C.A. No. N13C07-330-MMJCCLD http://courts.state.de.us/Opinions/Download.aspx?id=242380.

[B] Earn-Out Period

Earn-out periods are usually between one and three years and occasionally up to five years or more. In general, the longer the period, the more likely a dispute; in a longer earn-out period, there tend to be more changes to the target entity's business and, as time passes, the seller has less responsibility for developments after closing.

Changes to a business during the earn-out period can affect the ability to measure and report earn-out metrics on a consistent basis. The following are examples of changes that may affect the earn-out basis after closing and cause problems:

- A strategic buyer integrates the target business into its group operations to achieve synergies.
- A PE sponsor merges the target business with another portfolio company's operations for similar reasons.
- A target business shares overhead functions and cost allocations with those of other companies.

It is not difficult to see how, in any of the above circumstances, the target entity may no longer be in a position to report profits on a basis comparable with when it was a stand-alone company. It is therefore advisable for the target entity to continue to report on a stand-alone basis during the earn-out period, or for an appropriate pro-forma basis of accounts preparation to be agreed and specified in the SPA. However, allocating costs on a pro-forma reporting basis can be problematic and lead to disputes over the earn-out basis.

In view of this, earn-outs can be less problematic for financial (PE) buyers who do not plan to merge operations, than for many strategic buyers (particularly earn-outs based on profits alone). For strategic buyers, successful earn-outs may be best linked to metrics that are not affected by the integration of the target entity into its owner's operations. Examples include prices charged by a specific supplier, or non-financial metrics that are key drivers of the business plan.

[C] Preparation of the Earn-Out Statement

In principle, the process for the (annual) preparation and finalisation of the earn-out statement and calculation is somewhat similar to the preparation of the completion accounts. In a typical process, once the buyer (who is usually responsible for the preparation) delivers the draft earn-out statement to the seller, the seller has the opportunity to review. The preparation and review periods are contractually predetermined. As the buyer is in control of the business during this time, the SPA should include access rights to the accounting records of the target company.

If the seller agrees with the draft earn-out statement, it becomes final. If the seller takes the view that an earn-out statement has not been prepared in accordance with the terms of the SPA, then it prepares a written objection notice. Following the objection notice is a period for negotiations during which the parties attempt to reconcile their differences on the items in dispute. If they cannot reach agreement, the dispute may be submitted to an independent expert.

[D] Purchaser's Covenants

The SPA usually includes purchaser's covenants to protect the seller from unforeseen changes to the company that would reduce or eliminate the earn-out. These may include a combination of the following: the target company will not engage in M&A activity, enter into new lines of business not related to its business activities at closing, alter its financing structure, voluntarily be dissolved or liquidated, or deviate from specified business plan measures.

[E] Conclusions

Well-structured earn-out clauses reduce the likelihood of disputes by taking account of the following considerations:

- A comparatively simple structure is advantageous. As a general rule, complexity increases the ability to manipulate the earn-out basis. The simpler it is to measure, the less scope there is for disagreement.
- A short earn-out period is generally preferable.
- A close relationship of the earn-out metrics to value (of the target entity) is generally important. Even if it is not possible to identify metrics that measure value perfectly, it may be useful to think about the earn-out in such a way that its purpose is to ensure that any incremental change of the earn-out metric is directly and proportionately linked to the parties paying more or less.
- A general rule is that the higher up the income statement performance is measured (moving from sales at the top to net income at the bottom), the fewer opportunities there are to 'manage' the earn-out basis. Sales (or volumes sold, or prices) tend to be less dispute-prone than profit.
- It is advisable to require the use of consistent accounting policies and ensure access rights.
- Use example calculations in the SPA Exhibits.
- Consider carefully how best to leave as little as possible to the buyer's discretion when preparing the earn-out figures.

CHAPTER 9

Revenue Recognition

§9.01 OVERVIEW

Revenue recognition is a central theme in post-M&A disputes for two reasons. First, it is an important link between a target company's accounting information and its valuation: Additional (profitable) sales increase the reported earnings in a period, and earnings are often the basis for the valuation of the target business. In transactions where the purchase price is determined as a multiple of a measure of earnings (such as EBITDA), the incentive to overstate earnings is magnified, possibly by as much as the multiplier. Even when a buyer values the target using a DCF method, inflated historical revenues may mean expectations of future revenue growth are too high and, in turn, affect the buyer's valuation. Second, revenue recognition is a significant judgment area in accounting.

When to recognise revenue is typically associated with two key uncertainties: whether the product or service has been provided and whether cash will be collected. Revenue recognition criteria that address these uncertainties are that revenue should only be recognised when (a) it is earned and (b) it is realised or realisable. Both may require significant judgment. This creates scope for disagreement over the timing of recognising sales and earnings and the amounts to recognise.

The IASB and US FASB have recently issued IFRS 15 as a new revenue recognition standard that will replace almost all existing revenue recognition rules in IAS (in particular, IAS 18 and IAS 11) and US GAAP. IFRS 15 were effective from 1 January 2018. The standards will be identical in IFRS and US GAAP, with some exceptions. The new revenue recognition standards are discussed in §9.02.

The basic principle in IFRS 15 is that an entity recognises revenue to depict the transfer of promised goods or services to customers in an amount that reflects the consideration to which the entity expects to be entitled in exchange for those goods or services. The standard applies to revenue recognised both at a point in time and over a period of time, in particular for long-term contracts.

Management judgment and estimates play a key role in revenue recognition for long-term contracts where revenue is recognised with the degree of completion (which requires judgment about the extent to which the earnings process is complete). The accounting for long-term contracts and related disputes are discussed in §9.03.

Revenue recognition does not usually give direct rise to a purchase price adjustment (with the exception of a net debt deduction for deferred revenue (see §4.04[F])). Disputes involving revenue recognition therefore often relate to misrepresentations or warranty breaches. One such dispute is *Sycamore Bidco Ltd v. Breslin & Dawson.*[93]

Example Dispute about Revenue Recognition (High Court of England and Wales)

The central figure in this case was 'total revenue'.[94] The buyer and claimant, Sycamore Bidco, a PE-owned company, acquired Gissings Advisory Services Ltd from two sellers and claimed damages for misrepresentation against the sellers in relation to the inclusion of a monthly reduction in the charges by an IT supplier (granted as compensation for previous problems with the supplier's services) in revenue of the target company. Net income and cash flow in the relevant period were not affected by this error. However, the buyer argued - successfully - that its valuation model meant that the inflated revenue led to an overstated valuation. The SPA included the following accounts warranty:

> 4.1: The Accounts:
> 4.1.1 show a true and fair view of:
> (a) the state of affairs;
> (b) the assets and liabilities; and
> (c) the profit or losses
> of each Group Company to which they relate and the Group (on a consolidated basis) as at the Accounts Date;
> 4.1.2 have been prepared in accordance with relevant generally accepted accounting practice ...

The relevant accounting standard in this case was UK GAAP. The relevant definition of 'turnover' was defined as:

> The revenue resulting from exchange transactions under which a seller supplies to customers the goods or services that it is in business to provide.[95]

The judge found that the reduction should not have been included in turnover, as there was no evidence that there was any un-recouped expenditure or any unremunerated provision of services at the date of the agreement, and it could not be treated as compensation in respect of any such matters. Accordingly, the turnover figure was overstated. Further, the judge found that the compensation should probably have been treated as 'other income', and that including the supplier's compensation sum in

93. *Sycamore Bidco Limited v. Sean Breslin/Andrew Dawson* [2012] EWHC 3443 (Ch).
94. *Ibid.*, para. 116.
95. *Ibid.*, para. 216.

turnover for the relevant year failed in a material way to present a true and fair view of the state of affairs of the company or its profit and losses.

The question of damages in this case is discussed below in §9.03.

§9.02 NEW REVENUE RECOGNITION STANDARDS

IFRS 15, applicable to accounting periods beginning on or after 1 January 2018, has been developed in parallel with equivalent changes to US GAAP.[96] The purpose of the new standard is to remove inconsistencies in current revenue recognition practice, provide a more robust framework for addressing revenue issues, and improve comparability of revenue reporting across sectors and jurisdictions.

In the short and medium term, the transition between the old and new rules is expected to create challenges in an M&A context. For example:

- Under the new rules, revenue recognition may be accelerated or delayed, affecting reported profitability, working capital, net debt, or other deal metrics, potentially impacting the closing balance sheet or earnings adjustment mechanism.
- Forecasts stated using the new rules may differ materially from those provided during due diligence, or those forming the basis for the transaction price.
- Changes in earnings could impact profits available for distribution or could result in non-compliance with loan covenants, triggering indemnity clauses.
- Earn-out clauses negotiated using accounts prepared under the old rules may result in materially different compensation when the agreed earn-out methodology is applied using accounts prepared under the new rules.

In the long term, there is no reason to expect that revenue recognition will be less relevant to M&A-related disputes. The new standard continues to have important areas of judgment (even if different from those in existing standards). For example, IFRS 15 has the following requirements:

- For long-term contracts where revenue may be recognised over time, the percentage of the performance obligations satisfied will be subject to estimates, including appraisals of results achieved, surveys of work completed, time elapsed, milestones reached, units produced, costs incurred, or labour hours expended. Appraisals, surveys of work completed and estimation of total hours or costs of a project involve technical knowledge and judgment.
- For contracts with variable consideration or where some goods are expected to be returned by customers, estimates will be required. These and other estimates of probabilities or amounts can be biased or, in hindsight, turn out to be incorrect.

96. This section draws significantly from 'This is How IFRS 15 will Impact M&As', Financial Director, 32 May 2017, Phil Hersey, Heiko Ziehms and Anna Hartley.

IFRS 15 will not only lead to different accounting treatments once the transition to the new standard has occurred, but also to uncertainty during the transition itself. Beyond affecting reported earnings, IFRS 15 may require wider changes to customer contracts or loan agreements – legal matters that may not receive sufficient attention during busy negotiations.

The motivation behind the changes is improved comparability in financial reporting between companies and across industry sectors. This is a desirable objective. However, in the short and medium term, the changes introduce additional complexity into the financial and accounting aspects of M&A transactions. In the long term, revenue recognition issues will likely continue to play a prominent role in M&A-related disputes.

§9.03 REVENUE RECOGNITION FOR LONG-TERM CONTRACTS

[A] Accounting Rules

When a performance obligation is satisfied over time, a firm may, under certain conditions, recognise revenue before the obligation has been performed in full, by measuring the progress towards completion (IFRS 15.39). The degree of completion may be assessed using either an output or an input method.

Output methods measure revenue on the basis of direct measurements of the value to the customer of goods or services transferred to date, relative to the remaining goods or services promised under a contract. Input methods recognise revenue on the basis of the entity's efforts or inputs to the satisfaction of a performance obligation; for example, costs incurred relative to the total expected costs for the satisfaction of that performance obligation. In both cases, the firm recognises a profit margin along with revenue. Two key estimates enter into reported profitability when reporting earnings: the degree of completion and the overall contract profit (of which a fraction is realised). Both are open to bias.

IFRS 15.4 requires a company to update its estimates continuously relating to the measure of progress. In case long-term contracts are expected to be loss-making, IAS 37 requires the immediate recognition of a loss.

[B] The Degree of Completion and Cost to Complete

Estimating the degree of completion of large projects and the remaining costs to complete requires both technical engineering expertise and judgment. It is easy to overestimate the degree of completion or an entire contract's expected profitability before it has been completed, only to find at its end that actual profits are much less (or the contract was loss-making).

The unbiased exercise of judgment would mean that new information that comes to light during long-term contracts would increase or decrease contract profitability in an approximately equal number of cases (all else being equal). As IFRS requires the immediate recognition of expected losses in full, a typical pattern would be that entities recognise losses earlier rather than later. In fact, the opposite may be more often the case. To illustrate, Figure 9.1 shows a summary of cumulative profits reported (under IAS 11) over the lifetime of a portfolio of four long-term contracts for an undisclosed target company. While each contract had a different term, the terms were scaled here to be comparable.

Figure 9.1 Evolution of Reported Contract Profitability over Time

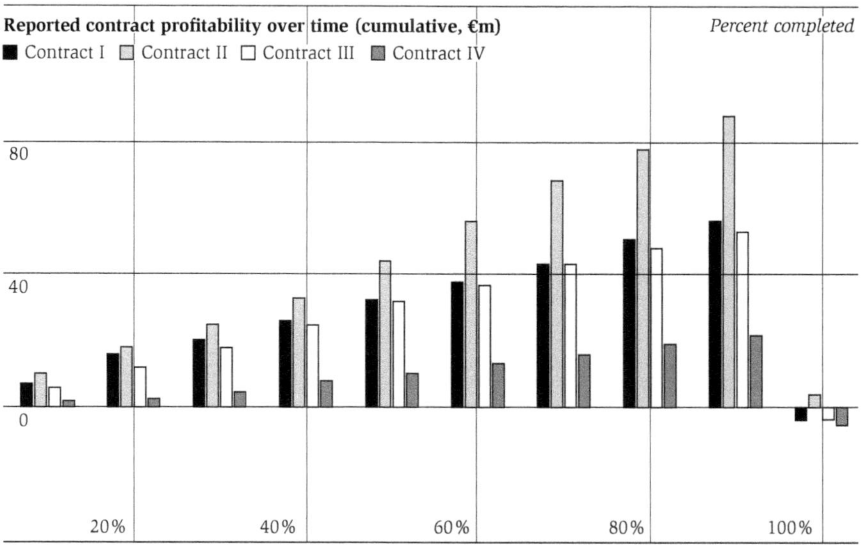

Over the contract terms, management was consistently too optimistic about total contract profitability. This led to overstated profits up until completion of each contract. Only at the end of each contract, with no future periods were available to defer losses to, did the company report the losses actually incurred. In three out of four cases, these cumulative losses exceeded all previously (incorrectly) reported profits.

Earnings of long-term contracts can generally be overstated in two ways:

- Underestimating the costs to complete work under the contract. In this case, the real costs were only reflected in the accounts when no further periods were available and the contract was completed, and the costs associated turned out to be much higher than the previous estimate suggested.
- Overstating the degree of completion in the periods up until the last reporting quarter. This moves the recognition of contract profitability ahead in time (e.g., into a financial year on which the valuation is based) even when the estimate of overall profitability is correct. In this case, it moved (non-existent) profits into earlier reporting periods.

Prematurely recognised gains are not part of recurring earnings and should not be included in the basis of valuation of a business if the basis is a historical EBITDA or other earnings figure. Identifying bias in the earnings recognition process is a step towards removing non-recurring components of earnings from the basis of valuation. The type of analysis as above is a financial due diligence tool for companies with long-term contracts that can serve to quantify appropriate adjustments to EBITDA.

Example Dispute over Revenue Recognition for Long-Term Contracts (International Arbitration)

A buyer acquired a company engaged in the construction of a power plant. The buyer was in the process of building numerous plants at the time of the acquisition, and the average construction period was well over one year. The buyer valued the business using the income method (a DCF valuation). The projected cash flows used in the valuation were based on the target's business plan to which the buyer had made certain adjustments. The projections included the cash receipt from a customer of GBP 15 million upon the expected completion of a milestone in relation to the power plant in 2017, two years after closing.

Table 9.1 Valuation Model and Working Capital Adjustment

Enterprise Valuation

in GBP million	2016	2017	2018	2019	2020	2012	Terminal value
	Plan	Plan	Plan	Plan	Plan	Plan	Plan
EBIT	70	74	77	80	82	85	
Depreciation	12	12	13	14	15	15	
Change in working capital	-2	-5	-9	0	-8	-8	
Change in POC receivables	-12	15	-8	-8	0	0	
Change in other net operating assets	5	-12	3	-6	-2	2	
Operating cash flow	73	84	76	80	87	94	
Capital expenditure	-20	-23	-20	-20	-20	-22	
Free cash flow	53	61	56	60	67	72	78
WACC	10%	10%	10%	10%	10%	10%	10%
TV growth rate							3%
Terminal value (undiscounted)							1,114.29
Discount factor	1.00	0.91	0.83	0.75	0.68	0.62	0.56
Present value of free cash flow	53.00	55.45	46.28	45.08	45.76	44.71	628.99
Enterprise value	**919.27**						

Working Capital Adjustment

in GBP million	Reference value	Closing date	Difference
		Actual	
Trade receivables	70	64	-6
POC receivables	11	25	14
Inventory	50	57	7
Trade payables	-80	-84	-4
Net working capital	50	62	12

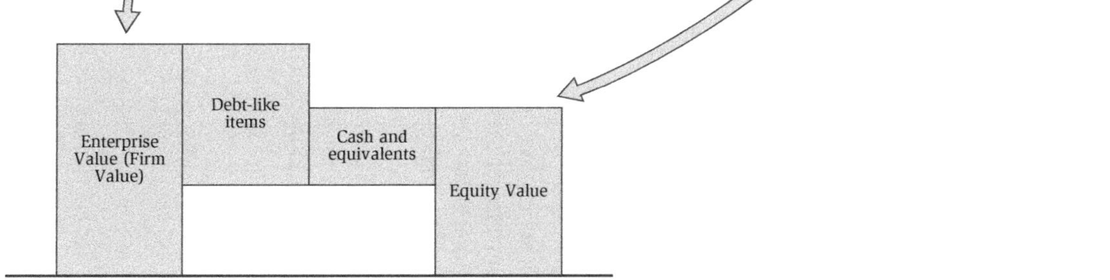

The expected cash receipt of GBP 15 million is visible in the cash flow statement in Table 9.1 as a reduction of the POC receivable (a credit) in 2017. This cash inflow, discounted, led to an increase in enterprise value. The definition of working capital in this transaction included POC receivables. The original recognition of the POC was still included in working capital at closing, as it had not yet been invoiced at closing. The expected cash inflow and the working capital item related to the same underlying transaction.

Table 9.1 shows that working capital at closing was GBP 14 million higher than it would have been without the POC receivable, and this led to closing date working capital exceeding the reference value (which did not reflect a POC receivable of this magnitude). All else being equal, this led to an additional working capital adjustment of GBP 14 million - however, the same underlying transaction had already been included in enterprise value. The buyer argued, (unsuccessfully) that the information had not been available to them that the POC receivable related to the same project for which the cash inflow was included in the seller's projections.

The problem of double counting illustrated is not limited to POC accounting. Work in progress (WIP) inventory is similar to a POC receivable, except that inventory usually does not include capitalised expected profits. In principle, the kind of double counting in the example above could have occurred with the WIP inventory instead of a POC receivable (the difference being the profit margin). The reason this problem does not occur more frequently is that individual components of inventory are often not as significant relative to overall working capital as the item in the example above, and the average time for them to convert into cash is usually shorter. However, large construction projects that are accounted for using the (more conservative) 'completed contract' method of revenue recognition in which all revenue and profit are recognised only upon completion can be exposed to similar risks of double counting.

Different teams had worked on the valuation and on the completion mechanism in this transaction. They had not communicated sufficiently to be aware of the risk that an item in working capital may already have been reflected in enterprise value.

CHAPTER 10

Fraud

§10.01 INTRODUCTION

Fraud can have many different meanings, depending on context and the law that governs it. In the US alone, fraud has been described by courts as being 'infinite in variety'.[97] Fraud is defined by Black's Law Dictionary as:

> A knowing misrepresentation of the truth or concealment of a material fact to induce another to act to his or her detriment.[98]

The definition of the Association of Certified Fraud Examiners (ACFE) is as follows:

> any intentional or deliberate act to deprive another of property or money by guile, deception, or other unfair means.[99]

The ACFE definition is broad and encompasses corruption, asset misappropriation and financial statement fraud, each of these three, in turn, have numerous subcategories.[100] Of these, financial statement fraud and corruption are perhaps the most important in an M&A disputes context. The ACFE defines financial statement fraud as:

97. *Reddaway v. Banham*, [1896] A.C. 199 (H.L.) 221 (Eng.)., cited in: That Pesky Little Thing Called Fraud: An Examination of Buyers' Insistence Upon (and Sellers' Too Ready Acceptance of) Undefined 'Fraud Carve-Outs' in Acquisition Agreements By Glenn D. West, The Business Lawyer; Vol. 69, August 2014, p. 1054.
98. Bryan Garner, ed., Black's Law Dictionary. 8th Ed. (2004), s.v., 'fraud.'.
99. Association of Certified Fraud Examiners, What is Fraud? Fraud 101. Available at https://www.acfe.com/fraud-101.aspx.
100. The Fraud Tree, ACFE, http://www.acfe.com/fraud-tree.aspx.

> the deliberate misrepresentation of the financial condition of an enterprise accomplished through the intentional misstatement or omission of amounts or disclosures in the financial statements to deceive financial statement users. Note that financial statement fraud, much like all types of fraud, is an intentional act.[101]

High profile fraud cases show the variety of ways fraud can enter into a transaction. Examples include:

- The acquisition of Autonomy by HP in 2012, the second-largest acquisition in HP's history, in which HP executives alleged that they were misled by Autonomy which accounted for most of a USD 8.8 billion write-down after the transaction.[102] In a public statement, Hewlett-Packard announced that '... some former members of Autonomy's management team used accounting improprieties, misrepresentations and disclosure failures to inflate the underlying financial metrics of the company, prior to Autonomy's acquisition by HP. These efforts appear to have been a wilful effort to mislead investors and potential buyers, and severely impacted HP management's ability to fairly value Autonomy at the time of the deal'.[103]

  In early 2018, Autonomy's former CFO was convicted of fraud in the US after being found guilty of artificially inflating the firm's financial position before it was sold (he intended to appeal against the judgment).[104] (Other lawsuits were ongoing at the time of writing).
- The acquisition of mobile operator EE by BT from Deutsche Telekom and Orange, the French telecoms group. The transaction closed in early 2016. Part of the consideration of GBP 12.5 billion was paid in BT shares. Orange and Deutsche Telekom became shareholders of BT in 2016 as a result (Deutsche Telekom owned 12%). In early 2017, BT issued a profit warning after discovering a complex fraud in its Italian business unit that led to a GBP 530 million write-down at BT. This triggered a decline in BT's share price by almost 25% in the first half of 2017.[105] Deutsche Telekom wrote down its interest in BT by EUR 2.2 billion, and subsequently by a further EUR 1.1 billion. In order to avoid a potential dispute, BT struck a GBP 225 million settlement that ruled out further legal disputes with Orange and Deutsche Telekom.[106] This case is similar in the following respect to the *The Hut Group Ltd v. Nobahar-Cookson and another*, discussed further below.[107] In both cases, the consideration consisted in part in shares in the buyer's group, and it

101. ACFE's 2015 Fraud Examiner's Manual.
102. Autonomy deal is a lesson for managers, Financial Times, 2 Dec. 2012.
103. HP Issues Statement Regarding Autonomy Impairment Charge, HP, 20 Nov. 2012, http://www8.hp.com/us/en/hpnews/press-release.html?id=1334263#.UnPvQPleY4k.
104. BBC Business News 1 May 2018, Autonomy ex-executive guilty of fraud, https://www.bbc.co.uk/news/business-43959468.
105. Financial Times, Deutsche Telekom takes further EUR 1.1 billion hit from BT stake, 3 Aug. 2017.
106. *Ibid.*
107. *The Hut Group Ltd v. Nobahar-Cookson and another* [2016] EWCA Civ 128, discussed in §10.03.

emerged after closing that financial statement fraud had occurred that dated from the time before the transaction which meant that the consideration shares – the acquisition currency – were worth less than the seller had expected.

- Caterpillar Inc's USD 677 million acquisition in 2012 of ERA Mining Machinery Ltd, the holding company for Zhengzhou Siwei Mechanical & Electrical Equipment Manufacturing Co Ltd, one of China's biggest makers of hydraulic coal-mine roof supports. The purchase was billed as a coup for Caterpillar, the world's top maker of tractors and excavators, and Caterpillar's advisors even received an award for 'cross-border deal of the year'.[108] Shortly thereafter, Caterpillar announced that it had discovered 'deliberate, multi-year, coordinated accounting misconduct' at Siwei and Caterpillar took a goodwill impairment charge of USD 580 million, 86% of the value of the deal.[109]
- Numerous cases of (alleged) fraud In Chinese reverse mergers on American exchanges.[110]

While these types of disputes tend to make prominent headlines, fraud is not the most common cause for M&A-related disputes. According to a recent survey, misrepresentation – whether deliberate or not – was named as the most common area of disputes by only 17% of respondents, behind earn-out clauses and completion accounts disputes (33% each).[111] Misrepresentation in the survey included fraud cases, but likely also cases of unintentional misrepresentation (though the survey does not indicate how many), so that the share of disputes involving fraud is likely lower than 17%. An analysis of the cases in the sample of disputes (*see* §1.04), though not representative of all M&A disputes, suggests that in approximately 10% of cases at least one claim related to fraud.

Financial statement fraud often relates to misrepresentations by the seller or the target entity's management about the target business. The seller may withhold information during the transaction process, or the target's financial statements may be misrepresented. As a consequence, the buyer acquires unknown liabilities or later discovers that the target business has in fact less earnings potential than it assumed. However, misrepresentations may also be made by the buyer, not the seller.

Another type of fraud risk is corruption, a type of occupational fraud for which the ACFE distinguishes four major categories: bribery, conflicts of interest, illegal gratuities, and economic extortion. Of these, allegations of bribery have received

108. The M&A Atlas Awards Asia Pacific Middle Markets, 8 Nov. 2012, Category: Asia Pacific Deal Award Winnder Cross-Border Deal of the Year – Large.
109. Special Report: How Caterpillar got bulldozed in China, Reuters World News, 23 Jan. 2014, https://www.reuters.com/article/us-caterpillar-china-special-report/special-report-how-caterpillar-got-bulldozed-in-china-idUSBREA0M03720140123.
110. Fraud In Chinese Reverse Mergers on American Exchanges – And We're Surprised?, Forbes, 8 Apr. 2011.
111. Grant Thornton, A smarter way to get deals done International Survey: Identifying international market practice for equity value adjustments and Sale and Purchase Agreements, November 2017, p. 18.

significant press coverage in recent times as enforcement of anti-foreign corruption statutes has been stepped up in numerous countries.

§10.02 THE FRAUD TRIANGLE

[A] Introduction

The fraud triangle is a framework for analysing fraud that was first introduced by the American sociologist Donald Cressey.[112] Cressey's original hypothesis from which the fraud triangle originated is as follows:

> Trusted persons become trust violators when they conceive of themselves as having a financial problem which is non-shareable, are aware this problem can be secretly resolved by violation of the position of financial trust, and are able to apply to their own conduct in that situation verbalizations which enable them to adjust their conceptions of themselves as trusted persons with their conceptions of themselves as users of the entrusted funds or property.[113]

The factors identified by Cressey that cause someone to commit occupational fraud are usually summarised as in Figure 10.1: The circumstances present in M&A transactions can be a fertile breeding ground for all three factors.

Figure 10.1 The Fraud Triangle

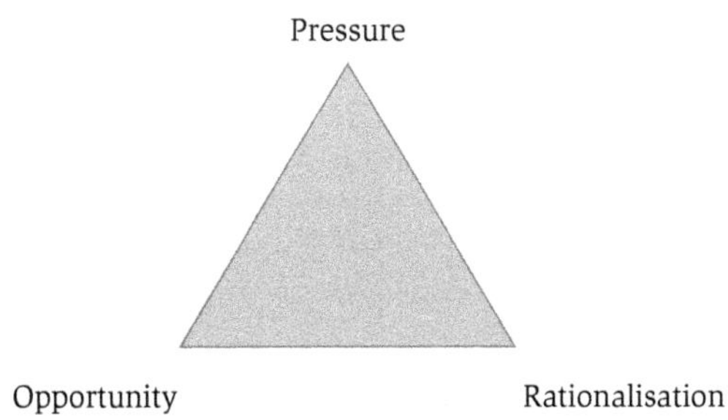

[B] Pressure

The parties in an M&A transaction are often subject to a variety of pressures: Sellers naturally want to make the target business look as good as possible. There can therefore be the temptation to conceal obligations that would expose a less favourable financial situation of the target entity or that the buyer would have otherwise deducted from the purchase price. As the transaction progresses, sellers may come under

112. Donald R. Cressey, *Other People's Money* (Montclair: Patterson Smith, 1973) p. 30.
113. *Ibid.*

pressure to withhold new information such as disappointing earnings numbers or the loss of a key customer. As pressure builds, a downward spiral begins.

A seller who stays silent about recent adverse developments (e.g., the loss of a key customer) may be guilty of fraudulent misrepresentation if the buyer relies on information presented to him or her. This happened in *Erlson Precision Holdings Ltd v. Hampson Industries plc* in which the buyer learned on the day following the sale that a key customer would be terminating all business with the target.[114] This information meant that various forecasts which the seller had provided to Erlson over a period of ten months prior to the transaction were incorrect. It transpired that the seller's CEO had been informed of the customers' decision much earlier. The judge held that the seller was guilty of fraudulent misrepresentation.

The principals working on a transaction may be the first to feel pressure. However, pressure can be passed on to the target's management or the seller's or target's accountants, and even outside advisors who prepare the financial information or assist in the sale process. Exit bonuses or success fees may be linked to achieving specific results. The pressure is both obvious and implicit.

Finally, it is not just the sellers who feel pressure, but also buyers. For example, buyout firms that face limited fund terms may come under pressure to deploy funds. Or consider *The Hut Group Ltd v. Nobahar-Cookson and another*, discussed in detail below in §10.03, in which the sellers received consideration shares valued on the basis of the buyer's accounts (which later turned out to be misstated). The buyer's senior management allegedly put its finance team under pressure to hit figures which were consistent with the 'growth story' which the buyer wished to present to the outside world, whether or not it reflected reality.

[C] Opportunity

The natural opportunity to commit fraud in an M&A process follows from the asymmetry between the buyer and seller in a transaction. The seller usually knows far more about the business it is selling than the buyer, and it is the seller who can decide to influence accounting choices or disclosures pre-closing, or withhold information.

Buyers attempt to level the playing field by conducting comprehensive due diligence, but access is limited, in particular in a competitive auction. And a seller who is attempting to deceive will often make sure that access is even more restricted than usual. In *Erlson Precision Holdings Ltd v. Hampson Industries plc* the seller not only withheld information of a customer loss from the buyer, but, in fact, had gone to some length to ensure that the buyer did not learn of these developments, including asking the relevant customer to keep the information confidential.[115]

Detecting fraud is not the focus, nor even within the scope, of standard buy-side financial due diligence. Only when concerns over the numbers arise, or 'red flags' are

114. *Erlson Precision Holdings Limited (formerly GG132 Ltd) v Hampson Industries plc* [2011] EWHC 1137 (Comm), 20 Apr. 2011.
115. David v Goliath, New Law Journal, 22.7.2011, Available at https://www.newlawjournal.co.uk/content/david-v-goliath.

starting to emerge during the negotiations does this typically trigger further analysis by the buyer. If the buyer then decides to bring forensic expertise and fraud examination tools to the buy side financial due diligence, the transaction is no longer following a normal process. A discussion of red flags that may suggest potential fraud is in §10.03.

[D] Rationalisation

The third element of the fraud triangle, rationalisation, is the ability of the person who commits the fraud to convince him- or herself that their actions are acceptable or justifiable.

In a transaction context, this may develop out of a (tacit) understanding that sellers are expected to 'dress up the bride', or that 'earnings management' is what all sellers do. It may also appear that the sums involved are immaterial (from the perspective of a seller who commits fraud), or that a customer who announces its intention to leave does not really mean it.[116]

It is generally true that sellers do their best to present the target company in the best possible light, and purchasers in most situations accept that the lily is often gilded. Consider *The Hut Group Ltd v. Nobahar-Cookson and another* again, in which the buyer submitted that 'there is nothing wrong in principle with presenting your numbers in the best possible way, though of course you must do so honestly rather than dishonestly'.[117] However, intentional misstatements are a different matter.

§10.03 RED FLAGS FOR FRAUD

Identifying fraud before signing is made all the more difficult when, as is the case with fraudsters, the other party is actively attempting to conceal it. A seller who intentionally conceals fraud will also attempt to restrict access during the due diligence phase as much as possible. Even without such efforts, access and time are limited.

The following is a list of common 'red flags' to look out for:

(1) The analyses of cash flow and profitability:
   - (i) sales that do not turn into cash - red flags include deteriorating collection ratios, receivables ageing, inventory turns, and sustained cash outflow from operations despite profit growth;
   - (ii) pressures on profitability as evidenced by declining profit margins;
   - (iii) straight line or 'hockey stick' earnings/profit growth; and
   - (iv) high financing costs compared to debt levels.

(2) The analysis of organisational structure:
   - (i) impending/recent flotation or buy-out;
   - (ii) high level of related party transactions;

116. *Evlson Precision Holdings Ltd v. Hampson Industries plc*, CMS eAlerts, Share sale unwound for fraudulent misrepresentation, 11.10.2011, available at http://www.cms-lawnow.com/ealerts/2011/10/share-sale-unwound-for-fraudulent-misrepresentation?cc_lang=en.

117. *The Hut Group Ltd v. Nobahar-Cookson and another* [2014] EWHC 3842 (QB), para. 253.

(iii) unnecessarily complicated corporate structure or financing arrangements;
(iv) dominant, overbearing, or bullying CEO/Chairman;
(v) weak finance function;
(vi) consistent adoption of 'racy' but acceptable accounting policies; and
(vii) involvement of non-financial management in accounting.

It is useful to distinguish between fraud itself and the triggers that lead to its discovery. Once the transaction closes, the new owner takes control and has ample opportunity to find out more about the target's financial statements and disclosures. A trigger for detecting fraud is often that the target entity is in need of additional liquidity soon after closing. This, mostly likely, comes as a surprise to the buyer. In such circumstances, it is often appropriate to conduct post-closing due diligence. If this reveals unknown off balance sheet liabilities or that the seller's accounting for the target company has gone beyond optimism, then there might be a case for fraud. This is the start of a difficult process: unpicking financial statements can be a complex task and sometimes requires a combination of expertise of transaction specialists, forensic accountants, fraud examiners, and even intelligence professionals. In the absence of a trigger event, there is often no effort to uncover fraud, and it is, therefore, safe to assume that many frauds remain undetected.

Example: *The Hut Group Ltd v. Nobahar-Cookson and another* (High Court of England and Wales)[118]

In May 2011 the Hut Group Ltd (THG), acquired an online sports nutrition business known as 'MyProtein', the trading name of a company, Cend, owned by the defendants. The purchase price amounted to GBP 58 million, of which GBP 30 million was paid in cash and GBP 28 million in shares in THG. The sellers were the founder and manager of Cend and the family trust.

The SPA included sellers' warranties in relation to Cend's management accounts and warranties by THG, the buyer, that its draft statutory accounts gave a true and fair view of its state of affairs, assets and liabilities and profit and loss as at 31 December 2010 (the THG Accounts Warranty) and that THG's management accounts fairly presented its assets and liabilities and profits and losses for the period from 31 December 2010 to 31 March 2011 (the THG Management Accounts Warranty). The SPA limited the parties' liabilities for claims for breaches of warranty 'save insofar as it results from the fraud of [THG]' or '... the fraud of any of [the sellers]'. The relevant limitation was GBP 7.24 million for claims by Sellers against THG.

The sellers' warranties will be discussed in Chapter 12.

Shortly after closing, THG commenced preparations for an initial public offering (IPO). As part of the IPO preparations, THG's group audit firm carried out a half-year audit of THG's accounts. In September 2011, it came to the auditors' attention that there had been a falsification of documentation provided to it in its capacity as the

118. *The Hut Group Ltd v. Nobahar-Cookson and another* [2014] EWHC 3842 (QB).

Group auditors. The Financial Controller had been manipulating monthly profitability, by overstating off-line stock and debtors, and understating liabilities. In addition, an initial review revealed a number of occasions where it was apparent that the external auditor had been misled by the finance team.

The external auditor then switched its focus to the audit of the preceding year end, 31 December 2010, and identified a number of further issues. Before corrections, EBITDA had been GBP 4.1 million. Following corrections, the figure was restated as an EBITDA loss of GBP 1.5 million. There was also an adjustment to the 2011 management accounts, though no definitive revised accounts for the quarter are in evidence. The IPO process was halted.

In summary: a series of documents had been falsified during the audits of the year ended 31 December 2010 and the six months ended 30 June 2011, and the external auditors had also been misled as to the recoverability of certain assets and the extent of unrecorded liabilities. The three key areas of manipulation were:

- Offline stock: On 31 December 2010, an entry had been booked to recognise GBP 1.6 million of 'off-line' stock which was either double counted within the system stock balance, or which had been sold prior to 31 December.
- Unrecorded liabilities: There were a number of unrecorded liabilities on 31 December 2010 and members of the finance function (including the wider purchase ledger team) had falsified a number of supplier statements and withheld certain invoices and supplier statements from the external auditors. The Financial Controller had also released a significant number of smaller accruals which would be below the audit materiality threshold.
- Recoverability of debtors: On 31 December 2010, a number of debtors were either recognised early or were not recoverable, despite formal representations from senior members of the finance team to the contrary.

It was not in dispute that THG was in breach of buyer's warranties.

The issue between the parties was that while THG accepted that its breach of warranty results from the fraud of the financial controller, it submitted his fraud was not to be attributed to THG with the result that a contractual cap on damages of GBP 7.24 million would apply, whereas, in the sellers' view, the fraud was to be attributed to THG.[119] The judge observed that there was an atmosphere within the finance department which allowed fraud to flourish.

In an email chain between the financial controller and THG's Finance Director (FD), the FD asked the controller and others about the timing of booking a sale in June in respect of goods still in the warehouse at the beginning of July.

THG accepted during the trial that the email exchange that followed made 'uncomfortable' and 'unfortunate' reading.

Many professionals have had the same sinking feeling of discomfort as THG in this age of emails. The lesson here goes beyond fraud. Professionals should never do anything, write anything, or say anything that they would not be happy to see printed in the *Financial Times* or raised in a court of law. Business confidentiality cannot

119. *Ibid.*, para 285.

always be relied upon, especially not to cover wrongdoing and unprofessionalism. On top of that, the public, clients, and judges do not consider 'banter' to be an appropriate defence.

The judge found that his fraud was to be attributed to THG. As a consequence, the warranty cap did not apply to the claim.

CHAPTER 11

Damages Valuation in M&A Disputes

§11.01 INTRODUCTION

So far in this book the focus of the discussion has been on the mechanics of transactions and their completion, including which items lead to purchase price adjustments, how these items are accounted for, and the process of how adjustments are determined. This section deals with the measurement of damages if a breach of contract (usually the SPA) has occurred.

The basic compensatory principle is that the monetary award should restore the claimant to an economic position equivalent to the position but for the breach. This has been expressed as follows:

> [A]s regards pecuniary loss, the claimant should be awarded the total of revenue (less costs) that would have been earned, less the total of revenue (less costs) actually earned.[120]

'Revenue' and 'costs' are accounting terms, and a claim for lost profits references an accounting metric (profit). The measurement of damages in M&A disputes often starts from accounting figures, for the reason discussed above in §4.02 [C]. Indeed, the accounts have been called the 'building blocks of quantum'.[121] However, accounting values (book values) need not have anything to do with commercial value, and often do not: Historical cost accounting which is used as a basis for the book value of many (though by no means all) assets is backward-looking and measures value differently from a commercial valuation, which tends to be forward-looking. Accounting is by fiat. As a consequence, how something is accounted for may have no relevance to the

120. Adam Kramer, *The Law of Contract Damages* (2nd ed., Hart Publishing, 2017), p. 496.
121. Gervase MacGregor, Andrew Maclay, and David Mitchell, *Overview of Damages and Accounting Basics* in John A. Trenor (ed.), *The Guide to Damages in International Arbitration*, 160 (2nd ed., Global Arbitration Review 2017).

commercial basis of value. This commercial basis has not yet been discussed, and that is the subject of this chapter.

Valuation can relate to non-contentious or contentious situations. Valuations in contentious situations may become necessary in the following cases:

- a warranty breach when an asset does not have the attributes that were promised (e.g., a 'true and fair view' or minimum EBITDA warranty);
- when a party has been deprived of an asset or the basis of its operations, or an asset has been expropriated;
- when an asset has been harmed;[122]
- when a joint venture agreement is terminated; or
- when the buy-out of an asset or of a minority shareholder is enforced, for example under a partnership separation.

As relates to M&A transactions, contentious valuation plays a role in the small minority of transactions that end up in disputes. While contentious valuation uses the same methods as non-contentious valuation, it is used in different contexts and often measures different things. This chapter provides a high-level overview of the valuation approaches commonly used in damages valuation and discusses specific questions arising in M&A-related disputes. It does not intend to summarise the vast body of literature on valuation.[123]

Finally, this book also deals with the topic of value of the target and price paid. In case of a warranty breach, for example, the price paid in a transaction may be (rebuttably) presumed to be the value as warranted. A measure of loss that courts and tribunals often consider is therefore the difference between price paid and the actual value of the shares acquired. However, price is not necessarily the same as value. Why bidders may pay more, or less, than an asset is worth can be a complicated question that is outside the scope of this book. Even so, in order to discuss valuation, it is useful to start with the question of what constitutes value.

§11.02 WHAT DO VALUATION MODELS MEASURE?

All valuation models start from the premise that individuals are concerned with consumption, and that cash buys consumption. An investor gives up consumption today in the expectation of more consumption in the future.[124] The value of an investment is based on the cash flows it is expected to deliver. As valuation is concerned with future cash flows, it is therefore forward-looking. Despite recent

122. Phil Haberman and Liz Perks, *Overview of Methodologies for Assessing Fair Market Value* in John A. Trenor (ed.), *The Guide to Damages in International Arbitration*, 176 (2nd ed., Global Arbitration Review 2017).

123. For further reading on these topics, *see* Elizabeth A. Evans, Joseph J. Galanti, and Daniel G. Lentz *Developing Damages Theories and Models* in Weil, Lentz, Hoffman, *Litigation Services Handbook* (5th ed., Wiley, 2012).

124. Stephen H. Penman, *Valuation Models: An Issue of Accounting Theory* (Columbia Business School, Columbia University, 2, in *Routledge Companion to Financial Accounting Theory* (Routledge 2015).

developments in behavioural economics, it is fair to say that this rationalist view is a non-controversial basis of damages valuation.

§11.03 STANDARDS OF VALUE

[A] Introduction

A contentious valuation requires a standard of value (sometimes called basis or bases of value), i.e., a statement of the fundamental assumptions of how value is measured, for example, the nature of the hypothetical transaction that is assumed in the valuation, the relationship and motivation of the parties to this transaction, and the extent to which the asset being valued is exposed to the market.[125] This chapter covers standards of value commonly used in disputes.

[B] Fair Market Value

Fair market value is generally considered the most commonly used and accepted business valuation standard and is often referred to by tribunals as the relevant measure of damages.[126]

Fair market value can be defined as:

> [T]he price, expressed in terms of cash equivalents, at which property would change hands between a hypothetical willing and able buyer and a hypothetical willing and able seller, acting at arm's length in an open and unrestricted market, when neither is under compulsion to buy or sell and when both have reasonable knowledge of the relevant facts.[127]

A definition for US tax purposes is:

> [T]he price at which the property would change hands between a willing buyer and a willing seller, neither being under any compulsion to buy or to sell and both having reasonable knowledge of relevant facts.[128]

Both definitions of fair market value refer to a willing buyer and seller in a hypothetical transaction as opposed to specific, identified parties.[129] A valuer determines fair market value by assessing the positions of the population of hypothetical parties and arrives at an average that represents the likely price at which a transaction would be expected to take place.[130] This price can be different from the price of an actual transaction between specific parties: A specific seller could be forced to divest (a 'distressed' sale), or a specific acquirer may have an ability to achieve cost savings

125. International Valuation Standards 2017 IVS 104 Bases of Value.
126. Weil, Lentz and Hoffman *supra* n. 123, at 10.6.
127. *International Glossary of Business Valuation Terms*, American Society of Appraisers, ASA Business Valuation Standards, 2009.
128. Regulation §20.2031-1.
129. Haberman and Perks, *supra* n. 122, at 177.
130. *Ibid.*

from synergies after an acquisition that may not be available to a hypothetical, generic acquirer. Synergies that are unique to a particular buyer are therefore generally included under the fair value standard (see below), and not the fair market value standard. On the other hand, synergies that are available to the average market player are included both under the market value standard and under the fair value standard.

Both definitions of 'fair market value' are also very similar to the International Valuation Standards (IVS) definition of 'market value' (discussed below in section [D]), and fair market value has been considered to correspond to the IVS-definition of 'market value'.[131]

[C] Fair Value

The meaning of the term 'fair value' differs when used in a general corporate finance context (where it is also referred to as 'equitable value') from its use in an accounting context. As both can be relevant in disputes, they are discussed separately.

[1] General Meaning

In a general corporate finance context, an authoritative source is the International Valuation Standards Council (IVSC). The IVSC has recently retitled the previously defined 'fair value' as 'equitable value', in order to avoid confusion with other definitions of fair value. It defines the term as:

> [T]he estimated price for the transfer of an asset or liability between identified knowledgeable and willing parties that reflects the respective interests of those parties.[132]

In contrast to fair market value and market value, the definition references specific identified parties and their particular interests and circumstances.

[2] Accounting Meaning

The accounting meaning of 'fair value' can come into play in M&A disputes, for example, in completion accounts disputes. An example is *Mihail Tartsinis v. Navona Management Company* (the dispute discussed in §3.04 above).[133]

The authoritative source of definition in an accounting context is the relevant standard setter. In IAS, the term 'fair value' is defined by the IASB as:

131. For example, *see ibid.*, 177.
132. International Valuation Standards (IVS) 2017, 104 para 50.
133. *Mihail Tartsinis v. Navona Management Company* [2015] EWHC 57 (Comm). The court stated in para. 45: For present purposes, the concept of 'fair value' can be treated as synonymous with 'market value'.

> The price that would be received to sell an asset or paid to transfer a liability in an orderly transaction between market participants at the measurement date.[134]

The measurement under this definition can raise complex questions related to the valuation premise (stand-alone asset or liability, or in combination with other assets or liabilities), the condition and location of the asset, the principal market, and estimating fair value when there has been a significant decrease in the volume or level of market activity, to name a few.[135] IFRS 13 introduces a fair value hierarchy that categorises the inputs used in the valuation:

- Level 1: Unadjusted quoted prices for identical assets and liabilities in active markets.
- Level 2: Other observable inputs for the asset or liability, such as quoted prices in active markets for similar assets or liabilities, or quoted prices for identical assets or liabilities in markets which are not active.
- Level 3: Unobservable inputs developed by an entity using the best information available where there is little or no market activity for the asset or liability at the measurement date.

The standard setter prefers observable market prices wherever available over mere unobservable inputs (the preparer's estimates). Where available, the first level is therefore the preferable method. However, where observable inputs are not available, unobservable inputs can be used to measure fair value. Examples of assets that may be valued using Level 3 inputs where no active markets exist include long-dated currency swaps, interest rate swaps, and cash-generating units.[136]

The use of Level 3 inputs is sometimes labelled 'mark-to-model' accounting. It has been criticised in academic research[137] on the basis that, among other things, reliance on managerial assumptions in the valuation process gives significant discretion and opens the door to intentional bias, rendering mark-to-model estimates potentially misleading.[138] A similar concern was expressed by the investor Warren Buffett as follows:

> Errors will usually be honest, reflecting only the human tendency to take an optimistic view of one's commitments ... [O]ften there is no real market ... and 'mark-to-model' is utilized ... In extreme cases, mark-to-model degenerates into what I would call mark-to-myth.[139]

Given the discretion that goes into Level 3 inputs, this is an area of potential disputes when accounting numbers are used as the basis of a purchase price adjustment.

134. IFRS 13.
135. Applying IFRS 13 Fair Value Measurement, EY, November 2012, 21, 23, 24, 26, 46, 62.
136. *Ibid.*, 146.
137. Kalin Kolev, 'Do Investors Perceive Marking-to-Model as Marking-to-Myth? Early Evidence from FAS 157 Disclosure', Working Paper (NYU Stern School of Business 2009), with further references.
138. *Ibid.*, with further references.
139. Berkshire Hathaway Annual Letter to Shareholders 2002.

[D] Market Value

Market value is defined in the IVS as:

> The estimated amount for which an asset or liability should exchange on the valuation date between a willing buyer and a willing seller in an arm's length transaction, after proper marketing and where the parties had each acted knowledgeably, prudently and without compulsion.[140]

This definition is similar, although not identical, to that of 'fair market value' as defined by the US Internal Revenue Service for tax purposes. 'Fair market value' is often considered to correspond to (the IVS-defined) 'market value'.[141] Others, however, draw a distinction between the two.[142]

[E] Conclusion

Choosing the appropriate standard is usually a legal question. The standard of value used can make a significant difference to the quantum. Performing a valuation once the appropriate standard has been decided is often the responsibility of a damages expert.

A commonly used and accepted business valuation standard is the fair market value. This standard is also frequently referred to by tribunals and courts as a relevant measure in their consideration of damages. There is, however, no single authoritative definition of fair market value, and there remains some uncertainty over the exact meaning of the term.[143]

§11.04 VALUATION APPROACHES

[A] Introduction

There are generally three approaches used to value a company, an ownership interest, or any other asset. In normal circumstances, these alternative approaches are also available for the measurement of damages. However, as will be shown there can be important differences between contentious and non-contentious valuation. Each valuation approach is discussed below.

140. IVS 104, para. 30.
141. In its US sense, *see* Haberman and Perks, *supra* n. 122, at 177.
142. Herfried Wöss et al., *'Damages in International Arbitration Under Complex Long-Term Contracts'*, Oxford International Arbitration Series (Oxford University Press 2014) 260.
143. Haberman and Perks, *supra* n. 122, at 177.

[B] The Income Approach

[1] Overview

The most commonly used form of the income approach is the DCF method.[144] This is, in a sense, the most explicit application of the premise set out above (§11.02), where the value of an asset is equal to the present value of the future cash flows it is expected to return. Under this method, free cash flows are projected and discounted to a present value at an appropriate discount rate. The discount rate reflects both the time value of money and the risk associated with the expected cash flows.

According to a recent PwC survey of published arbitration awards, DCF and other income approaches were the most common valuation methodologies used by tribunals.[145] However, this has not always been the case, and the acceptance of these approaches has increased significantly in recent years. Most cases in which the income method was not accepted by tribunals related to new ventures that were considered speculative or too uncertain.[146] While the majority of cases in the sample analysed by PwC related to investment treaty arbitration, the findings appear relevant to awards in international commercial arbitrations as well.

As discussed in §2.01, enterprise value (or firm value) is the value of the firm's net operating (including investing) activities. It is the present value of the future free cash flows, the cash surpluses a firm generates from its operations, less cash investments. If positive, free cash flow is divided between the different providers of capital – the debtholders and shareholders. If negative, the deficit of the operating activities must be funded, for example by issuing new debt or equity securities in the capital markets. Cash flows below free cash flows are financing cash flows. They concern returning cash to equity or debt holders (if the operations have generated a surplus), or raising cash from them (if a deficit).

The equity bridge also showed that enterprise value is always equal to the value of the debt plus the value of the equity. It is unaffected by the financing structure of the firm (assuming perfect capital markets, without taxes).

The value of the equity can be calculated directly by projecting, discounting and adding up cash flows to equity holders (dividends and any other equity capital changes). However, this approach – the dividend discount method or cash flow to equity method – is not commonly used in practice for non-financial businesses. In a theoretical corporate finance sense, secondary effects aside, dividends reduce the value of the enterprise dollar-for-dollar (otherwise there would be arbitrage opportunities),

144. *See* David Saunders, Amit Arora, and Joe Skilton, *The Applicable Valuation Approach*, in John A. Trenor (ed.) *The Guide to Damages in International Arbitration*, 187 (2nd ed., Global Arbitration Review 2017), for references of empirical research.
145. PwC 2015 – International Arbitration Damages Research, Closing the Gap Between Claimants and Respondents, p. 8, and 2017 update, p. 6.
146. PwC 2015 – International Arbitration Damages Research, Closing the Gap Between Claimants and Respondents, p 3.

that is, dividend payout is a zero-net-present-value activity.[147] Discounting projected dividends can be viewed to represent a conundrum: Value is based on expected dividends, but forecasting dividends is irrelevant to valuation.[148] Dividends themselves are not the fundamental to valuation, and forecasting them means analysing the distribution of value generated by the operations. The conundrum does not exist when one forecasts free cash flows to determine enterprise value as this requires looking inside the firm and analysing the generation of value, not merely its distribution.

An alternative to discounting cash flows is to discount accrual earnings. This can take the form of discounting residual operating income and adding it to the book value of net operating (before deducting net debt to arrive at equity value). Residual operating income is the operating income in excess of a required income on net operating asset, also referred to as 'economic profit' or 'economic value added'.[149] The method is one form of the residual income method (RIM).[150] It is an accounting-based valuation method that uses the profit and loss account and information in the balance sheet. Earnings reconcile to free cash flow according to the accounting equation, so that (in theory) for an infinite forecast horizon, the DCF model and residual earnings model get to the same value of the equity if consistent assumptions are used. As residual income models do not play a significant role in damages valuation, the book focuses on the DCF method. However, the author is hopeful that residual income models will play a greater role in the future.

[2] The Separation of Operating and Financing Activities in a DCF Valuation

An important distinction when using the DCF method is that between operating cash flows to the firm and financing cash flows. Operating cash flows (including capital expenditure) are part of free cash flow and hence become part of enterprise value. Financing cash flows are below free cash flow. An example where this distinction was crucial was with respect to reverse factoring cash flows reported by Carillion within operating cash flows as discussed above in Chapter §4.04 [A] [5].
The valuation model should treat cash flows consistently with the SPA where SPA definitions relate to net debt or net working capital. Projected cash flows that relate to items treated as net debt in the SPA, such as debt service payments, should also be included in financing cash flows in the valuation model. If they are not, then there is a

147. Penman (Accounting for Value), *supra* n. 37, at 18. This property is called the dividend irrelevance proposition *see* Merton H. Miller and Franco Modigliani, *Dividend Policy, Growth, and the Valuation of Shares*, The Journal of Business 34(4) (October 1961), 411–433.
148. This requires certain assumptions, in particular perfect capital markets. Merton H. Miller and Franco Modigliani, *Dividend Policy, Growth, and the Valuation of Shares*, Journal of Business 34 (1961), 411–433
149. Stephen H. Penman, *Financial Statement Analysis and Security Valuation* (4th ed., McGraw-Hill Education 2009), p. 433.
150. The residual income method can alternatively be levered and discount net earnings to determine equity value without deducting (net) debt.

risk that the same item may be deducted twice. Similarly, if the definitions do not interact seamlessly, the same item could not be captured at all.

For example, cash flows related to working capital should generally be included within free cash flow. The criteria that suggest that an asset or liability is working capital are discussed in §5.03 above. One of these criteria was that working capital arises from *operating activities*, i.e., activities connected with the production of goods or services which are the object of the enterprise. It is consistent with this definition that changes in working capital generally correspond to operating cash flows: the collection of a trade receivable, the payment of a trade creditor, or the sale of an item from inventory all lead to operating cash flows that should be part of free cash flow to the firm. Only if a cash flow that affects working capital is not due to an operating but to a financing activity, such as factoring of trade receivables (discussed above in §4.04 [A]), then the related cash flow should also be classified as a financing cash flow (provided the financing activity is also treated as debt in the SPA as argued above). Otherwise, there would be double counting.

Projecting cash flows usually amounts to preparing a set of pro forma financial statements for the future. These pro forma statements are often modelled on historical accounting numbers taken from the audited financial statements or management accounts. There are a number of areas where accounting numbers - and the subtotals they show for net operating cash flow, investing cash flow, and financing cash flow - are not necessarily consistent with operating, investing, and financing cash flow in a corporate finance sense. Further, the valuation should also be consistent with the way in which these terms are used in SPA definitions. Examples of potential inconsistencies include:

- Interest and dividends received or paid may be classified as either operating, investing, or financing cash flows, provided that they are classified consistently from period to period (IAS 7.31). In a corporate finance sense, and, crucially, in SPA definitions, these cash flows would normally be considered to be financing cash flows (for a firm that is not a financial institution for which dividend or interest income represent part of the operating business) as they concern the distribution of surpluses generated by operations or the funding of operating cash shortfalls rather than the creation of value.
- Cash flows arising from taxes on income are normally classified as operating, unless they can be specifically identified with financing or investing activities (IAS 7.35). This may collide with an SPA definition that includes certain tax liabilities in net debt.

US GAAP knows numerous comparable inconsistencies.[151]

It is important to restate, where appropriate, and to reformulate historical financial statements when performing a DCF valuation.

151. *Ibid.*, 124 for further discussion.

[C] The Market Approach

The market approach uses market data from comparable companies or transactions to value a company or an ownership interest in a company. It can be based on two types of transactions in the shares of comparable companies:

- Transactions in shares of comparable companies that trade on a stock exchange ('trading comps').
- M&A transactions involving substantial interests in comparable companies ('transaction comps').

In both alternatives, the value of the business that is to be valued is derived from the market valuation of comparable companies, or the 'peer group'. This is a relatively simple way of measuring and comparing company valuations. Differences in scale between the firm to be valued and the peer group are adjusted by expressing value in relative terms to certain metrics of the peer group. The use of ratios to market price, or valuation multiples, therefore allows for comparison between different sized firms (as long as the size difference itself does not render the firms insufficiently comparable)

The metrics used in the market approach are often taken from the financial statements: sales, EBITDA, EBIT, operating cash flow, net income or the book value of equity. From these, the valuer calculates, respectively, EV-to-sales, EBITDA-, EBIT- and cash flow to operations (CFO)-multiples; net income (P/E) and price-to-book (P/B) ratios. Sales-, EBITDA-, EBIT- and operating cash flow-multiples are enterprise value multiples. Net income and price-to-book multiples are equity value multiples.

Earnings-based multiples can be based on historical earnings (e.g., of the last financial year), current earnings (the 'current' financial year at the given valuation date), or projected earnings (usually the financial year following the acquisition or valuation date). When earnings-based multiples are used, the analysis of the quality of earnings and the identification and elimination of one-off or non-recurring elements to determine normalised earnings often takes centre stage during the financial due diligence. To get a sense of the capacity of large corporates to manage earnings, consider the following example.

Example of Earnings Management: Acquisition of Kidder, Peabody by GE

GE acquired Kidder, Peabody, one of Wall Street's oldest investment banks, in 1986. In 1994, it was discovered that a trader had created false entries over a number of years that artificially boosted Kidder's income. The SEC later concluded that the trader had committed securities fraud and banned him from the industry. Just after the discovery of the fraud (two days before a quarterly earnings release) GE determined that it was necessary to write off USD 350 million. This is how the CEO, Jack Welch, described the reaction of the senior business leaders upon hearing the news in his autobiography (it is not suggested that this should have given rise to a dispute):

> The response of our business leaders to the crisis was typical of the GE culture. Even though the books had closed on the quarter, many immediately offered to

> pitch in to cover the Kidder gap. Some said they could find an extra $10 million, $20 million, and even $30 million from their businesses to offset the surprise. Though it was too late, their willingness to help was a dramatic contrast to the excuses I had been hearing from the Kidder people.[152]

Multiples can also relate market prices to non-financial metrics, especially for industry-specific valuations where certain metrics are important drivers of performance and cash flows. For example, energy companies can be valued on the basis of hydrocarbon reserves, and hotel operators on their number of rooms.[153]

A limitation of the market approach is that it only provides information relative to other, comparable firms. It adopts the view that similar firms should have similar valuations and, therefore, similar multiples, and that markets are efficient at setting the price of the peer group. The market approach itself is not based on fundamental analysis of intrinsic value. It derives a valuation implied by the given market valuation of other firms, and it cannot be used to challenge market prices.[154]

Another limitation of this approach is that no two companies are exactly the same. Even comparable companies, usually in the same industry, trade at different multiples. This can be due to geographical differences, differences in expected growth rates, different accounting rules, different risk profiles (and therefore cost of capital), and so on. In efficient markets, market prices reflect these differences. However, when valuing a firm using other firms' multiples, it is often not clear how to adjust for these differences, other than by narrowing the peer group.[155]

Nevertheless, the market approach is widely used in M&A-related valuation.

In damages valuation, the limitations of the market approach often make it unsuitable as the sole valuation method. It has even been called 'generally inappropriate for post-M&A damages disputes'.[156] However, it is frequently used at least as a cross-check on other valuation approaches.[157] Further, there are instances in which it is, in fact, the sole approach to the valuation of damages. One example of this is in the following case.

Example of Market Method Used in M&A-Related Damages Valuation (High Court of England and Waltes)[158]

This is the same case as above in Chapter 7 in which a misrepresentation resulted in a breach of buyers' warranty. The case also considers a claim by the buyer, THG, for breach of the sellers' 'true and fair view' warranty of the target's accounts. This claim is interesting not only because it was common ground between the parties that the

152. Jack, Jack Welch, *Headline Book Publishing*, London, 2001, p. 225.
153. Saunders, Arora and Skilton, *supra* n. 144, at 191 for further discussion.
154. Penman, *supra* n. 37, at 77.
155. *Ibid.*, n. 28, p. 264.
156. Gerhard H. Wächter and Christoph Wollny, *A Proposal for the Calculation of Damages in Post-M&A Disputes*, 2, SchiedsVZ, Heft 2, pp. 80, 89 (2018).
157. Saunders, Arora and Skilton, *supra* n. 144, at 191.
158. *The Hut Group Ltd. v. Cookson & Barclays Private Bank Ltd* [2014] EWHC 3842 (QB). (There was an unsuccessful appeal from this decision in relation to issues unrelated to the quantum calculation: [2016] EWCA Civ 238).

market method was the sole method on which the damages valuation should be based, but also because of the discussion as to whether the value as is should reflect a reduction in the multiple used due to concerns over the reliability of the accounts or for other reasons.

In short, the following was agreed between the parties in relation to the calculation of quantum:

- The target's value as warranted ('warranty true' enterprise value) was GBP 58 million, the purchase price, which consisted of GBP 30 million in cash and GBP 28 million in shares of the buyer.
- The appropriate valuation methodology on the 'warranty false' (i.e., actual position) basis was based on a multiple of EBITDA.
- A 'starting' EBITDA (i.e., prior to any adjustments for the true position given the breach of warranty) amounted to GBP 5.442 million.
- As a starting point basis of quantifying loss, it was appropriate to apply the transaction multiple, 10.7x EBITDA. However, this was subject to a 'reduced multiple' contention advanced by THG (*see* below).

Further, the treatment of certain one-off adjustments was undisputed.

The judge observed that, using the multiple method, arriving at the 'warranty false' valuation of the target business was in essence an 'arithmetical exercise'.[159]

The buyer's quantum expert argued for a reduction of approximately 18% in the transaction multiple on the basis that the 'existence of errors [...] [which] would call into question the accounts as a whole and the concern that further issues would arise would lower the value of the business to the acquirer'.[160] This reduction in the multiple would make a significant difference - to the loss of GBP 5.6 million based on the then 'base' multiple, the expert added a further loss of GBP 5.3 million based on the 'reduced' multiple.

The sellers argued that this was not a legally coherent position. They contended that the true value of the target business, with fairly stated management accounts, would not have been discounted by a purchaser to reflect a (false) hypothesis that those fairly stated accounts might be unreliable. If anything, because the accounts would (*ex hypothesi*) have been entirely accurate, they would have withstood all due diligence probing and would have enhanced a purchaser's confidence.[161]

In a subsequent submission, the buyer's expert changed the discount to produce a multiple of approximately 9.9. Of the revised damages claim of GBP 8.6 million, about GBP 4 million was attributable to the reduced multiple. The rationale for the reduction in the multiple had also changed. It was this time 'justified by an assumption of a stable gross margin with a sustained high growth in revenues, the combination of which is necessary to give to a high growth in projected EBITDA', and by reference to comparisons with long-term growth forecasts that had been provided by the seller in 2011. The buyer's submission was that the 'elastic had snapped' such that a reasonable

159. *Ibid.*, para 161.
160. *Ibid.*, para 164.
161. *Ibid.*, para 166.

hypothetical purchaser and a reasonable hypothetical seller would have had to revisit the multiple as well as the EBITDA. Only by the reduced multiple could the further deterioration in the target business's growth rate and shortfall against its forecast growth be fairly reflected.[162]

The judge did not consider that the justification of a discount to the multiple based on the target's growth prospects had real force in the light of the factual evidence as to those prospects. He found that a reasonable hypothetical purchaser and a reasonable hypothetical seller would not have had to revisit the multiple as well as the EBITDA reduction, and that the application of a discount to the multiple would produce an unrealistic valuation of THG's loss. The judge held that the application of the agreed multiplier of 10.7 reached a number which is solidly based on an agreed methodology.

[D] The Cost or Asset-Based Approach

The cost or asset-based approach assesses a firm's value by identifying and adding up the market values of its assets. As assets are reported in the balance sheet at book values, an asset-based approach effectively converts these book values into market values. The value of the equity is then determined by deducting the firm's debt.

The asset-based approach must deal with the fact that many assets are not recognised on the balance sheet. For example, brand or knowledge assets and other intangibles may account for much of a firm's overall value, but may not be on the balance sheet. They may also not trade in liquid markets. Those assets and liabilities that are on the balance sheet may be accounted for using different valuation bases – historical cost accounting, or fair value, for example. Even if all operating assets and liabilities were accounted for at fair value, the net total of all these fair values may not correspond to the value of the firm, as the fair value of the assets when they are put to use jointly may be different from the sum of individual fair values.

One purpose of the asset-based approach is to provide a floor to a valuation of a firm. This is because of the implicit break-up option inherent in any going concern: the owner always has the option of discontinuing operations and liquidating the company and may exercise it if the liquidation value exceeds the present value of the going concern's expected returns.[163] Other than in this context, asset-based valuations are also used for specific types of companies. These include, for example, companies that hold income-generating assets (instead of trading entities). The approach is also used in specific situations such as orderly liquidations.

162. *Ibid.*, para 171. Note that the value as is is discussed in hypotheticals.
163. Haberman and Perks, *supra* n. 122, at 182.

CHAPTER 12

Damages for Breaches of Representations and Warranties and Quantum of Indemnities

§12.01 OVERVIEW

[A] Breach of Warranty

The SPA in every transaction contains representations and warranties from each party to the other. The principal purposes of representations and warranties include:

- the allocation of risk between the buyer and the seller as representations and warranties identify which party is responsible for which item, including the party that will assume the risk of unknown conditions and liabilities;
- to force disclosure;[164]
- to serve as a closing condition (bring down of representations and warranties).[165]

A warranty is a promise made in a contract by one party to another that a state of affairs exists.[166] A breach arises when the state does not exist.[167] Alleged breaches of warranties in SPAs are a common cause of post-deal disputes. Alleged breaches of warranties that relate to the financial statements also explain why many purchase price

164. Representations and warranties are typically qualified by reference to any matters disclosed to the other party, including in a formal 'Disclosure Letter' typically sent by the buyer to the seller. Any matters fairly disclosed in the Disclosure Letter or other circumscribed disclosure cannot found a claim for misrepresentation or breach of warranty.
165. Latham & Watkins, *Key Provisions of Acquisition Agreements*, February 2016, p. 10, available at https://www.lw.com/admin/Upload/Documents/OilAndGasMandA/General%20Concepts/Consolidated_General_Concepts_Part_II_Key_Provisions.pdf.
166. Kramer, *supra* n. 120, at 225
167. *Ibid.*

adjustment disputes that would otherwise have been resolved in an expert determination end up in litigation or arbitration.

SPA warranties typically relate to the title to shares, insolvency, commercial contracts, intellectual property, litigation, employees, pensions, environmental damages, taxes, compliance with law, and the financial statements, among others. The focus in this chapter is on SPA warranties that relate to the financial statements - usually (though not necessarily) those of the target company.

Financial statement warranties can relate to the target company's historical accounts giving a true and fair view of the state of affairs as at the end of the period, and the profit or loss for the period (or similar wording). This is a 'true and fair view' warranty. Financial statement warranties can also relate to particular elements contained in or derived from (historical) profit and loss accounts, such as a minimum EBIT or EBITDA for a certain period, or specific balance sheet line items, such as trade receivables, working capital, minimum equity, total assets, or total debt figures. In legal terms, these kinds of warranties are considered to be similar to a warranty of quality, i.e., a warranty as to the characteristics of the business and its past.[168]

Warranties can also be promises that reasonable care was taken when financial information (e.g., a business plan) was prepared. 'Warranties of reasonable care' are legally different from 'warranties of quality', and damages are measured on a different basis. These are discussed separately in §12.02.

The following case concerns an alleged breach of a 'true and fair view' warranty.

Example: *Macquarie Internationale Investments Limited v. Glencore UK Ltd*[169]

Approximately three months after Macquarie acquired Corona Energy Holdings Limited ('Corona'), one of Corona's main suppliers presented an invoice for GBP 2.4 million relating to meter charges that had been missed previously by the supplier due to an error that occurred during an IT system change. The charges were unknown to both the seller and the target, and the target's liability could not reasonably have been discovered before signing. The seller was not at fault by reason of their failure to disclose the existence of the liability.

The SPA included the following warranty:

> The Accounts:
>
> (a) have been prepared in accordance with Relevant Accounting Standards and in a manner consistent with that adopted in the preparation of the annual accounts of the Group and/or the Company or Subsidiary to which they relate (as the case may be) for the Financial Years ended 31 December 2003 and 31 December 2004;
> (b) give a true and fair view of the assets and liabilities of the Group and/or the Company or the Subsidiary to which they relate as at the Accounts Date and the profits and losses of the Group and/or the Company or the Subsidiary to

168. *Ibid.*
169. Court of Appeal of England and Wales: *Macquarie Internationale Investments Limited v. Glencore UK Ltd* [2010] EWCA Civ 697.

> which they relate (as the case may be) for the Financial Year ended on the Accounts Date (including all related party transactions) ... .[170]

The buyer argued that the seller had breached the 'true and fair view' warranty on the basis that accounts which did not include the liability (unknown or not) could not show a 'true and fair view' of the target group. The Court of Appeal held that, unless there are exceptional circumstances, accounts would show a 'true and fair view' if they have been prepared in accordance with all relevant accounting standards. The relevant accounting standards did not require provision to be made for the unknown liability, and the accounts in question had therefore been 'true and fair'. The court stated that the accounts warranty, as its title indicates, 'is concerned with accounts, not with retrospectively perceived commercial value'.[171] The buyer's claim for breach of warranty failed.

[B] Misrepresentations

A representation is a statement of fact made by one person to another which induces the other to enter into a contract. If a representation is false, and it was relied on by the buyer when entering into the contract, then this may entitle the buyer to unwind the contract and/or claim damages.[172]

The general principle for calculating damages for misrepresentation is to put the parties in the position they would have been in prior to the contract being made. This is a different basis from damages for breach of warranties, in which damages should be assessed so as to put the claimant in the position they would have been in had the contract been properly performed (i.e., had the warranty been true).[173]

[C] Indemnities

An indemnity is a promise to reimburse the claimant in respect of a specified loss suffered by the claimant. Indemnities are often appropriate for specific matters which are known to the parties, such as liabilities arising from environmental risks, litigation, product liability, or taxes relating to the seller's period of ownership.

The quantum of an indemnity depends on its terms.[174] It is important that the SPA sets out clearly the terms of the indemnity. In general, if a seller undertakes to indemnify a buyer for loss suffered as a result of a particular event then if the event occurs (subject to thresholds and other conditions) the seller has to reimburse the buyer dollar for dollar for the loss suffered as a result of the event in question. There is

170. *Ibid.*, para. 23.
171. *Ibid.*, para. 84.
172. Such damages will typically be recoverable in the law of tort/delict, not the law of contract (which is concerned with breaches of contract terms), although many SPAs exclude most claims for misrepresentation and resulting rights to avoid the contract, confining the parties to claims for breach of warranties.
173. Kramer, *supra* n. 120, at 237.
174. *Ibid.*

no obligation to prove that any loss has occurred as a result of any inaccuracy in the information that the seller provided.[175]

§12.02 COMPENSATORY DAMAGES AND THE BUT-FOR FRAMEWORK

[A] Overview

The award of damages is the principal remedy granted by courts and tribunals for breach of contract.[176] A modern formulation in European law for the basic measure of contract damages is:

> [S]uch sum as will put the aggrieved party as nearly as possible into the position in which it would have been if the contract had been duly performed. Such damages cover the loss which the aggrieved party has suffered and the gain of which it has been deprived.[177]

This award is referred to as 'expectation damages' (in contrast to 'reliance damages'), as the claimant is entitled to be put in the same position as he or she 'expected' to be in had the contract been performed as promised.[178]

The general principle is that the expectation measure must put the claimant in the same position he or she would have been in but for the breach. The basic compensatory calculation is a factual comparison between what actually happened (the breach position) and what would have happened but for the breach (the non-breach position).[179]

[B] The But-For Framework

The but-for framework is a method to measure the loss by comparing the position the aggrieved party would have been in had the contract been performed properly with the actual position it found itself in as a result of the breach. This was expressed by a High Court judge as follows:

> I take the governing principle to be that damages should be such as will restore the plaintiff, so far as a monetary award can do so, to the position it would have occupied had the breaches found to have been committed by the defendants not

---

175. Although there may be additional terms ensuring that the seller has some oversight over or involvement in the handling of the dispute that has emerged between the target company and a third party, in order to protect the seller from a buyer whose motivation to fight the liability is reduced by knowledge of the indemnity.
176. Kramer, *supra* n. 120, at 4. For example, it was set out by *Baron Park Robinson v. Harman* in 1848 and cited many times. Kramer, *supra* n. 120, at 13 with further citations.
177. Article 9:502 of the Principles of European Contract Law. There is a similar principle in bilateral investment treaty (BIT) arbitrations, based on Chorzow Factory (1928), which states that compensation should 'wipe out all the consequences of the illegal act and re-establish the situation which would, in all probability, have existed if that act had not been committed'. *See* Wöss et al., *supra* n. 142, at 6.26.
178. Kramer, *supra* n. 120, at 13 with further citations.
179. Kramer, *supra* n. 120, at 249.

> occurred. On that basis an inquiry into damages should therefore normally take the form of a comparison, in financial terms, between the events which have actually happened and those which would have happen[ed] had the relevant breach not occurred, the former being susceptible of direct evidence, the latter being necessarily hypothetical.[180]

A graphical depiction of the factual comparison between what actually happened and what would have happened but for the breach is shown in Figure 12.1.

Figure 12.1 The But-For Framework

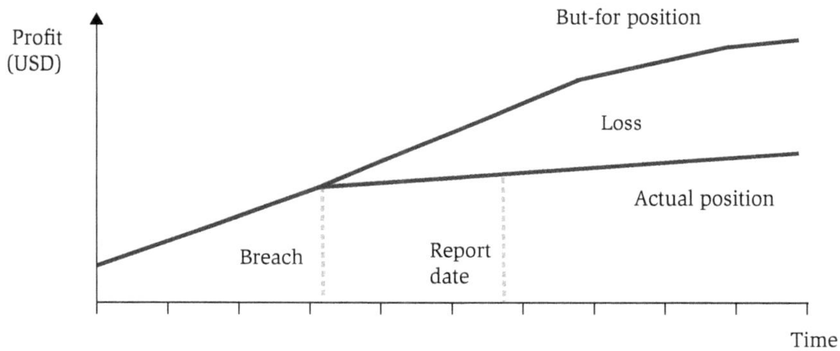

This is a representation of the two positions, expressed by two paths representing (e.g.,) actual and but-for free cash flows. The actual and hypothetical paths diverge from the date of breach, and they remain separate. They could alternatively diverge only at some point *after* the breach, or the damages period could be finite and the two paths could converge after some time.

[1] The Actual Position (The Breach Position)

The actual position, or breach position, is what in fact happened. As damages should be assessed so as to put the claimant in the position he or she would have been in had the warranty been true, the actual position measures what the ownership interest was really worth (the value as is).

It has been stated that in general terms when considering a claim for breach of contract the actual position is normally relatively straightforward to develop and what is more difficult is to calculate what would have happened had the contract not been breached.[181] In a warranty case, however, it is the actual position that is usually the more difficult to establish (whereas the parties themselves have already valued the non-breach position, thinking that was reality). This is because the actual position is

180. *Stephenson Blake (Holdings) Ltd v. Streets Heaver Ltd* [2001] Lloyd's Rep PN 44 para. 159 (Hicks QC).

181. MacGregor, Maclay and Mitchell, *supra* n. 121, at 160.

what the company was really worth on the basis of corrected (or restated) accounts. Consider the case of a minimum EBITDA warranty where the buyer's valuation was based on reported EBITDA of a historical period. It turns out that the EBITDA was overstated. The value as is what the company was really worth, not what the buyer assumed it was worth on the basis of an incorrect EBITDA figure.

Another area where establishing the actual position can be complex is when the actual scenario extends into the future, beyond the time at which the valuation takes place. In Figure 12.1, this is the part of the line for the actual position to the right of the report date.

A basis for establishing the actual position may be the last available historical (interim) financials at the time of the damages valuation, and, if available, management's expectations for the business.

[2] The Hypothetical Position (The Non-breach Position)

The hypothetical position is what would have happened had the breach not occurred. Establishing this position is necessary in order to put the claimant in the same situation but for the breach. The assumptions used to establish this position must be realistic.[182] The following sources are often used as a basis for the hypothetical position:

- Trend extrapolation from historical financial statements, in particular for companies with a stable track record of trading.
- The company's projections (ideally prepared just before the time of the breach - that is, unaffected by the breach), possibly adjusted to reflect new information.
- Profitability and balance sheet ratios of a group of comparable companies (a peer group).
- Analysts' expectations about market growth rates, market shares, and other developments.

When the income approach is used to value damages, the non-breach position is often represented by hypothetical free cash flows. In order to project them, they are usually broken down into their constituent parts: projected profit and loss, working capital and other balance sheet movements, and capital expenditure. Costs are usually dissected into their variable and fixed components. The damages expert usually prepares an integrated set of projected financial statements from which hypothetical free cash flows are derived.

When, as a result of the breach, the target company discontinues operations, the actual free cash flows of the company may go to zero after liquidation. This situation is depicted in Figure 12.2.

182. *Ibid.*

Figure 12.2 The But-For Framework: The Actual Position Goes to Zero

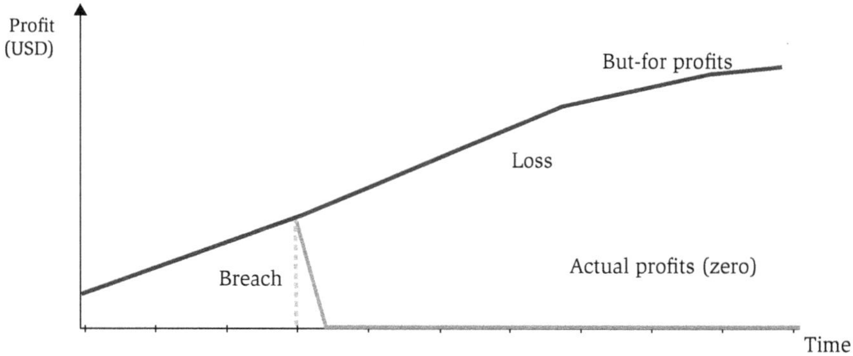

Example: Joint Venture Dispute over Lost Profits (International Arbitration)

Two joint venture partners entered into an agreement over the production and distribution of technology used in shipbuilding. Party 1, a start-up, contributed patented technology that it had recently developed. Party 2, a mid-sized manufacturer and distributor of similar products, contributed access to its existing international distribution network as well as financing during the start-up phase (in which the joint venture entity was expected to be loss-making). The parties agreed to split the profits from the joint venture evenly over an initial term of several years. At the inception of the joint venture, Party 1 licensed the technology to the joint venture entity, and Party 2 provided start-up funding.

Shortly after inception of the joint venture entity, while the entity was still ramping up its operations, Party 2 was acquired by a large corporate. The acquirer had its own technology which competed with the technology which Party 1 had licensed to the joint venture. Shortly after the acquisition, Party 2 withheld any additional financing from the joint venture entity, which was soon forced into liquidation.

Party 1 argued that the joint venture agreement was breached as Party 2 had withheld the promised funding. It claimed damages as the difference between the actual value of its share of the joint venture company (close to zero other than some proceeds from liquidation) and the hypothetical value had the joint venture continued to operate. The hypothetical position was largely based on a business plan which the two joint venture parties had agreed a short time prior to the acquisition of Party 2.

[3] Loss of Business Value Versus Lost Profits

The term 'loss' has been used so far to mean both lost profits and a reduction in the value of the shares. In theory, when the income method is used, the value of an asset is the present value of future cash flows. When damages experts refer to 'lost profits', they usually mean lost cash flows.[183] Even if lost profits refer to a measure of accrual earnings, these earnings should reconcile to cash flow according to the accounting equation (for an infinite forecast horizon). Every USD of lost operating cash flow, discounted to a valuation date, therefore translates into a reduction of enterprise value at the same date. In concept, therefore, 'lost profits' means a reduction in the value of the business, and the terms 'lost profits' and 'lost business value' can be redundant.[184]

However, there can be differences between lost profits and lost business value. One difference relates to the valuation date and the use of hindsight. The valuation of a business (or an ownership interest) at the time of breach often means that the valuation should reflect only what was known to the parties at the time. In contrast, a claim for profits that would have been generated after the date of the breach (but were lost) may incorporate additional information.[185] Also, if a company itself is the claimant, it may be able to claim a loss of profits, but not the diminution of its own value. In contrast, shareholders in a company may only be able to claim a diminution in the value of their shares. These are however legal considerations outside the scope of this book.[186]

[4] Damages Related to Warranties of Quality

A warranty of quality is a promise that the goods are in a specific state.[187] An example of a warranty in this sense in an SPA is a 'true and fair view warranty', or a warranty that the target entity's reported EBITDA in a certain period up to closing was at least a particular amount.[188] If a warranty of quality is breached, the question becomes what the target's share capital would have been worth had the target company indeed achieved the EBITDA as promised in the SPA by the seller. This is shown in Figure 12.3, which refers to EBITDA as 'profit' to be consistent with the earlier figures.

183. Evans, Galanti and Lentz, *supra* n. 123, at 4.16.
184. *Ibid.*, 4.17.
185. For example, this was the issue in the Canadian case *RBC Dominion Securities Inc. v. Merrill Lynch Canada Inc.* [2004] B.C.J. No. 2337.
186. For further discussion *see* Kramer, *supra* n. 120, *at* 497.
187. This relates to English contract law. *See ibid.*, at 225.
188. *Ibid.* 226.

Figure 12.3 Breach of Warranty of Quality

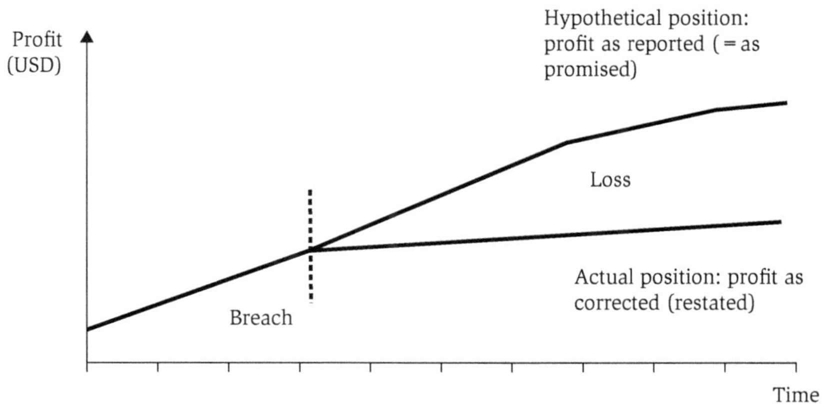

Note the difference to Figure 12.1, which showed the general contractual damages scenarios: while the two lines still reference the hypothetical (upper) and actual (lower) scenarios, the reported profits are now part of the hypothetical position, and the (usually lower) corrected profit figures make up the actual (non-breach) position. The hypothetical value is the value on the basis of the profits (EBITDA) as warranted. In the case of a true and fair view warranty, this is the value on the basis of the financial statements as presented. This is the non-breach position.

The actual position, on the other hand, is the value of the company on the basis of a corrected EBITDA and restated financial statements. This is the breach position. In contrast to other breaches, one cannot say in these cases that nobody knows what would have happened in the hypothetical (non-breach) position; in fact, the hypothetical is the known position because the acquirer (and possibly other bidders/market participants) determined and paid a price based on the incorrect financials presented to him. The value as warranted in this case will rebuttably be presumed to be the price actually paid.

[5] The Valuation Date

The normal approach is to assess loss at the date of the breach and on the basis of the information available to the parties at that date. In M&A disputes, this is often the transaction date. However, the question may arise whether subsequent events should be taken into account in assessing loss. This can have a significant effect on damages. This was a central issue in *Ageas v. Kwik-Fit & anr* which concerned the breach of an accounts warranty.[189] After closing, it emerged that the warranted accounts on which the buyer had based its valuation of the target contained errors in the treatment of bad

189. *Ageas (UK) Ltd v. Kwik-Fit (GB) Ltd & anr* [2014] EWHC 2178 (QB).

debt: an incorrect treatment of 'Time on Cover Bad Debt' (TOCBD) had resulted in the overstatement of both profits and assets of the target. The judge stated:

> Damages for breach of contract will normally be assessed by reference to the position at the date of breach. But a later date may be used for the assessment if in all the circumstances of the case to do so would more accurately reflect the overriding compensatory principle.[190]

The judge held that in this case under the terms of the SPA, the buyer had assumed the risk connected with the bad debt TOCBD post-acquisition. The judge referred in particular to the fact that the purchase price was a fixed price. The bargain embodied in the SPA was the allocation of risk to the buyer of any benefit or loss arising either as a result of the way the buyer chose to run the business or as a result of external influences on the success of the business.[191] The court could not therefore cut across this allocation of risk by allowing hindsight to influence the calculation of damages.

In cases such as these, where the contractual allocation of risk may be of relevance, parties should examine whether a backdated acquisition date, such as in a locked box SPA, could affect the valuation date.

[6] Measure of Damages Related to Warranties of Reasonable Care

A different measure of damages applies for warranties of reasonable care. This type of warranty is a promise that the seller has taken reasonable care in preparing financial information.[192] An example is *Esso Petroleum v. Mardon*. A warranty of a forecast was found not to be a warranty of the forecast being true, but a warranty of the seller having taken reasonable care in preparing the forecast.[193] The measure of damages was not the 'loss of bargain', but compensation for having been induced to enter into a contract which turned out to be disastrous for the claimant. The Court of Appeal found that the damages were to be measured by the loss the claimant suffered, as:

> he can say:
>
> > I would not have entered into this contract at all but for your representation. Owing to it, I have lost all the capital I put into it. I also incurred a large overdraft. I have spent four years of my life in wasted endeavour without reward: and it will take me some time to re-establish myself.

For all such loss he is entitled to recover damages. It is to be measured in a similar way as the loss due to a personal injury. You should look into the future so as to forecast what would have been likely to happen if he had never entered into this contract: and contrast it with his position as it is now as a result of entering into it. The future is necessarily problematical and can only be a rough-and-ready estimate. But it must be done in assessing the loss.[194]

190. *Ibid.*, para. 30.
191. *Ibid.*, para. 50.
192. Kramer, *supra* n. 120, at 233.
193. *Esso Petroleum v. Mardon* [1976] QB 801, discussed in Kramer, *supra* n. 120, at 233.
194. *Ibid.*

§12.03 DAMAGES MATTERS SPECIFIC TO M&A DISPUTES

This section discusses aspects of damages valuations that frequently play a role in M&A-related disputes. While these topics are not unique to M&A-related disputes, they are frequently encountered in these types of disputes.

[A] Which Cost of Capital?

Non-contentious Valuations

In the (non-contentious) valuation of the target company before an M&A transaction, a purchaser who uses the income approach must decide on a rate of return at which to discount future income streams of the target company. As with other capital investment decisions, the investor's required return will depend on the perceived level of systematic risk, and the discount rate he or she uses must reflect this risk appropriately. As different companies have different risk profiles, acquirers will require different returns for different target companies.

A question for acquirers is whether to discount projected income streams at the cost of capital of the stand-alone target or the cost of capital of the target when it is part of the acquirer group after the acquisition.

A similar question arises when the market approach is used: should an acquirer who uses a multiple-based valuation limit the peer group to companies comparable only to the target (e.g., in terms of the type of the business or geography) or include peers of the acquiring group as it is expected to be after the acquisition?

The cost of capital or peer group used can have a considerable effect on the outcome of the valuation. The effect is possibly most pronounced in cross-border transactions involving emerging markets and acquisitions of young, high-growth businesses by more stable, larger acquirers. In both cases, there is often a significant difference between the cost of capital of the acquirer and the target entity.

In non-contentious M&A valuations, many acquirers, as a matter of policy, use the target's cost of capital and not the acquirer's.[195] The reason usually given, and consistent with corporate finance theory of capital investment decisions, is that the objective is to discount at a rate that appropriately reflects the systematic risk of the investment, not the investor.

An acquirer who uses the market approach for valuing the target and who selects a peer group on a set of criteria that relate solely to the target, not the acquirer or the combined group, essentially takes the same view of how to consider systematic risk in the valuation.

The systematic risk of an acquisition target will be influenced by the acquirer's plans once the deal has closed. These plans include the extent of integration of the target into the acquiring group. In many PE transactions, the target effectively

195. For example, *see* James R. Hitchner, *Financial Valuation: Applications and Models, 858 (Wiley* 2003).

continues to operate as a stand-alone business after an acquisition. Neither its operations nor the financial structure will be merged into those of the acquirer (even though the stand-alone financial structure often changes after an acquisition with debt pushed into the acquired entity).

On the other hand, strategic buyers and PE buyers in bolt-on acquisitions often plan at least a partial integration of the target entity after an acquisition. This means that the acquired entity may share corporate functions or participate in a group cash pooling arrangement. The target is embedded in the acquirer's financing structure, and financial markets may, as a consequence, consider that the target's lenders are effectively secured (either explicitly or implicitly) by the acquiring group's assets or cash flows. On the other hand, even if integrated, the target may remain a distinct division with a distinct risk profile.

If an acquisition reduces the risk profile of the target, the target benefits. This benefit is similar to other synergies. In fact, a reduction in the cost of capital for a target entity after an acquisition is one type of synergy.[196] As with other synergies, the extent the buyer is willing to share them with the seller impacts the price it offers. The ability to offer a share of synergies can be central to the bidding strategy of corporates, and PE bidders may find it difficult to compete with synergies available to corporate buyers.

Contentious Valuation

The measure of contract damages is different from that used in a non-contentious situation when valuing an acquisition target. Compensatory damages mean that the claimant should be put in the position it would have been in but for the breach.

In the context of compensatory damages in an M&A dispute, the question could be whether to use the same cost of capital in the actual and hypothetical scenarios if the income approach is used. If the optimal leverage structure is assumed in both scenarios, then the debt and equity weights in the WACC calculation (assuming free cash flows are discounted) may be different. For example, the target may generate more cash in the hypothetical scenario, and this additional cash would affect the capital structure (relative to the actual scenario), leading to different weights in WACC. Further, if the target company is composed of different activities each with their own different systematic risk, and the breach affects one of these disproportionately, then the overall systematic risk may be different in the hypothetical scenario from the actual scenario. For example, if a target company consists of a portfolio of commercial real estate and solar projects, and the breach affects only the solar operations, then the risk profile of the overall target business may change as a result of the breach.

The standard of value may also affect the extent to which synergies specific to a buyer are reflected in the damages valuation. As discussed in §11.03, a standard of value commonly used is that of 'fair market value'. This is the value at which property would change hands between a hypothetical willing and able buyer and a hypothetical willing and able seller, acting at arm's length in an open and unrestricted market, when

196. Aswath Damodaran, *The Value of Synergy*, Working Paper, 29, (Stern School of Business, October 2005).

neither is under compulsion to buy or sell and when both have reasonable knowledge of the relevant facts.[197] The generic, hypothetical buyer this standard refers to will not usually reflect synergies of a specific buyer.

In contrast to 'fair market value' and 'market value', the term 'fair value' references specific, identified parties and their circumstances. If this standard of value is used, then the discount rate may reflect synergies a specific buyer may realise.

[B] Taxes

The general principle is that the claimant should be restored to the position it would have been in had the breach not occurred. This is a position after taxes - in relation to both lost profits and the award. With marginal tax rates in many countries being above 20% (many significantly higher),[198] notwithstanding the multitude of potential deductions from the tax base when calculating taxable income, taxes can have a significant impact when calculating loss in the context of an award for damages.

There are two distinct aspects when considering taxes in damages: the corporate income tax on lost profits (often those of the acquisition target), and taxes on the damages award payable by the claimant (if any). These two may be subject to entirely different tax rules, deductions, and so on.

The corporate income tax on lost profits is the difference between taxes on taxable income in the hypothetical and in the actual development. As the wrongful act may affect the tax base, the tax rates applicable as a percentage of taxable income are not necessarily the same. Estimating future corporate income tax payments can be a complex area of the damages claim and, for example in cross-border cases, may require specialised knowledge of local tax rules. Estimating future taxes further requires assumptions in respect of (future) tax rates, depreciation and amortisation, the appropriateness of transfer prices, the treatment of tax-loss carryforward, and future changes to the tax basis (such as the availability of deductions and allowances), to name a few.[199] This is often an area of significant complexity.

In general it is appropriate to consider taxes on operating earnings in the damages valuation as operating costs, no different in this respect from the cost of purchasing supplies, or the cost of rent, salaries, or wages. Conversely, corporate income taxes on financial income are financial expenses. If the income approach and a DCF model are used to measure damages, then taxes on operating income reduce free cash flow, whereas tax effects related to financial income or expenses are below free cash flow.

Separately, it is necessary to consider any taxes the claimant pays on the award itself. If the award does not reflect these, a claimant who is taxed on the award would

197. *International Glossary of Business Valuation Terms*, American Society of Appraisers, ASA Business Valuation Standards, 2009.

198. *See Corporate Income Tax Rates around the World, 2016*, https://taxfoundation.org/corporate-income-tax-rates-around-world-2016/#_ftn5 (accessed in June 2018).

199. James Nicholson, *The Impact of Corporate Taxation on Economic Losses*, FTI Consulting White Paper, 2, (January 2018).

be undercompensated. However, in case these taxes are considered in the award but that the claimant is ultimately not liable for them, the claimant would be overcompensated. Taxes on lost profits should therefore be considered separately from taxes on the award.

One approach some quantum experts use is to omit all corporate income taxes from the damages calculation.[200] This means determining damages on the basis of pre-tax lost profits while also not considering taxes that may be payable on the award. This approach implicitly assumes perfect symmetry between the tax rates at which each of the two would have been taxed, so that the benefit to the claimant from omitting taxes in the calculation of lost profits (which are therefore higher) is exactly offset by the taxes payable on the award. However, there is usually no reason to assume that this should be the case in post-M&A disputes, and the tax situations of the claimant and of the target entity may in fact be very different.

It is also not straightforward to move a DCF valuation from a post-tax to a pre-tax basis. Stock market returns used in the Capital Asset Pricing Model (CAPM) are on a post-tax basis, and investors' return expectations are generally after taxes. An approach sometimes used to calculate pre-tax cash flows by grossing up post-tax cash flows at a rate equal to one minus the marginal corporate tax rate. However, this will usually not give the same result as discounting post-tax cash flows at post-tax discount rates as it ignores the difference between accrual accounting taxable income (on which the tax payable is based) and cash flows (which are grossed up). It can be shown that, except in no-growth perpetual cash flow scenarios, post-tax cash flows are not equal to pre-tax cash flow multiplied by a factor equal to one less the marginal corporate tax rate.[201] It is therefore important to use post-tax cash flows and post-tax discount rates in DCF valuations.[202]

[C] Value Versus Price

In the case of a warranty breach, the price paid in a transaction is often presumed to be the value as warranted. However, there are situations in which bidders pay more, or less, than an asset is worth – worth not to others, but to themselves. An example of a situation where value and price are not the same is an irrational escalation of commitments, also called a 'bidding war'. Bidding wars can result in prices that may not be justifiable by reasonable assumptions.[203]

Why someone is willing to pay more or accept less than an asset is worth can be a difficult question that is in the domain of behavioural economists. It is however

200. *See* the discussion in James Nicholson, *Taxation and Currency Issues in Damages Awards*, in: *The Guide to Damages in International Arbitration*, 265 (2nd ed., Global Arbitration Review 2017).
201. See Wayne Lonergan, Pre and Post Tax Discount Rates and Cash Flows – A Technical Note, THE JOURNAL OF APPLIED RESEARCH IN ACCOUNTING AND FINANCE, Volume 4 Issue 1 2009, p. 41 to 45.
202. Ibid., p. 45.
203. Max H. Bazerman and Don A. Moore, *Judgment in Managerial Decision Making*, 123 (8th ed., Wiley 2013).

instructive to consider the case of Guidant, a medical products manufacturer, to show that value and price are different things. This transaction escalated into the biggest and most contentious takeover battle at the time in the medical devices industry.[204] In December 2004, Johnson and Johnson (J&J) made a bid of USD 25.4 billion for Guidant. About six months later, before the transaction closed, the *New York Times* uncovered a flaw in one of Guidant's products, an implantable defibrillator, that caused it to malfunction in some instances. Guidant had not disclosed this deficiency, and this news therefore surprised J&J. The US Food and Drug Administration (FDA) opened an investigation into Guidant. The company announced a product recall.

A short time later, in November of 2005, J&J reduced its offer to USD 21.5 billion over concerns about the FDA investigation and Guidant's new outlook. J&J later raised its offer again, to USD 23.2 billion.

On 5 December 2005, Boston Scientific, a competitor of J&J, fearing to be at a competitive disadvantage in the event J&J acquired Guidant, offered USD 24.7 billion for Guidant. The FDA investigation progressed, and Guidant's situation worsened. On 11 January 2006, Guidant tentatively accepted a revised bid by J&J of USD 23.2 billion. Boston Scientific raised its bid to USD 25 billion within a day, and J&J increased its bid yet again to USD 24.2 billion which Guidant provisionally accepted. On 25 January, Boston Scientific raised its bid yet again to USD 27 billion. Guidant accepted this revised offer, pending the approval of shareholders and regulators. J&J decided not to follow suit. Its share price had fallen every time it had raised its bid for Guidant.[205]

The day after Guidant accepted Boston Scientific's bid, Boston Scientific's share price dropped to USD 23.15, a decrease of approximately 15% since the company first announced the bid, and by June 2006, after Boston Scientific had been forced to recall 23,000 Guidant pacemakers, it had fallen below USD 17.

Boston Scientific's winning bid of USD 27 billion was *higher* than the original bid by J&J of USD 25.4 billion, before any of Guidant's technological problems had emerged, and which later developed into significant legal and reputational problems. All else being equal, these problems would suggest a significant reduction in the value of Guidant, not an increase.

Behavioural economists have examined the conditions under which escalations of commitment such as this occur.[206] One scenario is a bidder who - in the event it lost in an auction process - would face a loss in market share or competitive position. Such a bidder can face a trade-off between accepting this loss and winning the auction and overpaying, which can then be a natural outcome.[207] An escalatory battle can lead to both sides losing.[208] Other explanations include 'competitive irrationality', including

204. B. Feder, *Quiet End to Battle of the Bids*, New York Times, C1 (26 Jan. 2006). The bidding war was discussed in Bazerman and Moore *supra* n. 203, at 125-126.
205. Feder, *supra* n. 204, at C1.
206. Bazerman and Moore, *supra* n. 203, at 126.
207. *Ibid.*
208. *Ibid.*, 127-130.

the motive to 'win' rather than to seek one's own gain.[209] Yet other explanations refer to a misalignment of management and shareholders' interests.

[D] Valuation Provisions in the SPA

There are situations in which the SPA may include a clause that governs the valuation of assets or liabilities (other than for purchase price adjustment purposes). It is also sometimes proposed to agree the method of damages valuation in the SPA, even though these clauses are the exception.[210]

As with other contractual valuation clauses, it is difficult even in concept to agree a valuation approach before signing that does not leave significant discretion to the valuer. The more precisely the SPA prescribes the damages valuation, the less it may fit the (hitherto unknown) circumstances at the time it may become relevant. It may lead to the removal of the option to use a specific valuation approach, even though it turns out that the approach would have been more appropriate than the method prescribed in the SPA. Consequently, damages valuation clauses for breach of contract are rarely used. On the other hand, the more generic the method, the greater the scope for disagreement. The following is an example of a generic valuation clause (albeit not damages valuations in an SPA) which led to a dispute.

Example: Valuation Method of Shares Subject to a Put Option

The example relates to the valuation of an ownership interest on the exercise of a put option by the seller.

The parties were two European companies that had entered into an SPA under which Respondent sold to Claimant 51% of the share capital of a Swiss target. The Claimant (buyer) also received a put option entitling it to require Respondent (seller) to purchase any shares in the target company held by Claimant during the seven years following the third anniversary of the SPA. The shares were to be sold at their fair market value. Fair market value was to be determined by an independent expert having regard to the following criteria:

- The target's existing and historical financial performance over the preceding three-year period.
- an analysis of relevant market factors existing during the same period including multiples of relevant financial indicators (i.e., turnover, net profits, cash flow, net assets) paid for comparable companies in recent M&A transactions in comparable countries and industries.

209. *Ibid.*, 131.
210. However, it is common that the SPA sets the terms of the indemnity and how to measure loss. It is also common for SPAs to define damages (compensation for lost profits, other consequential damages, and at the level of which entity damages are to be determined. The author has also come across a case in which misrepresentation damages were to be measured as the book value of the accounting error.

- An analysis of trading multiples of any existing comparable companies trading on the local stock exchange or other relevant stock exchanges.
- An analysis of the status of the subsector in the country where the target was located and its expected future development, with consideration given to any relevant market information and recent or expected legislative and regulatory developments which would bear on the market value if the company.
- And a DCF analysis.

Claimant exercised the put option, and the parties disagreed over the price of shares concerned. They appointed an audit firm to determine their fair market value, however, as the audit firm's valuation was not considered binding on the parties, the case went to arbitration. The tribunal performed a detailed analysis of twenty-seven valuation issues over which the parties disagreed and applied the criteria of the SPA.[211] The valuation provisions in the SPA references different valuation methods and criteria without defining their relationship to each other. Consequently, experts could arrive at vastly different valuations. It is difficult to pre-agree on a valuation method in the SPA in a way that does not grant significant discretion to the valuer. What can be useful, however, is to carve out that the damages valuation in the case of a warranty breach should be performed by an independent expert (expert determination).

[E] Event Studies

An event study can be used to value damages that relate to a company whose shares trade on a public stock exchange. As the market constantly values the shares of a public company, by extension, it constantly establishes its market capitalisation. If a single wrongful act has occurred and investors are well informed, then the expected monetary impact of the act, once known to the market, will be reflected in a subsequent drop in share price and market capitalisation.

As markets move constantly, the price movement due to the wrongful act must be isolated from market events. This is what an event study does. An assumption on which it is based is that shares are traded in an 'informationally efficient market'.[212]

Event studies have been used in class action litigation for many years. They can be relevant in M&A disputes in which shareholders of the target company receive shares of the acquiring company as part of an acquisition, or in an exchange of shares in a merger. An example is the acquisition of mobile operator EE by BT from Deutsche Telekom (DT) and Orange, the French telecoms group, discussed in §10.01 above in early 2016.[213] On the day of the second announcement of accounting irregularities, 24

211. ICC Case 11786, in: The Arbitration of Disputes Relating to Mergers and Acquisitions: A Study of ICC Cases, Andrea Carlevaris ICC International Court of Arbitration Bulletin Vol. 24 Number 1/2013, p. 29.
212. Federal Securities Acts and Areas of Expert Analysis, Nicholas I. Crew, Kevin L. Gold, Marnie A. Moore, *supra* n. 123, at 24.16.
213. BT Group: BT Group plc Results for the second quarter to 30 Sep. 2016, 27 Oct. 2017, available at https://www.btplc.com/Sharesandperformance/Quarterlyresults/2016-2017/Q2/Downloads/Newsrelease/q216-release.pdf.

January 2017, BT's market capitalisation fell by GBP 7.9 billion, a 20.8% decrease against the prior day's closing position. The irregularities reportedly dated back to the time before signing (at least 2013). An event study would be a method to measure how much of the share price decrease on 24 January 2017 resulted from the disclosure in relation to the accounting irregularities, and how much of the change related to general market movements.

In the event, in order to avoid a potential dispute, BT struck a GBP 225 million settlement that ruled out further legal disputes with Orange and DT.[214]

If erroneously reported earnings have resulted in a share price that is higher than it would have been had the company reported earnings correctly, then the shares, used as acquisition currency, may be worth less than their price. Had the information been available at the time of receiving shares, then more shares would have had to be traded in exchange for the ownership interest. An event study measures how much of the inflation of the share price in these situations resulted from the allegedly false information.

Event studies use statistical regression analysis of a time series of security returns in order to isolate the effects of the event on the share price. They use a regression model to predict the normal return on a firm's daily stock price. The difference between the model's predicted return and the actual return is the abnormal, or excess, return. It represents the part of the total returns that cannot be explained by general market events. Statistical methods are used to calculate the significance of the event day-specific return.[215]

214. Financial Times, Deutsche Telekom takes further EUR 1.1 billion hit from BT stake, 3 Aug. 2013.
215. *Supra* (212)., 24.19 for further discussion.

CHAPTER 13

Lessons Learned

§13.01 INTRODUCTION

The focus of this publication is technical, with an emphasis on financial and accounting matters insofar as they affect deal mechanics. The discussion in earlier chapters offers a number of lessons as to how disputes might be avoided. These lessons are summarised below. Even so, any such discussion would be incomplete without mention (albeit brief) of other factors that influence a transaction and which - whether or not by design - contribute to creating the conditions for a dispute. These include behavioural aspects which can be important in understanding the real reasons behind the decisions that lead to disputes.

Anyone who has been involved in multiple M&A transactions will know that dealmakers are humans: individuals subject to various biases in negotiation or, in the words of John Maynard Keynes, 'animal spirits'.[216] While this is the domain of behavioural economics and outside the scope of this publication,[217] it would be insufficient to ignore behavioural biases entirely. They are therefore incorporated in the following practical considerations that may help avoid disputes.

216. John Maynard Keynes, The General Theory of Employment, Interest and Money, 1973 (1936), pp. 149–150, 161–162,, New York: Macmillan, quoted in: George A. Akerlof/ Robert J. Shiller, Animal Spirits, 2009, Princeton University Press, p. 3.

217. For further reading, we suggest Managerial Judgment and Decision Making by Max Bazerman and Don Moore and Raymond S. Nickerson, *Confirmation Bias: A Ubiquitous Phenomenon in Many Guises*, Review of General Psychology 1998, Vol. 2, No. 2, pp. 175–220 with further references.

§13.02 RECOMMENDATIONS

[A] Ensure the SPA is Specific and Unambiguous

Many of the examples in this book have shown that ambiguous wording or vague measurement concepts in the SPA are common causes of disputes and concluded that the parties and their advisors should ensure definitions of accounting policies and financial terms in the SPA are clear and unambiguous. If even specific wording leaves room for potential disagreement, the parties should consider using fixed values or a formula-driven approach. For example, accounting policies such as bad debt policies that require management judgment may be replaced with a formula-driven policy in the completion accounts.

It has been recognised that it can be difficult, even for experienced dealmakers, to choose the appropriate moment during the negotiations to raise sensitive topics. It may seem that the right time to discuss what could (theoretically) go wrong in the future never comes. For example, the question what constitutes a Material Adverse Change event can be a difficult subject to broach in the midst of high stakes negotiations. Avoiding such topics, and thereby accepting ambiguity, can make negotiations easier and increase the probability of a successful signing.

Ambiguity of this kind has been called 'constructive ambiguity'.[218] It is based on the idea that it creates opportunities for both parties to advance their interests in a negotiation by accepting ambiguously worded text. In M&A negotiations, constructive ambiguity can avoid potential disagreements *in the negotiations* and increase the probability of signing. However, this can be a temporary deferral, and the disagreement may come back in the shape of a post-deal dispute (*see* §8 above). However, the parties may feel that the benefit of getting to the finish line outweighs the increased probability of disagreement later.

Another kind of ambiguity refers to situations in which only one party to a transaction forms the view that a lack of precision is desirable for tactical reasons in the negotiations. For example, a buyer may believe that an ambiguous, rather than narrowly defined, MAC clause will allow it more scope to claim later that a MAC event has occurred. Similarly, the party that prepares the completion accounts may prefer ambiguous accounting rules over narrowly defined ones. In these cases, clarity protects the other party.

In any event, if the objective is to avoid disputes, then accepting ambiguity can be counterproductive, and thus precise drafting is generally preferable. The author recommends to set aside a time and place during the negotiations in which these matters will be discussed with the other party and to invest sufficient time to ensure SPA definitions are clear.

---

218. Khaled Elgindy, When Ambiguity is Destructive, 22 Jan. 2014, Brookings Institution, https://www.brookings.edu/opinions/when-ambiguity-is-destructive/.

[B] Employ a Diverse Range of Skills on the Deal Team

Deal teams, led by the CFO or head of M&A, often include lawyers, accountants, bankers and others with industry, technology, IP, valuation, and complementary areas of expertise.

A range of voices with varied qualifications and professional or cultural experiences can help bring important issues to the surface. Diverse teams approach a problem from different angles and are more likely to develop creative solutions.[219] For example, a forensic accountant involved in the wording of SPA working capital clauses will bring expertise on where things can go wrong.

However, diversity need not mean only a diversity of disciplines. It also means individual diversity, such as career stage or personality. It has been observed many times that diverse teams challenge assumptions and combat 'groupthink'. This helps to deal with problems at an early stage.

[C] Communicate Constantly

It is a reoccurring theory in this book that many issues that lead to M&A disputes originate at the interface of disciplines. It has been shown in §9.03, for example, that if the valuation team is not sufficiently aware of how the completion mechanism works, the same item may be captured twice in the purchase price.

Members of the deal team should, therefore, as a matter of routine throughout the transaction process, share findings with each other. The leadership should ensure there is a forum for such exchanges.

[D] Recognise Behavioural Biases

The M&A process consists of a series of decisions, large and small, that principals and their advisors continually face. Even highly intelligent and experienced dealmakers do not always reason rationally.

Behavioural scientists who have studied decision-making make a distinction between 'System 1' and 'System 2' thinking.[220] While System 1 thinking refers to intuitive thinking, which is fast, effortless, and emotional, System 2 thinking refers to slower, conscious, more considered and logical reasoning.[221] Studies suggest that people are more likely to rely on System 1 thinking when they are more rushed and have more on their minds.[222] The frantic pace of M&A negotiations means dealmakers and their advisors are therefore prone to rely on System 1 thinking. No matter how

219. *See* Shireen Meer, 28 Jul. 2017 Diversity needs to be more than skin deep, Management Today.
220. Bazerman and Moore, *supra* n. 203 at p. 3.
221. Stanovich, K.E. and West, R.F., 2000, *Individual Differences in Reasoning: Implications for the Rationality Debate.* Behavioural & Brain Sciences, 23, pp. 645-665; D. Kahnemann, *A Perspective on Judgment and Choice: Mapping Bounded Rationality*. American Psychologist, 58(9), pp. 697-720.
222. Bazerman and Moore, *supra* n. 203, at pp. 3 and 4 with further citations.

intelligent or qualified a person is, errors or biases are more likely to occur when System 1 thinking is engaged.[223] Consider the parties discussed in §12.04 [C] who engage in a bidding war in which prices could not be justified by a valuation when using reasonable assumptions. An escalatory battle can lead to both sides losing.

It is fair to say that biases in decision-making at the very least facilitate M&A-related disputes. One of the most common of these biases is overconfidence.[224] Overconfidence can lead to many types of irrational decisions, including the escalation of commitments, or the failure to ignore sunk costs, believing that time and resources already spent on a transaction mean that too much has been invested to walk away from a bad deal.

When overconfidence comes in the form of unrealistic optimism, it may lead to the consistent overestimation in accounting judgments.[225] Consider a seller who consistently (and possibly unintentionally) overestimates the degree of completion of a long-term contract for which the target accounts under the percentage-of-completion method. This means that the target's EBITDA in the year relevant for the valuation is overstated and may lead to a breach of a true and fair view warranty in the SPA.

Behavioural scientists have analysed the anatomy of decision-making and developed recommendations on how to keep biases in check. [226] These include recognising situations in which others' decision-making is vulnerable to biases, and 'debiasing' one's own judgment. Being appropriately humble about the quality of one's judgment and being open to feedback at all times play an important role in becoming less reliant on System 1 thinking and being less vulnerable to biases in decision-making as a consequence.

Lastly, cognitive biases are not limited to the negotiations before the deal is signed. A recent analysis of arbitral tribunals' awards shows a degree of correlation between the amount awarded and where claimants and respondents had positioned themselves on damages.[227] The outcome of arbitrations may be influenced, to some extent, by 'anchoring' the tribunal's thinking in the first quantifications of damages.[228] It is therefore appropriate to consider this.

[E] Provide Opportunities to Raise Concerns ... and Listen

Confirmation biases, overconfidence, or 'deal fever' can all present a hazard. If there is apparent consensus in a deal team, it can require courage for an individual to raise concerns and challenge the consensus: after all, the concern raised could (and often does) turn out to be unimportant.

While challenging assumptions can lead to uncomfortable situations, in our view it is an important part of a successful acquisition process. Successful teams give their

223. *Ibid.*, p. 4.
224. *Ibid.*, at, p. 11.
225. *Ibid.*, p. 24.
226. *Ibid.*, pp. 15, 216, 217.
227. PwC 2015 – International Arbitration Damages Research, Closing the Gap Between Claimants and Respondents, p. 5.
228. *Ibid.*

members a sense that it is ok to speak up. Senior leadership should therefore create an environment where members of the deal team are encouraged to challenge assumptions and ensure that all concerns are addressed.

[F] Consider How Unexpected Events Could Impact the Transaction

The parties should ask themselves how something unexpected, for example in the target's customer or supplier markets, or in the financial markets, could impact the deal. Where could volatility find its way into the purchase price adjustment, represent a material adverse change, or cause a breach of warranty? The potential effects of volatility should be carefully considered in particular when volatile events meet 'soft' accounting standards or vague measurement concepts.

One way to address this risk is to use fixed values in the completion mechanism instead of measuring at closing. This is the usual practice for pension obligations. However, the same may be considered for metrics to be used for restructuring provisions, in inventory valuation, or expected profit margins inherent in long-term contracts.

[G] Ensure Proper Documentation/Note Taking

It can often prove difficult to retroactively understand the basis on which a certain decision was reached or a particular action taken. Documenting financial information or important assertions made by the other party, as well as your own thought processes, serves as a valuable reference and can also support your case should a dispute result in litigation. For example, it may be helpful to preserve trial balances at a historical reference date. This will ensure a seller has access to this information in a dispute even when it can no longer access the internal reporting systems.

A court will, in considering a case, take into account the decision processes of the parties not only as given in oral evidence, but probably even more so in contemporaneous documents.

[H] Recognise the Constraints

There is never enough time or perfect data to identify and address every risk. We have yet to meet a purchaser who was entirely happy with the information provided by the seller. The objective, therefore, is to form sufficiently robust judgments as to risks involved, to protect against them contractually to the extent possible or to reflect them in price.

Successful dealmakers understand what can realistically be obtained, recognise the constraints, make the most of the available data, and thus make avoidable errors less likely.

Index

J

L

M

ARBITRATION IN CONTEXT SERIES

1. Jane Jenkins, *International Construction Arbitration Law, Second Revised Edition,* 2014 (ISBN 978-90-411-4985-5).
2. Alejandro I. Garcia & Trevor Cook, *International Intellectual Property Arbitration*, 2010 (ISBN 978-90-411-2725-9).
3. Heiko Daniel Ziehms, *M&A Disputes and Completion Mechanisms,* 2019 (ISBN 978-90-411-8625-6).

www.ingramcontent.com/pod-product-compliance
Ingram Content Group UK Ltd.
Pitfield, Milton Keynes, MK11 3LW, UK
UKHW020813290926
15470UKWH00003B/1125